MANAGING INFORMATION TECHNOLOGY IN SECONDARY SCHOOLS

All schools should have a whole school policy for the effective use of information technology across all subjects. This book, aimed principally at secondary schools, is designed to help schools devise and implement an IT policy. The book considers how the IT curriculum, assessment, recording and reporting, and hardware and software resources can be organised and managed effectively. It also explores the impact of various models of the IT curriculum, new GCSE IT syllabuses and use of the Internet.

The book includes details of training activities that are suitable for INSET, and for use in teacher training. These are designed to heighten awareness of IT issues, including the extent to which IT should be embedded within the curriculum and the roles and responsibilities of those who manage IT in secondary schools. It will be useful to all those involved in the management and use of IT in secondary schools, particularly IT co-ordinators, student teachers and advisers. It will also help governors and senior managers who are concerned that the organisation of IT should be effective and efficient.

Roger Crawford is currently a senior lecturer in IT in Education at the University of Huddersfield.

MANAGING INFORMATION TECHNOLOGY IN SECONDARY SCHOOLS

Roger Crawford

London and New York

First published 1997
by Routledge
11 New Fetter Lane, London EC4P 4EE

Simultaneously published in the USA and Canada
by Routledge
29 West 35th Street, New York, NY 10001

Typeset in Garamond by Florencetype, Stoodleigh, Tiverton, Devon
Printed and bound in Great Britain by T. J. International Ltd, Padstow, Cornwall

British Library Cataloguing in Publication Data

A catalogue record for this book is available from the British Library

Library of Congress Cataloguing in Publication Data

Crawford, Roger.
Managing information technology in secondary schools / Roger Crawford.
p. cm.
1. Computer-assisted instruction–Great Britain. 2. Information technology–Great
Britain. 3. Education, Secondary–Great Britain–Data processing. 4.
Education–Great Britain–Computer network resources. I. Title.
LB1028.5.C72 1997
371.33'4–dc21 96–40270 CIP
ISBN 0–415–10734–2
0–415–10735–0 (pbk)

CONTENTS

CONTENTS

CONTENTS

FIGURES AND TABLES

FIGURES

TABLES

PREFACE

This book will be of interest to all those involved with the management and use of Information Technology (IT) in secondary schools in the UK. It will be particularly useful to IT co-ordinators, student teachers, and advisers. It will help governors and senior managers who are concerned that the organisation and management of IT should be effective and efficient, and that the curriculum should provide pupils with a satisfactory experience of IT that meets statutory requirements. Classroom teachers of subjects other than IT may also find the book helpful in placing what they do in a whole school context.

How the IT curriculum, assessment and record keeping, and hardware and software resources can be organised and managed effectively, including security, and health and safety issues, is discussed. Various models of the IT curriculum are identified, and their impact on the school curriculum and resource provision considered. There is a concise summary of the new GCSE IT syllabuses, and a section on using the Internet. An organisational structure for managing IT is reviewed, and there is practical advice on writing a whole school policy for IT. Details of training activities are included that are suitable for INSET and for use in teacher training. These are designed to heighten awareness of IT-related issues, including the extent to which IT should be embedded within the curriculum, and the roles and responsibilities of those who manage IT in secondary schools.

The applications of IT in school administration and management are reviewed. A wide range of software is described and the distributors' addresses are given. This includes comprehensive suites of integrated software that provide complete solutions to schools' needs, and discrete items of software that focus on solving particular problems at an economic cost. The use of technical jargon has been avoided wherever possible, and a glossary has been provided to clarify technical terms used in the text.

The views expressed in this book are the author's. Where possible, these are supported by reference to research evidence, statistics and professional consensus. However, much of what is written is based on the author's experience as an IT co-ordinator in secondary schools, as a Chief Examiner for GCSE IT and as an OFSTED inspector specialising in IT.

ACKNOWLEDGEMENTS

I am grateful to Helen Fairlie, Cyril Poster and other Routledge editorial staff who made useful criticisms of the text, and have been otherwise supportive throughout its writing and production. Colleagues at Shirley Boys High School in New Zealand, and at Rhodesway Upper School and Queensbury Upper School in Bradford, also have my thanks for their support while I was employed at each school. I also acknowledge the help and assistance given to me by the School of Education at the University of Huddersfield where I am now employed as a Senior Lecturer in Education, specialising in Information Technology. My wife, Jennie, has my thanks for her patient support. Her comments have been both useful and illuminating. My mother has also played her part in producing this book, carefully proofreading the entire text. Without the support of colleagues, family and friends this book would not have been written.

Material from the National Curriculum documents is Crown copyright. It is reproduced by permission of the Controller of HMSO.

Roger Crawford
Senior Lecturer in Education, specialising in Information Technology
Chief Examiner for GCSE Information Technology
OFSTED Inspector

LIST OF ABBREVIATIONS

ALU	Arithmetic and Logic Unit
AOL	America On-line
AT	Attainment Target
BASIC	Beginners All-purpose Symbolic Instruction Code
BEd	Bachelor of Education
BIT	Binary digit
C&G	City and Guilds of London Institute
CAD	Computer Aided Design
CAL	Computer Assisted Learning
CAM	Computer Aided Manufacture
CBAC	Cyd-Bwyllgor Addysg Cymru
CD-ROM	Compact Disk – Read Only Memory
CEC	Commission of the European Communities
COBOL	Common Business Orientated Language
COM	Computer Output on Microfilm
CPU	Central Processing Unit
CU	Control Unit
DDE	Direct Data Entry
DfEE	Department for Education and Employment
DT	Design Technology
DTP	Desk Top Publishing
EDI	Electronic Data Interchange
EFT	Electronic Funds Transfer
EWO	Educational Welfare Officer
FE	Further Education
GNVQ	General National Vocational Qualifications
GSCE	General Certificate of Secondary Education
GUI	Graphic User Interface
HE	Higher Education
HENSA	Higher Education National Software Archive
HoD	Head of Department
ILS	Integrated Learning System

INSET	In-Service Training
IS	Information System
IT	Information Technology
ITE	Initial Teacher Education
ITT	Initial Teacher Training
K	Kilobyte
KS3	Key Stage 3
KS4	Key Stage 4
LAN	Local Area Network
LCD	Liquid Crystal Display
LEA	Local Education Authority
MEd	Master of Education
MEG	Midland Examining Group
MICR	Magnetic Ink Character Recognition
MIS	Management Information System
NC	National Curriculum
NCC	National Curriculum Council
NCET	National Council for Educational Technology
NDTEF	National Design and Technology Education Foundation
NEAB	Northern Examinations and Assessment Board
NSG	Non-statutory guidance
OCR	Optical Character Recognition
OFSTED	Office for Standards in Education
OMR	Optical Mark Reader
OPAC	On-line Public Access Computer
PC	Personal Computer
PDA	Personal Digital Assistant
PGCE	Post Graduate Certificate in Education
PIR	Passive Infra-Red Detector
PoS	Programme of Study
PTA	Parent–Teacher Association
QTS	Qualified Teacher Status
RAM	Random Access Memory
RCD	Residual Current Device
RoA	Record of Achievement
ROM	Read Only Memory
RSA	Royal Society of Arts
SAT	Standard Assessment Task
SCAA	School Curriculum and Assessment Authority
SEG	Southern Examining Group
SEN	Special Educational Needs
SIMS	Schools Integrated Management System
SMT	Senior Management Team
SOHO	Small Office and Home Office

SPaG	Spelling, Punctuation and Grammar
TA	Teacher Assessment
TSI	Technology Schools Initiative
TVEI	Technical and Vocational Educational Initiative
ULEAC	University of London Examination and Assessment Council
URL	Uniform Resource Locator
VDU	Visual Display Unit
WAN	Wide Area Network
WIMP	Windows, Icons, Menus and Pointers
WJEC	Welsh Joint Education Committee
WORM	Write Once Read Many
WWW	World Wide Web
WYSIWYG	What You See Is What You Get

1

WHAT IS INFORMATION TECHNOLOGY?

Information Technology (IT) is a powerful tool. It significantly extends what people can do and as a learning tool it is particularly effective. Pupils encounter different facets and levels of knowledge using IT. Learning experiences can involve learning about a topic, and learning how to use the IT tools required, at both operational and conceptual levels. Suppose a pupil is using IT in English to produce a magazine; the pupil would learn operational skills and knowledge associated with an understanding of English, for example, spelling, grammar, punctuation, and how to write for a particular audience. At this level the IT skills learnt would be those that were required to operate the software being used, i.e., page layout; using different text fonts and sizes; importing pictures; and printing the finished product. However, learning also takes place at a much deeper level. In common with all technology, IT embodies the accumulated understandings of its makers. IT hardware and software are the products of extensive human thought; they are physical and intellectual, and highly co-ordinated and structured. Unlike most other technologies, pupils using IT have interactive access to these operational and conceptual structures. In learning how to use IT they actively interrogate them and, as a result, pupils learn dynamically how knowledge is acquired and organised.

IT is an interesting teacher. It can make learning easier and more attractive; for example, a resource for learning about animals could include written information about their habitat, and pictures of it. There could be video clips showing the animal running, accompanied by animated diagrams of the operation of their skeletal structure and muscles. This could be done using multimedia software. Multimedia is a means of constructing flexible and attractive teaching and learning resources that integrate text, pictures, animation, video and sound.

IT is also a patient and responsive teacher. Software does not tire of waiting for a response. Computer Aided Learning software can give pupils immediate feedback. Pupils are rewarded as they make incremental progress. This can be particularly helpful where pupils have learning difficulties. Rewards can be structured so that pupils are motivated to learn. Many computer games are attractive to pupils for similar reasons. Concerns arise when this leads to addictive behaviour and dependence; however, care should be taken not to confuse such negative characteristics with the length of time spent at the computer. In common with other activities, it is not the duration of the experience that is important but its quality.

IT is pupil-centred. Unlike traditional didactic teaching, strategies for teaching IT will emphasise pupil-centred, resource-based learning. This helps IT teachers with the particularly exaggerated problems they have in planning and controlling continuity, progression, differentiation, and breadth and depth of learning. In addition, where IT resources are relatively immobile, pupils must move to use them. They may need to use them at any time. These features of IT teaching and learning contrast sharply with traditional teacher-centred, didactic approaches based on inflexible timetables and strict rules controlling pupils' movement about the school.

IT supports open, independent and flexible learning. This level of support will increase as hardware becomes cheaper and more portable. In the future, pupils might be expected to provide their own computer in the same way that they now bring other equipment to school. This computer would not be like the ones we are now used to, with the large screens and other bulky hardware components now in common use. It could be a small, portable device used for entertainment as well as education. This portable computer could be integrated with the stereo and TV at home, and with local, national and international learning networks at school. Access to these networks at home would reduce the need for pupils to attend school. Schools will need to ensure that the availability of IT and other resources in the home or else-where is adequate for all pupils.

IT gives access to on-line learning resources, for example, on the World Wide Web (WWW). The WWW is based on the Internet which is a network of networks. TV cable networks and telephone networks are part of the Internet, bringing the WWW to most homes and schools. Multimedia learning resources could be available nationally and internationally on the WWW. The WWW also supports e-mail and on-line conferencing. The development of video-on-demand will make the full range of educational programmes available on these networks.

IT is everywhere. In addition to their experiences of IT in school, pupils come into contact with a variety of access points to larger IT networks and systems, such as supermarket checkouts, libraries, and cashpoints. As adults, they will directly or indirectly access large IT systems, such as telephone banking, Gas Board customer enquiries, the National Lottery, and the Driver Vehicle Licensing Centre (DVLC). Many will work with automated control systems for warehousing and manufacturing. New IT systems will be introduced or become more accessible. IT systems will be used for road traffic management, and home banking. Electronic tagging is being evaluated for control of criminals. Swipe card registration systems for school pupils can give accurate information about attendance. An understanding of what these IT systems can and cannot do, and an awareness of their responsibilities and rights, will help pupils become more effective citizens. Schools need to know what rights pupils have in relation to their record-keeping systems, and what demands will be made of them.

IT promotes sharing and collaboration. As international networks are up-graded, schools may join virtual consortia and these could extend current collaboration with the community, commerce, industry, colleges and univer-sities. Virtual consortia will be the building blocks of a global village; they could be regional so that local collaboration is supported, or may be inter-national in scope. Virtual consortia will share resources; they will develop their own educational and training programmes. Students of all ages could have open access to independent learning materials for distance learning in all subjects at all levels and this could be as general or as specialised as is desired.

IT promotes diversity. There are opportunities to learn about world cultures, religions and political systems across international networks; for some this is interesting; to others it is a threat. Freedom of access to the WWW may be denied as governments and others seek to control informa-tion. Censorship can be beneficial; few parents would wish their children to have easy access to pornography. However, complete control of information is rarely entirely beneficial for all. It is often difficult for those who control information to resist the temptation to control it for their own benefit. The widespread distribution of information does not guarantee that it is true and comprehensive. Schools are not neutral agents as they have their own partic-ular values. Careful thought is needed about the impact of IT on the ethos of the school.

IT is blind to gender, race, age and disability. It is not unknown for people to adopt alternative persona when corresponding using IT networks. Personal characteristics communicated at a distance using IT are largely under the control of the originator. However, equal opportunities can be a major issue when IT is used in schools. Competition between pupils for the use of IT resources can lead to the emergence of the unpleasant prejudices that often arise in the wider community. To help prevent this, pupils' access to IT should be carefully supervised and constantly monitored.

IT affects employment. Teleworking will become more widespread as, in the future, more people work from home. This trend is already evident; the Small Office and Home Office (SOHO) market sector is predicted to expand rapidly. Increasingly, employers hire employees in a global labour market. Pupils leaving school in the UK will compete for jobs in this inter-national market and they will need good IT skills to enter the market. Their wages and conditions will be the same as those of employees in other coun-tries. These trends will tend to increase wages for skilled work but push down wages for unskilled work. The future well-being of our pupils and our country depends on raising skill levels throughout the community. Schools must ensure pupils leave school with good IT skills.

IT is a valuable resource. It is not now uncommon for schools to buy the same computers as commercial companies, and to teach pupils using industry standard software. Schools are often more technologically advanced than many small businesses and this helps sell training services to local companies, earning income that can be reinvested in schools. Unfortunately, this also makes schools' IT resources more attractive to thieves.

IT is unpredictable. It is very difficult to predict how it will develop and this uncertainty makes planning difficult. Many of the above developments could radically affect how IT is organised and used in schools, and its impact on them. There is still a lack of consensus regarding when, how, where and by whom IT should be taught in secondary schools, and the extent to which IT should be integrated into the whole curriculum. A flexible whole school plan for the development of IT is essential. This book offers some guidelines to the successful adoption of IT in secondary schools, including the writing of a whole school IT policy.

2

THE IT CURRICULUM AND ITS ORGANISATION

THE NATIONAL CURRICULUM

The National Curriculum (NC) reflects the age-related organisation of education in England and Wales. Pupils begin eleven years of compulsory education at the age of 5 and may leave school at the age of 16. These are identified as year 1 through to year 11 respectively, and are grouped into four key stages (see Table 2.1). The NC requires that pupils in Key Stage 3 (KS3) should study English, Mathematics, Science, Technology (Design Technology and IT), History, Geography, Art, Music, Physical Education, a modern foreign language and Religious Education. This requirement is reduced to English, Mathematics, Science, Technology (Design Technology and IT), Physical Education, a modern foreign language, and Religious Education at Key Stage 4 (KS4). In Wales, the KS3 requirements are the same as in England, with the addition of Welsh, but at KS4 there is no mandatory requirement to study Technology or a modern foreign language.

The subject content of each NC subject is described in the relevant statutory orders. For each subject, this subject content may be subdivided into one or more Attainment Targets (ATs). Within each AT, the relevant subject content may be presented as a Programme of Study (PoS) for each key stage. Pupils' achievements in each AT are assessed in relation to 'levels' of attainment and these levels are described by 'level descriptions'. Most pupils are expected to achieve one of the levels from level 1 (the lowest) through to 8 (the highest). Above level 8, pupils are said to have achieved 'exceptional

Table 2.1 The association between age, year, key stage and the expected range of levels to be achieved

Age	Year	Key Stage	Expected range of levels
5 to 7	1 to 2	1	1 to 3
7 to 11	3 to 6	2	2 to 5
11 to 14	7 to 9	3	3 to 7
14 to 16	10 to 11	4	4 to 8

performance'. There is an expectation that pupils will achieve within a range of levels during a particular key stage. The relationship between age, school year, key stage and the expected range of levels of attainment is shown in Table 2.1.

IT IN KEY STAGE 3 AND KEY STAGE 4

Whilst both IT and Design Technology are included in the NC as a part of Technology, they each have their own statutory orders (DfE, 1995a). The statutory orders for IT are quite separate from the orders for Design Technology, and refer only to IT. There are also general references to the need for pupils to 'develop and apply their IT capability' in the statutory orders for most of the other NC subjects. In addition, non-statutory guidance for IT is provided by the School Curriculum and Assessment Authority (SCAA) and the National Council for Educational Technology (NCET). This elaborates on the statutory orders, providing details of specific types of software that could be used and examples of activities that might be used in the classroom. GCSE syllabuses also influence the IT subject content to be taught, and provide a means of assessment at the end of KS4.

The statutory orders for IT

The mandatory requirements for the study of IT are specified in the statutory orders (DfE, 1995a). In the 'Common Requirements' section, pupils' IT capability is characterised as:

> . . . an ability to use effectively IT tools and information sources to analyse, process and present information, and to model, measure and control external events. This involves:
>
> - using information sources and IT tools to solve problems;
> - using IT tools and information sources, such as computer systems and software packages, to support learning in a variety of contexts;
> - understanding the implications of IT for working life and society.

There are separate PoS for each of KS3 and KS4 which indicate the range of curriculum activities that pupils should experience. The PoS describe what pupils should do in terms of opportunities and themes. These opportunities and themes are further subdivided into several elements. The titles of the themes are:

- Communicating and handling information
- Controlling, measuring and modelling.

In KS3, pupils' attainment is assessed as one of levels 1 to 8, or, beyond level 8, as being of 'exceptional performance'. Teachers assess a pupil's level of attainment in IT using 'level descriptions', which are general statements of the skills, knowledge and understanding of IT that a pupil might have acquired. The level description given for attainment at level 5, for example, is:

> Pupils use IT to organise, refine and present information in different forms and styles for specific purposes and audiences. They select the information needed for different purposes, check its accuracy and organise and prepare it in a form suitable for processing using IT. They create sets of instructions to control events, and are becoming sensitive to the need for precision in framing and sequencing instructions. They explore the effects of changing the variables in a computer model. They communicate their knowledge and experience of IT and assess its use in their working practices.
>
> (DfE, 1995a)

It is assumed that pupils will be assessed at the end of KS4 by being entered for GCSE, GNVQ or another assessment scheme which need not be an external examination.

Alterations to the statutory orders require parliamentary legislation. However, IT hardware and software change rapidly, consequently, in order to avoid frequent recourse to Parliament, there is no mention of specific hardware or software in the statutory orders for IT. Unfortunately, as a result, the orders may seem somewhat vague in places. For example, in the KS4 PoS, element 1.d. indicates that pupils should be given opportunities to 'apply and continue to develop their IT skills in order to enhance their work in a variety of subject or vocational areas'. Similarly, element 2.b. in the theme of Communicating and handling information, states that pupils should be taught to 'use IT to enhance their own learning and the quality of their work'. The non-statutory guidance provided by both SCAA and NCET interprets the statutory orders in more detail. This non-statutory guidance can be altered without parliamentary legislation. It is hoped that it will be amended regularly, as the underlying technology changes, so that the IT curriculum remains up-to-date.

References to IT in the statutory orders for other NC subjects

There are few specific references to IT in the statutory orders for other NC subjects. However, there is a common requirement which appears in all of the statutory orders for the NC subjects that are mandatory at Key Stage 4, excluding Physical Education, which states that 'Pupils should be given the opportunities, where appropriate, to develop and apply their IT capability in their study of [the relevant NC subject]'.

The non-statutory guidance from SCAA

The non-statutory guidance for IT in KS3 is presented in two forms (SCAA, 1995b,c). There is a booklet clarifying the mandatory requirements, and leaflets that show how IT can be used to support and enhance pupils' work in other NC subjects. There is no non-statutory guidance for KS4.

The booklet: Key Stage 3 IT: the new requirements

This booklet contains non-statutory guidance and advice in interpreting and putting into practice the statutory orders for IT in the NC. In particular, in contrast to the statutory orders, the booklet names or describes specific types of software and hardware that schools need to provide pupils with an adequate experience of IT. Thus, in the booklet, pupils who have IT Capability are seen as having 'knowledge about the applications of IT and IT tools, such as wordprocessors, databases, spreadsheets, software for processing sound and images, and software for simulation and modelling'. There are also examples of appropriate classroom activities.

The SCAA non-statutory guidance states that pupils should become 'critical and largely autonomous' users of IT. They should be aware of how the use of IT can help them in their work and can improve the quality of their learning. IT is seen as extending what pupils can do, giving them access to a range of information sources and other resources that can be used to support their learning in all subjects.

Themes and sub-themes

The non-statutory guidance identifies two themes, each with several sub-themes. These are described in the boxes below:

THEME: COMMUNICATING AND HANDLING INFORMATION

Sub-theme: Communicating information
Pupils use IT to create, develop and communicate ideas in the form of words, numbers, pictures and sounds. The work pupils produce takes into account the purpose of the communication and the nature of the audience.

Sub-theme: Handling Information
Pupils use IT to collect, sort, classify and store information, and to access, edit, search and analyse it.

THEME: CONTROLLING, MEASURING AND MODELLING

Sub-theme: Controlling
Pupils use IT to control what happens. Pupils design, test and improve solutions to control problems.

Sub-theme: Measuring
Pupils use IT to monitor, measure and record events, perhaps over an extended period of time.

Sub-theme: Modelling
Pupils use IT to investigate real or imaginary situations by exploring computer based models of them. Pupils create, evaluate and improve their own models.

Within each sub-theme, details are given of the specific types of software and hardware that might be used, and a range of appropriate activities are described. The sub-themes are described at length in the non-statutory guidance, which should be referred to for more detailed information.

The leaflets: Key Stage 3 IT and the NC

There are leaflets available for specific NC subjects offering guidance on appropriate activities (SCAA, 1995c). The leaflets briefly describe a selection of classroom activities that are suitable for pupils learning or using IT within other subjects. There are leaflets for English, Mathematics, Science, Design and Technology, History, Geography, Modern Foreign Languages, Art and Music. These do not materially add to the content of the non-statutory guidance for IT, in so far as IT is concerned, though they are likely to prove useful to teachers of other subjects seeking inspiration and ideas.

The non-statutory guidance from NCET

The non-statutory guidance from NCET looks at ways of putting the statutory orders for IT into practice throughout the school curriculum. There is a lead booklet on approaches to implementing the IT curriculum, and a range of booklets each covering a single school subject (NCET, 1995a), for example, there are booklets for each of English, Mathematics, Science, and Design and Technology. The lead booklet *Approaches to IT Capability* describes different ways that teachers can start to make use of IT, and several models for organising the IT curriculum. A variety of related issues are considered, such as the need for planning for continuity, progression and differentiation in pupils' experiences of IT; the use of IT with SEN pupils; assessment;

monitoring and reviewing; and staff development. There is a useful matrix showing in which NC subject each element of the KS3 PoS could be covered. This also shows how the PoS are covered in the accompanying subject booklets. NCET recommend using such a matrix as a mechanism for mapping IT across the curriculum.

The subject booklets each describe several activities that address the subject PoS, for example, the English booklet suggests that pupils might use 'word-processors, graphics packages, and audio and video editing facilities' to 'explore the most effective ways of combining words, images and/or sounds' to produce a page for a magazine, or a short TV programme. NCET consider that these activities will help pupils achieve elements 1.b., 1.c. and 3.b. from the English KS3 PoS.

The NCET non-statutory guidance also suggests the general type of software and hardware that might be used. Again, these booklets should be referred to for more detailed information.

GCSE SYLLABUSES IN IT

GCSE IT syllabuses exert a major influence on teaching in KS4. Short Course and Full Course syllabuses are available. Both Short Course and Full Course GCSE IT syllabuses cover the KS4 PoS, however, a Full Course syllabus will contain additional IT subject content. A Short Course should be roughly half of a Full Course.

All GCSE syllabuses conform to the Mandatory Code of Practice (SCAA, 1995d) and are based on the GCSE criteria for IT (SCAA, 1995e). Consequently, they all have similar aims, objectives and subject content. However, the ways in which they conduct assessment may differ significantly (see Appendix 1, p. 143). In brief, the aims stated in the GCSE criteria are that:

- syllabuses must be consistent with the NC;
- pupils should have opportunities to use IT to solve problems;
- pupils should develop an understanding of the capabilities of a wide range of IT systems.

These aims are elaborated in the objectives. In full, the objectives state that pupils should be able to:

- apply their knowledge, skills and understanding of IT to a range of situations;
- analyse, design, implement, test, evaluate and document IT systems for use by others and develop understanding of the wider applications and effects of IT;
- reflect critically on the way they and others use IT;
- discuss and review the impact of IT applications in the outside world;

- consider the social, legal, ethical and moral issues and security needs for data which surround the increasing use of IT.

Pupils' IT capability is assessed for the GCSE by means of coursework and written examinations. The coursework is done throughout KS4, and is set, supervised and marked by pupils' own teachers. In contrast, the written examinations are taken by pupils at the end of KS4, and their setting and marking are the responsibility of the examination boards. Typically, coursework is 60 per cent of the final assessment, and the written examinations are 40 per cent. IT syllabuses are available from each of the GCSE examination boards. More information and copies of the syllabuses can be obtained from the subject officer for IT at the relevant examination board and the addresses of the examination boards are given in Appendix 4, p. 207.

In common with the non-statutory guidance from SCAA and NCET, GCSE syllabuses are unlikely to contain a definitive list of the software and hardware that are needed to ensure that pupils' experiences of IT in schools are satisfactory, which is surprising, since this would help schools ensure that their IT resources were adequate. A summary of the software and hardware needed is provided in the later chapters on practical considerations.

CURRICULUM MODELS

Whilst schools must cover the statutory PoS, the ways in which they organise their IT curricula are not mandatory. Schools choose to organise the delivery of the IT curriculum in a wide variety of different ways. In practice, three basic models of the IT curriculum have emerged. These are:

- the subject IT approach;
- the cross-curricular IT approach;
- the hybrid IT approach.

These different approaches to organising the IT curriculum are reviewed below.

Subject IT

This is the traditional approach taken by many schools. It is also referred to as the 'centralised' approach (NCET, 1996a). IT is taught as a separate subject; time is allocated on the timetable for IT in the same way that it is allocated for Mathematics, English, Science, and the other NC subjects. It is assumed that pupils will be taught IT, make use of IT, and be assessed in IT mainly in the timetabled subject of IT.

Prior to the implementation of the NC, many schools taught IT, or related subjects such as Computer Studies, as separate subjects in KS4. These appeared

11

as named subjects in the school's timetable and time was specifically allocated for them. They often covered a high proportion of the subject content of NC IT and it was therefore relatively easy for these schools to implement the NC. In these schools, the existing staffing, organisation of IT resources and curriculum structures were carried forward with few changes. The content of the courses changed with the introduction of the NC but the means of organising their delivery did not.

Unfortunately, this approach may cause serious resource problems. Current staffing and other resources may not be sufficient to allow all pupils to do IT. However, all pupils have an entitlement to follow a curriculum that includes the KS3 and KS4 IT PoS. If the traditional subject-based organisation is simply extended to accommodate all pupils, schools may find that they need to make a considerable investment in extra staffing and other IT resources. Alternatively, schools could decide to spread their existing resources more thinly. This might meet the statutory requirements, but may lead to a relatively insubstantial experience of IT for all pupils. This is particularly unsatisfactory for those pupils who might benefit from more in-depth studies. One solution is to offer all pupils a course that only covers the NC IT PoS, giving some the opportunity for more in-depth study. All pupils could follow a course leading to the GCSE IT (Short Course) at the end of KS4. A supplementary options course could be available leading to the more substantial GCSE IT (Full Course) for those pupils who choose to study IT in greater depth.

It has been suggested that the subject IT approach is unlikely to provide sufficiently rich contexts in which pupils can consolidate their IT skills (NCET, 1996a) but this is not necessarily so. IT skills are almost inevitably taught in context. These contexts may be satisfactory whether pupils experience them in IT or elsewhere. For example, when pupils are taught to use Desk Top Publishing (DTP) software, they may learn how to use it by producing a school newspaper and develop and consolidate their IT skills by doing this task. That the task is done in an IT lesson rather than an English lesson, or vice versa, need not influence the quality of their learning experiences.

Cross-curricular IT

In the cross-curricular approach, IT is taught and used only in the other NC subjects. There is no time allocated on the timetable specifically for IT as it is assumed that the teaching, use and assessment of IT will all take place in some, or all, of the other NC subjects. The cross-curricular IT model was recommended in the old non-statutory guidance (NCC, 1990a), and consequently, many schools adopted this approach.

The cross-curricular model can be organised in a variety of ways – for example, by mapping the sub-themes of the IT PoS to several other NC subjects. The sub-themes represent coherent groupings of the subject content. As there are only five sub-themes, the responsibility for teaching, using and assessing one or more entire sub-themes can be given to a particular subject. One possible arrangement is:

- The Communicating Information sub-theme is given to English.
- The Handling Information sub-theme is given to Geography.
- The Controlling sub-theme is given to Science.
- The Measuring sub-theme is given to Design Technology.
- The Modelling sub-theme is given to Mathematics.

This arrangement can help ensure coherence, continuity and progression in the IT curriculum, and simplicity of the associated planning and administration. However, the subjects given responsibility for delivering IT may find that the extra work is too great a burden in addition to their own subject teaching and other subjects may feel excluded. An alternative is to allow some of the subjects nominated to change or relinquish their sub-theme at the end of a key stage. Another possible arrangement is to allocate one sub-theme to a group of two or three associated subjects, allowing the subjects themselves to determine how they will share the responsibility.

Another means of ensuring that a comprehensive programme of IT is delivered across the curriculum is to design a number of coursework tasks that, taken together, cover the NC IT PoS. This approach has been tried at Rastrick High School with some success, following completion of a project funded by Calderdale and Kirklees TEC (Crawford, 1994b). Teacher trainees on a BEd course at the University of Huddersfield developed independent learning materials for cross-curricular IT to be done in English, Mathematics and Technology. These learning materials helped pupils prepare coursework tasks that, taken as a whole, covered the NC IT PoS. Where possible, the coursework tasks also met GCSE coursework requirements in both IT and the other subject.

Another possibility is for classroom teachers in other subjects and IT specialists to team teach. The IT specialist identifies a coherent programme of opportunities to study IT derived from the whole curriculum. The IT specialist then teaches and assesses IT skills while the other teacher concentrates on teaching the other subject. This approach can be successful but it is very expensive and it is not unusual to find that too little IT support is provided and that its availability is constrained. There is also an assumption that detailed forward planning is possible across a range of subjects but this may not be the case.

The teaching, use and assessment of IT across the curriculum can lead to overly complex organisation and administration. There is concern that pupils may not be taught IT effectively by non-specialist teachers; that too little specialist support will be available; and that assessment of pupils' IT skills may be of a variable standard. IT hardware may be spread thinly throughout the school so that whole class teaching of IT skills is not possible. Consequently, the cross-curricular approach is rarely entirely successful and in extreme cases it may lead to the effective disintegration of the IT curriculum.

Although cross-curricular IT can deliver the statutory PoS in KS4, it is unlikely that pupils will be adequately prepared for GCSE assessment. For GCSE IT, pupils will need to produce IT coursework, and will need to be prepared for the terminal examinations. However, as there is no time allocated in the timetable for IT, this must happen within the time allocation for other subjects, and may be neglected. Pupils' IT coursework tasks could be done in another NC subject, and jointly assessed for IT and that subject. Even so, time will need to be found for pupils to do revision specifically related to their IT examinations and it may prove difficult to ensure that this is done thoroughly.

The cross-curricular approach is unlikely to cover adequately the subject content of the GCSE IT Full Course. The cross-curricular model needs to be extended if pupils are to be prepared for Full Course assessment. This can be done in various ways, for example, a school could provide all of its pupils with their NC entitlement through an entirely cross-curricular programme of IT. In addition, pupils who choose to or who can benefit from further study may follow a supplementary taught course leading to GCSE assessment. This should require only 5 per cent of timetabled time for IT subject studies.

Hybrid IT

The hybrid approach is the most common in schools (Fox and Selwood, 1992; Yeomans *et al.*, 1995). There are a variety of hybrid models used in practice. The extension of the cross-curricular model described in the previous paragraph is one such variant. NCET (1996a) identify two variants: the 'kick start' approach and the 'skills core' approach. The kick start approach offers 'skills training only at the beginning of KS3, with all further development being through cross curricular use'. The skills core approach offers 'a central core of IT running through each year and aimed at developing skills which can then be used across the curriculum'. This approach attempts to combine the advantages of both the subject IT and cross-curricular IT models. It is similar to the 'ideal' hybrid model referred to throughout this book.

In the 'ideal' hybrid model, pupils are taught and assessed by IT specialists in IT subject classes, and use IT across the curriculum wherever possible. A course in IT, taught by a specialist teacher, could prepare pupils for assessment in the GCSE IT Short Course, and for using IT in other NC subjects. Such a course could occupy 5 per cent of timetabled time. Pupils are assessed by the IT specialist who teaches them. Pupils' use of IT across the curriculum will still need to be planned and recorded. However, teachers of other NC subjects will not need to teach and assess IT skills as this will be done in

IT subject studies; these teachers can give due priority to their own subjects, making use of IT when appropriate. Having acquired adequate IT skills in IT subject classes, pupils have the opportunity to make use of them in the variety of rich contexts provided by other NC subjects, and will need a minimum of support when they do so. As the teaching of pupils' IT skills is done in IT subject studies by a specialist, adequate coverage of the NC IT PoS can be ensured. Administrative and organisational difficulties are reduced, and the co-ordination of assessment is simplified.

Extending this hybrid IT approach, so that some pupils can undertake further study leading to a GCSE IT Full Course, will require extra timetabled time. However, an additional 5 per cent may not be required as pupils will have opportunities to consolidate their IT skills in other NC subjects.

Which model?

Schools must cover the statutory NC IT PoS but how they organise this is their responsibility. However, they are given considerable guidance from SCAA, NCET and OFSTED, although much of this is implicit. On the whole, the hybrid model is acknowledged to be the most practical approach for schools.

The SCAA non-statutory guidance states that 'time needs to be allocated to teaching IT skills ... as well as to practising and consolidating them' (SCAA, 1995b). It is recommended that time should be available for the teaching of IT skills as well as for using IT to enhance learning in other subjects. The non-statutory guidance describes pupils' entitlement to develop specific IT skills, and to use IT to support and enhance their learning in other subjects. IT skills should be developed, practised and consolidated in a 'variety of contexts'. What is recommended can be put into practice either by delivering IT entirely across the curriculum, or by a combination of IT subject teaching and its use throughout the curriculum; that is, there may be lessons in the subject of IT or its equivalent, in conjunction with well-planned opportunities to use IT across the curriculum.

NCET (1995a) consider that discrete IT courses may lead to 'thorough but sterile coverage, whilst delivering IT entirely across the curriculum may result in incomplete coverage of the PoS, or 'not making any progress beyond learning rudimentary skills'. They suggest that schools should 'develop a carefully designed IT course together with appropriate consolidation across the curriculum'.

OFSTED use inspection evidence collected in 1993/4 from 240 secondary schools as a basis for their comments (OFSTED, 1995). They remark that cross-curricular delivery of IT 'works only where subject teachers are also confident in IT, pupils' progress is monitored, and structures are in place for motivating and effectively coordinating delivery'. In contrast, where IT is taught as a subject 'coverage of the PoS is more rigorous; but often there are insufficient opportunities to apply the IT skills so acquired to work in other subjects. Absence of such opportunities deprives pupils of the benefits of rigorous training.' This leads them to conclude that the delivery of the IT PoS is most effective when there is 'some timetabled teaching of IT' combined with 'well supported opportunities to apply skills in other subjects'.

SUMMARY

The statutory orders for IT define what must be taught. There are separate PoS for KS3 and KS4. Level descriptions are given so that teachers can assess pupils' IT capability throughout KS3. The non-statutory guidance from SCAA and NCET elaborates the subject content of the statutory orders, and reviews related issues. GCSE IT Full Course and Short Course syllabuses provide more detail of what should be taught in KS4. They are the main means of assessing pupils' IT capability at the end of KS4.

Schools can choose how they organise the delivery of the IT curriculum and a variety of different ways are possible. Three models of the IT curriculum have emerged:

- the subject IT approach;
- the cross-curricular IT approach;
- the hybrid approach.

SCAA, NCET and OFSTED implicitly recommend the hybrid model as the most practical approach for schools. There are many variants of this hybrid model. The author advocates that pupils should be taught and assessed in specialist IT subject lessons, and use IT to support their learning throughout the curriculum.

3

ASSESSMENT, RECORDING AND REPORTING

Assessment is an essential part of good teaching. There should be regular assessment of pupils' IT capability. Properly planned and co-ordinated formative assessment will be helpful in clarifying what needs to be taught. This should be recorded in such a way that it is clear how the whole assessment process leads to the summative assessment reported to parents. Moderation ensures that assessment is consistent, and can provide fruitful opportunities for professional development. The IT curriculum model adopted will have some impact on the process of assessment, recording and reporting.

KEY STAGE 3

Schools are currently required to report pupils' progress in IT in years 7 and 8 to parents, and must report a NC level for IT at the end of KS3. The NC IT orders contain programmes of study and level descriptors. It is almost implicit that all a pupil's work in IT will be collected together before a summative assessment of a pupil's level of attainment is made, though this is not a statutory requirement.

Organising the collection of the evidence to be assessed and its summative assessment are relatively straightforward for the subject IT approach to the curriculum. In this case, IT will be taught and assessed by a specialist IT teacher. This teacher can reasonably be expected to take responsibility for the assessment and reporting requirements of the classes he or she teaches. Most of the evidence to be assessed will be the work pupils will do in their IT class. The process of assessment, recording and reporting is likely to be similar to that of other subject departments, such as Mathematics.

If the cross-curricular IT approach is adopted, pupils may be taught, use or be assessed in IT in almost any NC subject. If all the evidence pupils generate is to be assessed, there will need to be procedures for collecting it together for each pupil, assessing it, and recording and summarising the assessments made and this must be done thoroughly and systematically if pupils are to be credited with all the work they have successfully completed.

17

Either pupils themselves will need to take responsibility for collecting their evidence or there will need to be systematic procedures for teachers to do this. Pupils could be asked to record their experiences throughout the curriculum using log books and put all their work in a file. However, some pupils cannot be relied on to do this thoroughly. Consequently, schools may adopt procedures that involve teachers in collecting and assembling the assessment evidence. This process can easily become quite complex, laborious and time-consuming. For example, suppose a pupil learns to use DTP software in English; evidence of this achievement will need to be assembled and assessed, and the pupil's achievements recorded and summarised, for both IT and English. The evidence may need to be accessible to both the IT co-ordinator and the English teacher. All the evidence a pupil has produced in all subjects must be assembled before that pupil's IT capability can be assessed using the NC level descriptors and this evidence may then need to be returned to the subject where it originated. As there will be many items of evidence per pupil per year drawn from a variety of subjects, the task of collecting, assessing and summarising all the evidence for every pupil in the school could be overwhelming.

It is almost always easier to collect together and summarise teachers' assessments of pupils' IT capability in a range of subjects than to collect all the assessment evidence they have produced in these subjects and assess it. Collecting together and summarising teachers' assessments should be done by a group of teachers. These could be IT specialists, or form or house tutors. The latter alternative is worth considering; it is not unusual for schools to adopt a procedure for preparing school reports which consists of teachers writing a separate report for each pupil in their subject. These separate reports, each for one pupil in one subject, are sent to the form or house tutor. These tutors then organise pupils to collect their separate subject reports and assemble them into their school report booklet to be sent home to their parents. Where schools have this or a similar procedure well established, it is relatively easy to extend and adapt it to collect together teachers' assessments of each pupil's IT capability in their separate subjects. This method also has the advantage of keeping pupils well informed regarding their progress.

One possibility is shown in Form 1 (see Figure 3.1); this could be used to record a pupil's attainment in IT in a particular subject such as English. Similar records could be produced for each subject a pupil studies and these could be assembled and Form 2 (see Figure 3.2) used to summarise them. The level of attainment could be recorded as an NC level if required; or this might be adapted to give better discrimination, for example, by using a decimalised level such as 4.1, 4.2, etc.; or might be recorded in some other way devised by the school. This system may be particularly useful where a clear mapping of the IT curriculum to specific subjects is based on a distribution of the sub-themes.

Name	Form	Year

Sub-theme/subject	Level of attainment	Teacher	Date
Communicating Information in English			
Description of evidence produced			

Figure 3.1 Form 1: a form that could be used to record a pupil's attainment in IT in a particular subject

Name	Form	Form

Sub-theme/subject	Level of attainment		
Communicating Information in English			
Handling Information in Geography			
Controlling in Design Technology			
Measuring in Science			
Modelling in Mathematics			
Overall level of attainment is		Teacher	Date

Figure 3.2 Form 2: a form that could be used to summarise the assessments made using Form 1

This mapping of the sub-themes is shown in the example:

- The Communicating Information sub-theme is given to English.
- The Handling Information sub-theme is given to Geography.
- The Controlling sub-theme is given to Design Technology.
- The Measuring sub-theme is given to Science.
- The Modelling sub-theme is given to Mathematics.

19

Name		Form	Year

Element	KS3 IT 'Opportunities' and 'Communicating Information' in English	Brief description of evidence	Level of attainment	Teacher	Date
	Opportunities				
1.a	uses IT autonomously				
1.b	considers purposes of using IT				
1.c	designs, evaluates and improves IT				
1.d	investigates problems using IT				
1.e	considers the limitations of IT				
	Communicating Information				
2.a	creates presentations for different audiences, integrating several forms of information				
2.b	selects appropriate IT resources				
2.c	conducts systematic searches				
2.d	collects, inputs, processes and analyses information				
2.e	interprets and displays information, checking its accuracy and validity				

Figure 3.3 Form 3: a more detailed version of Form 1

The advantage of this system is that the actual evidence produced by a pupil does not need to be assembled as it is assessed in the subject where it originates and remains there. The disadvantages are that the evidence is not available when a summary assessment is made; that many teachers will be involved, making consistency hard to achieve; and that not all the teachers involved in assessing the evidence will be specialist IT teachers.

It might be argued that this system lacks detail as it does not ensure assessment has taken place in all the elements of the opportunities and themes described in the NC PoS. However, to do so may result in assessment and record keeping that is far too detailed. Forms 3 (see Figure 3.3) and 4 (see Figure 3.4) are more detailed versions of Forms 1 and 2 respectively. A slightly different version of Form 3 would be needed for each subject.

Whatever system of record keeping is adopted, it should be both manageable and realistic; assessment and record-keeping should not become an intolerable burden to teachers and schools. Effective assessment and record-keeping systems devised for the cross-curricular IT approach are likely to be more complex, laborious and time-consuming than those for the IT subject approach. Consequently, many schools have found it difficult to meet their responsibilities with regard to assessment, recording and reporting pupils' levels of attainment in IT where the cross-curricular IT approach has been adopted.

Name			Form		Year

KS3 PoS	Cl in En	Hl in Ge	C in DT	Me in Sc	Mo in Ma
1.a					
1.b					
1.c					
1.d					
1.e					
1.f					
2.a					
2.b					
2.c					
2.d					
2.e					
3.a					
3.b					
3.c					
3.d					
3.e					
3.f					

Overall level of attainment is		Teacher	Date

Figure 3.4 Form 4: a more detailed version of Form 2

The hybrid IT approach straddles both the subject IT and cross-curricular IT approaches. Procedures for assessment, recording and reporting are likely to be determined by the particular curricular hybrid constructed, and will have some of the advantages and disadvantages of each extreme. One

21

way is to do almost all the assessment, recording and reporting necessary within the subject IT component of the curriculum with evidence from other subjects being reported internally to IT teachers on Form 1. This can then be used to enrich external reporting.

KEY STAGE 4

There is currently no requirement to report pupils' progress in IT to parents during or at the end of KS4. However, as pupils must follow the NC IT PoS throughout KS4, many schools will wish to do so. In particular, parents are likely to want pupils to acquire some qualification in IT as this will help their future careers.

Procedures for assessment, recording and reporting in KS3 could be carried forward into KS4. However, conformity to the regulations for the public examinations that pupils will be entered for at the end of KS4 is of great importance to teachers of pupils in years 10 and 11. It would therefore seem sensible to design a record-keeping system, which relates closely to that required by the external examination boards. However, the assessment and record-keeping methodologies of external assessment can be radically different from that of the NC. Consequently, schools may abandon NC-style assessment and record-keeping during KS4, possibly at the end of year 10, and adopt the methodology of their chosen GCSE or other external examination board.

Form 5 (see Figure 3.5) is similar to the assessment and record-keeping form for GCSE IT adopted by the SEG. The 1998 SEG syllabus takes a 'problem-solving' approach to the assessment of IT coursework that closely follows the strategies adopted when IT is applied in commerce and industry. The required record-keeping supports this approach.

All GCSE examination boards require that records of the assessment of pupils' coursework should be sent to them in the format they specify. Such records do not need to show progression or relate directly to the curriculum organisation of the school. Pupils do the coursework in school and it is assessed by their teachers who record their pupils' results on the forms provided by the examination board. The marking of the coursework is then moderated by the examination board and the coursework mark is later combined with the mark for the written examination to arrive at an overall grade for GCSE.

MODERATION

Whatever strategy is used for collecting and assessing pupils' work, there will need to be some well-understood mechanism for moderation. Moderation is necessary as different teachers will be involved in the assessment of pupils' coursework. It is a means of ensuring that all teachers apply the assessment

INFORMATION TECHNOLOGY – COURSEWORK

Name of Centre		Centre Number	
Candidate's Name		Candidate Number	

Criteria	Marks awarded
Choice of problem	
Description of problem	
Investigation and analysis of problem, and specification of solution	
Specification and Design of solution	
Implementation of solution	
I. Resources	
II. Data collection, data capture and input	
III. Data verification and validation	
IV. Data and program structures	
V. Output format	
Testing of solution	
Documentation of solution	
Evaluation of solution	
Spelling, Punctuation and Grammar	
Total mark	

Figure 3.5 Form 5: a form for recording the assessment of GCSE IT coursework, based on that used in the SEG IT syllabus

criteria in the same way, producing reliable, consistent judgements of the standards pupils achieve.

At Key Stage 4, coursework submitted for assessment for GCSE IT must be internally moderated in each school before being moderated by the relevant examination board as this ensures that standards in schools are consistent and in line with the standard set by the examination board. Further inter-board moderation ensures consistency at a national level. Other coursework assessments that are internal to the school should also be moderated to

23

ensure consistent standards. Moderation is essential if pupils' coursework is to be consistently assessed. A methodology for the moderation of IT coursework within the school should be agreed. If this subsumes the methodology that must be adopted for end of KS4 moderation, there will be no need to have different methodologies at each Key Stage.

Moderation involves teachers looking at each other's assessments of pupils' work, and agreeing that they too would have assessed the work as being of the same standard. A common methodology involves teachers re-marking a sample of each other's assessments (i.e. cross-marking); having discussed any discrepancies, they then arrive at agreed standards. This discussion takes place in a moderation meeting involving all those teachers who have assessed pupils' work. Cross-marking may be carried out before or during the meeting. Discussion at the moderation meeting is likely to focus on resolving the discrepancies that have arisen during cross-marking. Teachers later adjust their initial assessments of all the work they have marked to make them consistent with the standards agreed in the moderation meeting; in this manner, the meeting determines agreed standards.

A similar process may take place when GCSE coursework is externally assessed. Schools' representatives take samples of their internally moderated assessments to an area moderation meeting where regional agreement is reached. Similarly, representatives from the area meeting may attend a national moderation meeting; in this way, consistent standards may be achieved in and between schools.

There are many variations of this moderation methodology. The area moderation meeting is sometimes replaced by a regional moderator who is responsible for ensuring that all schools in the region are making assessments that are consistent with national standards. The coursework from each school, or a sample of it, may be sent by post to the regional moderator who re-marks it. Alternatively, the regional moderator may visit the school. Schools are then informed if their assessments conform to national standards, or must be adjusted in line with them.

Internal moderation is likely to be more complex and time-consuming where the cross-curricular IT approach is adopted in a school, as substantially more teachers, from a variety of different subject areas may be involved in assessing IT coursework. There is often less likelihood of immediate agreement between teachers from different subject backgrounds, as the cultures of their own subjects will influence their assessments of the IT coursework. In this case, it is likely that moderation meetings may need to be held for each subject grouping. There may need to be separate moderation meetings for IT in English, IT in Mathematics, and IT in Technology before the school moderation meeting can take place.

Moderation is easiest where only a few teachers are involved and these teachers are specialists in the subject being assessed. The subject IT and hybrid IT approaches lead to relatively straightforward moderation as all the assessment can be done by a few specialist IT teachers. Where only one teacher in the school is involved in making all the assessments, no in-school moderation is necessary.

Moderation may be assisted if there are examples of pupils' work available that represent agreed standards at different levels of achievement. A school portfolio of pupils' work might be assembled. Brief explanatory notes accompanying this portfolio could describe how the standards recorded in school relate to externally moderated standards year on year and this could include feedback from external moderators. Such a portfolio could be powerful evidence that the school is achieving, maintaining or improving standards of achievement in IT.

SUMMARY

Assessment should be fair and consistent. It should be carried out thoroughly and systematically so that pupils can be credited with all the work they have successfully completed. Where the cross-curricular IT approach is adopted, the arrangements needed to organise this may be more complex, laborious and time-consuming than for the subject IT and hybrid IT approaches.

Schools can organise assessment, recording and reporting in different ways. Whatever system is adopted, it must result in an individual summary of what each pupil can do, and it must meet statutory requirements. However, the system adopted should be both manageable and realistic. Assessment, recording and reporting should not become an intolerable burden.

Moderation is a means of ensuring that all teachers are applying the same assessment criteria reliably and consistently. This may be facilitated if there is a portfolio of pupils' work available showing representative standards. Moderation is easiest where only a few subject specialists are involved. The subject IT and hybrid IT approaches lead to relatively straightforward moderation, whereas, with the cross-curricular IT approach, this is likely to be more complex.

4

IT POLICY

Every school should have a policy for IT and a plan for its implementation.

(NCC, 1990a)

Schools should have a whole school policy for IT as it is both a cross-curricular skill and a NC subject in its own right. 'A whole school IT policy is a statement of the beliefs, values and goals of a school staff working co-operatively in the context of using IT in the operation of that school' (NCET, 1996d). This should be a working document well grounded in what is happening throughout the school. It should include a realistic implementation plan that enables the school to meet the requirements of the NC. The IT policy should also provide a clear vision for the future, providing targets for the overall development of IT within the school in the long term.

Headteachers would be right to assume that OFSTED inspectors will want to see evidence of thorough and effective planning of the IT curriculum, and a costed development plan for the provision of the necessary IT resources.

DEVELOPING A WHOLE SCHOOL IT POLICY

Writing an IT policy is not an exact, mechanistic process. Unique features of each school will find their expression in the IT policy. The following is not a prescription for writing an IT policy but some suggestions that will hopefully be helpful to those who attempt this task.

The first stage in developing an IT policy is to describe the long-term aims of the policy. Next, an audit of what is currently being done in the school should be carried out. When it is clear where the school is going and where it is starting from, an action plan can be developed that will help the school move forward.

The statement of the aims, the audit and the action plan is likely to cover:

- the management structure for IT;
- the IT curriculum and its organisation;

- the assessment, recording and reporting of pupils' work in IT; and arrangements for the moderation;
- provision of IT resources including hardware and software, and arrangements for security, disaster recovery, and the implementation of the Data Protection Act;
- equal opportunities issues;
- staffing and staff INSET;
- funding.

It is unwise to plan the development of IT resources in detail more than one year ahead. The underlying technology, and its cost, change very rapidly and have an immediate impact on what schools are able to do and how they can do it. The development of an IT policy is an on-going activity; the printed policy can only be a snapshot of the school's resources and intentions at the time it was written. 'It is virtually impossible for a written school IT policy to remain up to date' (Harris, 1994). Consequently, it is essential that the written IT policy is reviewed and updated every year.

AIMS

The aims are developed within the IT policy as the long-term goals that the school seeks to achieve. For practical purposes, the 'long term' can be considered to be a period of about five years. The aims should be realistic and achievable within the given time span. This is not the place for speculation akin to science fiction but an opportunity to state what the school wishes to work towards. It is necessary to think seriously and carefully about the aims of the school. However, as they are long-term goals, they should not be regarded as inflexible; they are a statement of intent that inform planning in the short term. The IT policy might begin with a statement of the overall aims, that is, a 'mission' statement. This is a general statement of intent; more detailed aims will follow, perhaps organised under the sub-headings used in this chapter or aggregates of these where this is more meaningful (see the example IT policy on p. 46).

It is important that the aims should clearly represent the ambitions of the school with regard to the development of IT in the long term. If the IT policy is to engage the efforts of the whole school, the aims should reflect the views of the whole school. It is therefore important that the views of those who are closely involved with IT in the school are balanced by the views of others who have different perspectives. Whilst the IT Co-ordinator may have well-informed opinions about the direction that the development of IT in the school should take, it is probable that he or she will have (and probably should have) a highly partial viewpoint. If the IT Co-ordinator is asked to write the aims, it is essential that these are thoroughly evaluated by more impartial members of staff. The statement of aims determines how IT will be developed in the school. It is ultimately used to direct funding and other resources to particular teachers and departments and, therefore, it is prudent to ensure that the statement of aims represents as broad a perspective as is possible.

Management structure

Often, when a policy statement is required, the Headteacher will ask the person in charge of the relevant subject department, or the person who has the responsibility for the co-ordination of the cross-curricular theme, skill or dimension, to write it. Let us suppose that the Headteacher asks the HoD Mathematics to produce a written policy document showing how the Mathematics curriculum is to be implemented throughout the school and to outline forward plans for the department. The HoD Mathematics will know what will be taught, when it will be taught and who will teach it. Arrangements for assessment will relate to how teaching within the Mathematics department is organised. The HoD Mathematics can expect that all those timetabled to teach Mathematics can do so! Writing a policy document within a well-known and well-defined subject area, such as Mathematics, is not easy but who is able to write the policy and what issues it will address are relatively clear; this is not so when an IT policy is written.

When developing an IT policy, the need to organise some aspects of IT across the curriculum may be a complicating factor. Pupils' experiences of IT may happen in many, perhaps all, subjects of the NC. Management structures will be needed to support a whole school approach. Features such as planning of the curriculum; assessment, recording and reporting; access to IT resources; and INSET will all have to be co-ordinated throughout the whole school. Consequently, developing a whole school IT policy may be a somewhat more complex task than writing a policy that predominantly addresses issues within the relatively well-defined focus of a traditional subject department. Moreover, it may not be entirely realistic to expect that all the teachers who might be asked to teach, use and assess IT will already have sufficient skills to do so. The development of an IT policy will involve the whole school and, therefore, the IT Co-ordinator alone should not be left to write the school's IT policy.

A management structure will be needed that is sufficiently effective and authoritative to organise the development, implementation, monitoring and evaluation of the IT policy throughout the school. Whilst this will inevitably redefine itself as the IT policy is developed and put into practice, it is useful to have, at least, the foundations of a suitable management structure in place at the beginning.

The Non-Statutory Guidance (NCC, 1990a) recommended the following arrangements for ensuring a co-ordinated approach to IT throughout the curriculum. These remain a useful indication of the level of organisation required to manage IT effectively.

- Every school should have a Co-ordinating Group for IT. This committee should consider the school's IT policy and implementation plan, and review practice. The membership of the Co-ordinating Group should include the IT Co-ordinator, the IT Manager and two or three representatives from different subject departments. The subject department representatives will prevent important decisions affecting the curriculum being made by a few IT specialists. The Co-ordinating Group might also include a member of the Senior Management Team (SMT).
- Every school should have an IT Co-ordinator. The IT Co-ordinator should report direct to senior management. The IT Co-ordinator should be responsible for organising pupils' IT experiences throughout the curriculum into a coherent, integrated framework. The IT Co-ordinator should have the skills to work with other teachers.
- Schools may also have an IT Manager. The IT Manager will be responsible to the IT Co-ordinator. The IT Manager will have the technical skills required for the management of the school's IT resources and will have time allocated to do this task.
- Technician support for the IT Manager is desirable.
- Heads of subject departments are responsible for ensuring that their departmental schemes of work support the school's IT policy.
- Every teacher is responsible for teaching IT and using IT to support learning.

These arrangements are reasonable but not entirely satisfactory. Schools that have put these arrangements in place have still encountered problems in providing pupils with a coherent experience of IT throughout the curriculum.

Problems can arise because of the assumption that all teachers will be willing and able to incorporate IT in their lessons, and that they will have sufficient time to consider how this might be done. This may not be the case in practice. Teachers' willingness to incorporate IT into their lessons cannot be assumed. A teacher of English, for example, might well be more interested in teaching English than IT. Our English teacher is likely to be (and probably should be) more concerned about pupils' performance in English than in IT, especially in reported, national assessments. How, then, can we encourage teachers to make use of IT? Part of the solution is to raise the priority teachers give to developing their use of IT in the classroom. One way that this can be done is by increasing the imperatives to use IT that are implicit in the management structure. A specific member of the SMT should be given responsibility for whole school IT. Unless the IT Co-ordinator is also a member of the SMT, the responsibility for organising IT provision on a day-to-day basis will be delegated to him or her. The IT Co-ordinator will report to the designated member of the SMT who will retain overall responsibility for IT in the school.

The designated member of the SMT should chair the IT Co-ordinating Group. Membership of this committee should be extended to include a representative from every subject department, preferably the Head of Department. These subject representatives will have the responsibility for ensuring that decisions regarding the IT curriculum and resources reflect the needs of the whole school. They should also be given responsibility for ensuring that the school's IT policy is implemented within their own departments. This will ensure that at least some development is taking place within each department and that there is an adequate reporting mechanism to identify problems. It is then the responsibility of the IT Co-ordinator or the designated member of the SMT to take the appropriate action to ensure implementation of the IT policy.

Management structures should include arrangements for the monitoring of the effectiveness of management itself. This might include regular reviews of performance in relation to agreed targets with prior agreement on the action to be taken if there is under- or over-performance. Accurate, independent minutes of meetings will also help indicate whether management is functioning effectively.

The curriculum and its organisation

When writing the aims, a decision will have to be made regarding the approach to organising the IT curriculum that is desirable in the long term. A cross-curricular approach is often recommended. Whilst the cross-curricular approach has its attractions, many schools have found it difficult to implement in practice. The subject IT approach can give pupils guaranteed access to an entitlement curriculum. However, it cannot provide rich contexts in which pupils can explore the variety of uses of IT. The hybrid IT approach places the teaching and assessment of IT in subject specialist classes, and encourages pupils to make use of IT throughout the curriculum wherever this is appropriate. The issues affecting the IT curriculum and its organisation have been reviewed in an earlier chapter.

Assessment, recording and reporting

When it has been decided what curriculum model is to be adopted and how it will be organised, a means of assessing, recording and reporting pupils' attainment and progress should be planned. Whatever system is seen as desirable, it must result in at least an individual summary of what each pupil can do and the progress each is making so that this can be reported to parents. There will also need to be some well understood and clear mechanism for moderation of the assessments made by different teachers. Some possible arrangements have been reviewed in an earlier chapter.

IT Resources

Some aspects of the management of IT resources that should be dealt with in a comprehensive IT policy are reviewed below. They are reviewed at greater length in the later chapters.

Hardware

The ideal mix of hardware, and how it will be distributed throughout the school, may be described in the aims of the IT policy. As there is unlikely to be sufficient hardware to meet all requirements, schools should employ the hardware available in the way that best supports their approach to the IT curriculum.

If the cross-curricular IT approach is adopted, hardware should be distributed to easily accessible locations throughout the school. One or more computers could be located in each classroom. Whilst this makes IT hardware available to each class, there are considerable disadvantages associated with this particular strategy. A more realistic alternative is to distribute the hardware in clusters throughout the school. This may be done in a way similar to the distribution arising from the hybrid IT approach. However, in this case, it is likely that the specialist IT facility will be greatly reduced or even entirely absent.

In contrast, if the subject IT approach is adopted, all IT hardware can be concentrated into adjacent IT rooms with little or no hardware distributed around the school. Unfortunately, the hardware may then not be easily accessible to classes in subjects other than IT.

The hybrid IT approach leads to a distribution of hardware that is a compromise between centralising all the IT hardware in a few, adjacent IT rooms and distributing the hardware to every classroom in the school. The specialist IT facility is developed to a limited extent so that IT can be taught to large classes. Possibly two or three IT rooms will be needed. However, these IT rooms may be located in different parts of the school. Small clusters of computers are also maintained in various locations throughout the school, where access is easy. A cluster of computers located in the school library will be readily accessible and can be supervised easily. In some instances, one or two computers can be located in specific classrooms where they will be heavily used, for example, a few computers may be permanently located in science for data logging experiments. This approach can provide adequate facilities for specialist IT studies, and ease of access for all pupils in all subjects.

The decision to standardise on one type of hardware, to introduce a limited choice or make available the widest possible range of types of hardware is also important. With the same computers in use throughout the school, the cross-curricular IT, subject IT and hybrid IT approaches to the curriculum can be associated with the particular ways of distributing IT hardware described above. The introduction of even a limited choice of hardware affects this association. If a school has chosen the hybrid IT approach with the distribution of IT hardware described above, it is anticipated that pupils will be taught how to use IT in their specialist classes and will use IT throughout the curriculum. However, if pupils are taught IT on one type of hardware, and are then expected to use IT on a different type of hardware, it is unlikely that they will be able to do so without additional instruction from the subject teacher. Unfortunately, it is unrealistic to expect that pupils will learn how to use all the IT resources available to the school in specialist IT classes. This thwarts the intention of the hybrid IT approach that pupils will learn IT skills in specialist classes, and then use them throughout the curriculum without further specialist teaching.

Similarly, if the cross-curricular IT approach is adopted, pupils may not, in practice, have easy access to suitable hardware. They may not be able to use the hardware that is available because of all the different types deployed throughout the school. These problems are exacerbated if the school has decided to make available the widest range of IT hardware possible. However, there are good reasons to ensure that pupils do experience a range of different types of computers: it is unlikely they will always have available to them the type of computer they are familiar with at school; also, the underlying technology changes so rapidly that even the same type of computer may eventually be used in radically different ways.

With the subject IT approach, pupils' access to hardware can be more closely regulated. Standardised hardware could be used throughout pupils' planned IT curriculum or more variety introduced as and when this is seen as being desirable.

Software

How the school believes that continuity, progression and differentiation are best achieved in pupils' experiences of IT software should be written into the aims of the IT policy. Software should be easy to use and understand, for pupils working at different levels of ability. Using the software should make it more likely that pupils will make progress in both IT and the subject in which they are using IT. It should not make it more difficult, for example, if a spreadsheet is being used in Business Studies to generate graphs that show where the break-even point occurs, it should be easier to use the spreadsheet than draw the graphs by hand. Pupils who have difficulty understanding the concept of the break-even point, should be able to use the spreadsheet to explore this concept, easily generating the graphs that will help them understand it.

Pupils should have available to them a range of software that supports their learning as their knowledge and understanding of IT develops. A single piece of software with different levels of access of increasing difficulty is ideal. Alternatively, different pieces of the same type of software of increasing complexity may be made available as pupils progress. In each case, there is an assumption of planned access so that pupils learn to use progressively more complex software.

The decision to standardise on one type of software, introduce a limited choice or make available the widest possible range is also important. With standardised software in use on the same type of hardware, the three approaches to the curriculum characterised can be associated with the particular ways of distributing IT hardware described. The use of even a few different examples of the same type of software can affect pupils' ability to make use of IT easily. If a school has chosen the hybrid IT approach with the associated distribution of IT hardware described above, it is anticipated that pupils will be taught how to use software, such as a wordprocessor, in their specialist IT classes and will use it throughout the curriculum. However, if pupils are taught how to use one wordprocessor in their IT class and are then expected to use a different wordprocessor in another subject, it is unlikely that they will be able to do so without some additional instruction from the subject teacher. Once again, this thwarts the intention of the hybrid IT approach that pupils will learn how to use IT in specialist classes and then use it throughout the curriculum without additional specialist teaching.

If the cross-curricular IT approach is adopted, pupils may not have easy access to suitable software because they are unable to use that which is available to them. These problems are compounded if the school has decided to make available the widest range of IT software possible. The same reasons apply here for ensuring that pupils do experience a range of different types of software: it is unlikely that they will always have available to them the type of software they have been used to in school; even the same software may change considerably between different versions.

With the subject IT approach, pupils' access to software can be more closely managed. Standardised software could be used throughout the planned IT curriculum or more variety introduced as required.

The means of distribution of software throughout the school should also be decided. This can be done either using a network or on local hard disks or floppy disks, or a combination of all of these. A network can be used to make all the school's software available to any pupil using any computer anywhere in the school. The software available can be restricted to only a few approved examples or a wide variety of different software can be made accessible. A network can be controlled centrally by the network manager. Central control facilitates regulation so that the software available supports the planned curriculum. With a network, the network manager only sets up the software once, on the fileserver. Access is then given to the software from anywhere on the network. This reduces the work involved considerably and can make security much easier to maintain.

Installing software on a computer's local hard disk may be the best arrangement when software needs to be made available at a specialist or isolated location. For example, it may be better to set up software for music applications on the local hard disk of a dedicated computer as these applications may only be used in music. In addition, the computer can be used in various locations that may not have access points to the school's network, such as on the stage in the school hall.

If a single piece of software is used on a small number of computers, on a limited number of occasions, it may be easier to distribute the software on floppy disks rather than install it on a network or on local hard disks. However, distributing software more widely on floppy disks can be very cumbersome, for example, to use a database with a class sharing fifteen computers that are not networked, a teacher could need thirty or more floppy disks. These floppy disks may have to be carried to the IT rooms, distributed to pupils, supervised to prevent pupils damaging them, collected in at the end of the lesson, then securely put away. The database would not be available to pupils at other times unless they collect the required floppy disks from their teachers. This is a time-consuming, administrative task that should be avoided if at all possible.

A network is almost essential if the cross-curricular IT approach is adopted as it is the only practical means of distributing software so that it is easily available on demand throughout the school. Local hard disks are useful for the hybrid IT or cross-curricular IT approaches for highly specialist applications or remote locations. Distribution on floppy disks should be confined to software that is not often used. Software distribution over a combination of a school network, local hard disks and floppy disks, is probably the most practical approach. Each particular way of distributing software is useful in some but not all circumstances.

Security

An effective means of ensuring the security of IT resources may be described in the aims. IT resources are expensive, and often have a high resale value. Schools that do not carefully secure their IT resources are likely to have them damaged or stolen. It may be that the general security precautions implemented in the school are adequate, but additional measures may need to be taken.

Unfortunately, security measures will have an impact on pupils' access to IT resources, for example, pupils may be prevented from using IT resources because supervision is not available at the time access is required. Security is important in ensuring computer equipment is not damaged or stolen. However, it should be remembered that the school's IT resources are provided to help pupils learn. A balance must be found that allows reasonable access to IT resources when pupils need to use them, and that keeps them secure.

Disaster recovery

An IT policy may also include within its remit procedures for disaster recovery. All hardware and software may malfunction at some time. Schools would be advised to have in place appropriate procedures for replacement and recovery. These might include:

- backups of all software and data files on a regular basis;
- preventative maintenance of all hardware;
- arrangements to repair or replace broken hardware within agreed time limits;
- arrangements to run vital software elsewhere. If as a result of a fire or flooding, the school is destroyed, or otherwise inaccessible, some software may still be needed. Such software should be identified and arrangements to run it at another location should be made.

The Data Protection Act

A comprehensive IT policy may also include reference to the measures the school has taken to conform to the requirements of the Data Protection Act (1984). This Act stipulates that all organisations keeping computer-based files of personal information should register them with the Data Protection Registrar. The Act also regulates what can be done with these data files. Schools should consider the implications of the Data Protection Act very carefully when using computers to manage information about pupils and others. Data protection legislation is reviewed in detail in the later chapter on the use of IT in school administration and management (see Chapter 10).

Equal opportunities issues

Relevant aspects of the school's Equal Opportunities Policy may be restated, re-interpreted, and elaborated in the IT policy with reference to IT. This topic is dealt with more extensively in the later chapter on Equal Opportunities (see Chapter 8).

Pupils' access to IT resources affects their access to the curriculum. If all pupils do not have the same level of access to IT resources, they cannot have the same opportunities to develop their knowledge, skills and understanding of IT. This is not only a matter of making IT resources available to all; it is also necessary to monitor and supervise pupils' access to and use of IT resources to ensure that the arrangements made are effective in ensuring equal access.

Pupils' access to IT resources is apparently easiest when these resources are most widely distributed throughout the school. Initially, it might seem that making these resources available to pupils only in specialist IT rooms is highly restrictive. However, in timetabled classes it is not unusual to find that if there are only one or two computers in each classroom then they are rarely used. In addition, it is often difficult to arrange adequate supervision of widely distributed resources out of timetabled classes. If IT resources are not adequately supervised, some pupils' access to them will be limited by social factors, such as bullying and intimidation. Racist, sexist, ageist and other types of discriminatory behaviour by some pupils can limit the access of the groups of pupils it is directed at. It is still not unusual to see unsupervised access to IT resources being dominated by easily identifiable social groups, for example, large, white boys. Overt, fair rules and careful supervision of pupils' access to IT resources are important in ensuring that all pupils have equal opportunities to develop their knowledge, skills and understanding of IT. Ensuring adequate supervision is far more difficult for widely dispersed IT resources than for a few specialist IT rooms. The subject IT and hybrid IT approaches to the curriculum and their associated distributions of IT resources, with a centralised element, are easier to manage so that equal access for all pupils is ensured outside of timetabled time.

Staffing and INSET

Clearly, the ideal is that the all teaching staff in a school should be fully competent in a wide range of IT skills and knowledgeable about the full potential of IT. However, this is probably too ambitious to begin with. Stated aims should be more realistic estimates of what levels of skill are required to deliver the chosen approach to the IT curriculum.

If the subject IT approach is chosen, only a small number of staff need have IT skills and knowledge but they should have the full range of skills and in-depth knowledge. With the hybrid IT approach, in addition to these IT specialists, a larger number of staff will need to know how to use the IT resources relevant to their subject. With the cross-curricular approach, a much larger number of staff will need to be capable of using IT, teaching IT and assessing pupils' IT capability. However, these teachers may only need expertise relevant to their particular subjects, for example, an English teacher may only need to know how to use a wordprocessor and Desk Top Publishing software; how to support pupils' use of this software in the classroom; and how to assess pupils' competency in Communicating Information.

INSET will be needed to raise all teachers' IT skills to the required standard and this can be made available through a variety of mechanisms. IT skills are often self-taught; many teachers invest their own time in learning IT skills for themselves. Whilst individual teachers can make considerable progress in developing their own IT skills, small groups of teachers can often support each other more effectively. Skills learnt by individuals attending short day or evening courses can be cascaded to the group. Residential weekends can sometimes be helpful in sustaining impetus. The strategy for providing INSET in IT should be agreed and clearly stated in the IT Policy.

Funding

Estimates of the total cost of each element of the IT policy will help in evaluating the affordability of the proposed curriculum model. A realistic estimate should be made of the cost of establishing and maintaining the school's proposals for the management structure; the curriculum and its organisation; assessment, recording and reporting; hardware; software; security; disaster recovery; meeting the obligations imposed by the Data Protection Act; implementing equal opportunities policy; staffing and INSET. Such estimates should be expected to change, perhaps due to price differences over time or as markets fluctuate. Even so, well-grounded estimates will provide a measure of the magnitude of the investment that needs to be made by the school.

AUDIT

An audit is a statement of what is being done. It is essentially a descriptive process. In order to plan how to reach the long-term goals the school has set for itself when determining its aims, the starting-points must be known. An audit describes exactly what is being done so that the school can plan what it will do in order to achieve its long-term aims.

It may be useful to present the audit in at least two different ways. There should be a detailed audit which is thorough and comprehensive. Such an audit will be required to enable administrative control to be exercised so that, for example, insurance claims are accurate. There will also need to be a summary audit. The detailed audit, although necessary, is not often immediately meaningful to teachers and others involved in managing the curriculum.

In the detailed audit, a computer may consist of a mouse, a keyboard, a processor box and a monitor. Each of these would be described in detail; for example, a processor box, model Elonex PC-420X, containing a 486SX processor, 8 Mbytes of RAM memory, a 240 Mbyte hard disk and a 1.44 Mbyte floppy disk. The serial number and location would also be recorded. There may be separate sections in the detailed audit for processor boxes, keyboards, and other component parts. A detailed audit of this type does not always present a clear view of what is available for use in the classroom. Teachers may find it more useful to know, for example, that a 486 IBM compatible computer is available for use in Room 11. The summary audit should express the contents of the detailed audit in a form useful to teachers, curriculum planners, governors and others to whom a detailed audit would be confusing and, possibly, meaningless.

What the school needs to know

Below is a list of some of the questions schools may wish to ask when considering aspects of IT policy. It is not suggested that it is necessary or desirable to always include the answers to all of these questions. However, the answers should be known. They will often appear in more detailed appendices to the IT policy. The policy itself will be a meaningful summary which may be less comprehensible if too much detail is included.

Management structure

- What is the current management structure for organising the staff involved in delivering the IT curriculum?
- What roles and responsibilities have these staff in relation to IT?
- What are the strengths and weaknesses of the existing management structure?
- How is the effectiveness of management procedures monitored?

The curriculum and its organisation

- Do different groups of pupils have different IT curricula? If so, which groups of pupils have what curriculum?

For each different group of pupils in each year:

- How is the delivery of the IT curriculum currently organised?
- What timetable structures are used to deliver IT?
- In what subjects is IT taught?
- What IT is currently taught in these subjects?
- In what subjects is IT used?
- What use is currently made of IT in these subjects?
- What are the strengths and weaknesses of the existing curriculum?
- Are the requirements of the NC met?
- How is curriculum provision monitored to ensure that the full NC entitlement is delivered to each pupil?
- What external syllabuses are used, especially for assessment at the end of years 11 and 13?
- Which groups of pupils have access to which external syllabuses?

Assessment, recording and reporting

Assessment: for each different group of pupils in each year:

- How is IT assessed? Are log books, profiles, coursework and written examinations used in assessment?
- For what purpose does assessment take place? Is it formative or summative?
- In which subjects is IT assessed by which teachers?
- Are the requirements for GCSE and other external assessments met?

- What are the strengths and weaknesses of the existing arrangements for assessment?
- How is the effectiveness of assessment procedures monitored?

Recording: for each different group of pupils in each year:

- What assessment evidence and what records are collected? When are these collected?
- What administrative routines are used to collect together the assessment evidence?
- What summaries of the results of assessment are prepared? When are these prepared?
- What assessment evidence and what records must be retained and for how long?
- What arrangements are made for the storage of the assessment evidence and the associated records?
- Which teachers have what roles and responsibilities in collecting the evidence, summarising it and ensuring the safe and secure storage of it?
- What are the strengths and weaknesses of the existing arrangements for collecting the evidence?
- How is the effectiveness of procedures for collecting the evidence monitored?

Progress and attainment: for each different group of pupils in each year:

- How are pupils' progress and attainment reported? When are they reported?
- Are statutory requirements met?
- Which teachers have what roles and responsibilities in reporting progress and attainment?
- What are the strengths and weaknesses of the existing arrangements for reporting progress and attainment?
- How is the effectiveness of these arrangements monitored?

Moderation: for each different group of pupils in each year:

- What assessment evidence is moderated?
- How is moderation of assessment organised?
- What moderation is done for internal assessments?
- What moderation is done for external assessments?
- When is moderation done?
- What record of the moderation process is retained and for how long? Where are these records stored?
- Are the moderation requirements for GCSE and other external assessments met?
- Which teachers have what roles and responsibilities in the moderation process?

- What are the strengths and weaknesses of the existing arrangements for moderation?
- How is the effectiveness of moderation procedures monitored?

IT resources: hardware

- Is there an inventory of hardware?
- How regularly is the hardware inventory updated?
- Does the hardware inventory cover all the separate pieces of computer equipment in the school?
- For each piece of equipment, is there recorded on the hardware inventory, at least, the serial number, description, cost of purchase, location used and the name of the person responsible for it?
- What other information is kept on the hardware inventory about each piece of equipment?
- Is there a summary hardware inventory that gives the same information in terms that are readily understandable?
- Is there a detailed plan of the school's network showing exactly where the network cable is installed?
- Who is responsible for keeping the hardware inventory and network cable plan up-to-date?
- What are the strengths and weaknesses of the existing arrangements for keeping a detailed, complete and up-to-date hardware inventory and network cable plan?
- How is the effectiveness of these procedures monitored?

IT resources: software

- Is there an inventory of software?
- How regularly is the software inventory updated?
- Does the software inventory cover all the programs and data files owned by the school?
- What information is kept on the software inventory about each program or data file?
- For each piece of software, is there recorded, at least, the serial number, description, cost of purchase, licence conditions and location?
- Is there a summary software inventory that gives the same information in terms that are readily understandable?
- Who is responsible for keeping the software inventory up to date?
- What are the strengths and weaknesses of the existing arrangements for keeping a detailed, complete and up-to-date software inventory?
- What checks are made to ensure that unlicensed software is not used?
- How is the effectiveness of these procedures monitored?

IT resources: security

- What physical security precautions are taken to guard against unauthorised access and theft? For example, what locks, grills, laminates, alarms, anchors, and disk safes are used?
- Where are physical security precautions used?
- Who is responsible for checking that physical security precautions are satisfactory?
- What precautions are taken to restrict access to software to those authorised to use it?
- What system of passwords and user identity numbers is used?
- Who is given passwords and user identity numbers?
- How often are passwords and user identity numbers changed?
- Who is responsible for setting up new users and deleting old users?
- What access do unauthorised users have to network cables?
- What measures are taken to protect the network cable from physical misuse?
- What steps are taken to protect the computer system from viruses?
- Who has overall responsibility for all aspects of security?

IT resources: disaster recovery

- What backups of software are made?
- How often are backups of software made?
- What system of organising regular backups is used?
- Where are backups stored?
- Who is responsible for taking backups and organising the system of backups used?
- What preventative maintenance is carried out?
- How regularly is preventative maintenance carried out?
- What arrangements are made for repair or replacement of broken hardware?
- What arrangements have been made for software maintenance on a day-to-day basis and in the longer term?
- What arrangements have been made to run mission critical software if the school's computer system is unavailable?
- Who has responsibility for ensuring that suitable arrangements are made for disaster recovery?
- What are the strengths and weaknesses of these procedures?
- How is the effectiveness of these procedures monitored?

IT resources: the Data Protection Act

- What systems containing personal data are registered with the Data Protection Registrar?

- What arrangements are made to collect personal data?
- What is the purpose for which the personal data is collected?
- Is the purpose for which the personal data is collected clearly stated?
- Is the personal data collected relevant to its use?
- To whom is personal data disclosed and under what circumstances?
- How long is personal data kept?
- What arrangements are made for parents, pupils and others to look at personal data about them stored on computer files at the school? What charge is made?
- How are parents, pupils and others informed of these arrangements?
- What arrangements are made to ensure personal data remains accurate?
- What arrangements are made to have inaccurate data changed?
- Who is responsible for ensuring that the school meets the provisions of the Data Protection Act (1984)?
- What are the strengths and weaknesses of these procedures?
- How is the effectiveness of these procedures monitored?

Equal Opportunities issues

- What monitoring is done of access to IT resources?
- What details are recorded during monitoring?
- What rules and constraints are used to ensure equal access to IT resources?
- When is access to IT resources supervised?
- Who supervises access to IT resources?
- What gender, ethnic origin, and age are staff who teach and use IT on a regular basis?
- Are Equal Opportunities strategies in IT congruent with those elaborated in the school's Equal Opportunities Policy?
- Who is responsible for ensuring that equal opportunities issues are identified and appropriate action is taken?
- What are the strengths and weaknesses of these procedures?
- How is the effectiveness of these procedures monitored?

Staffing and INSET

- Who teaches IT, helps pupils make use of IT and assesses IT?
- What IT skills do they currently have?
- What IT skills do they need?
- What arrangements are made for IT INSET?
- Who provides the IT INSET?
- Who is responsible for ensuring that an adequate programme of INSET is available?
- What are the strengths and weaknesses of INSET provision?
- How is the effectiveness of this provision monitored?

Funding

- What are the current costs and sources of funding for each element of the IT policy?
- What procedures are used to ensure spending remains within budget?
- Who is responsible for spending the budget?
- What procedures are used to monitor the effective use of funds?
- What criteria of effectiveness are used?
- Who is responsible for monitoring the effective use of funds?
- What are the strengths and weaknesses of these procedures?
- How is the effectiveness of these procedures monitored?

How the school can find out what it needs to know

There are two basic strategies for the school to find out what it needs to know.

1 The SMT or persons nominated by the SMT can find out what the current situation is by asking administrators, teachers, pupils, parents, caretakers, and ancillary staff. The opinions of those involved can be sought through meetings, interviews, and questionnaires. Meetings and interviews should be recorded or notes taken so that points raised can be thoroughly investigated at a later date. Questionnaires should be carefully analysed and there should be opportunities for informal comments to be made. Those involved in collecting the evidence should meet together to discuss the results of their investigations. A detailed audit report and a summary should be produced.

2 A person involved with and well informed regarding the current situation can be asked to write a detailed audit report and summary.

The advantage of the first option is that a thorough, detailed and extensive audit report is likely to be produced. However, the process of producing the audit report will be very time-consuming. The second option will lead to the production of an audit report in a much shorter time but it is more likely that there will be omissions or bias in the report. In each case, the audit report and summary should be discussed by the IT Co-ordinating Group and revised accordingly. The whole staff should then have the opportunity to comment before the final version is agreed.

ACTION

The aims stated within the IT policy are an indication of the long-term goals of the school; the audit is a comprehensive, detailed statement of the current circumstances within the school; an action plan is a programme for immediate implementation. The action plan consists of a number of action statements. An action statement should say what will be done in the next school year, who will do it, and what constitutes success if this is not immediately obvious. As such, these action statements should be recognised as being immediately achievable by those who will be involved in their implementation.

The action statements will direct the school from the audit towards the aims. That is, the action statements will indicate what the school should do in the short term to achieve the aims of the IT policy in the long term, starting with current circumstances in the school. However, what can be done will be constrained by the resources available to do it. It is useful to write all the proposed action statements and estimate the cost of implementing them before considering the constraints that limited funding will inevitably impose. If all the desired progress towards the aims cannot be achieved within available funding, a costed list of action statements will assist in prioritising what can be done.

Some action statements will be attainable within existing resources, or with limited additional funding, for example, changing the management structure may only require some adjustment of existing responsibilities and the allocation of a limited amount of time for meetings. In contrast, some action statements will not be attainable without considerable additional expenditure: for example, developing and extending the IT curriculum to include groups of pupils who currently do not have an adequate experience of IT. This may require the purchase of large quantities of additional IT hardware and software, or the employment of extra teachers with IT skills.

It may be worth considering whether action statements can be implemented by extending the functionality of existing resources. This can often be done for relatively little cost; additional equipment or component parts could be purchased that extend the functionality of the school's hardware, i.e., more memory could be purchased for the computers, allowing a wider range of educational software to be run. Similarly, an intensive, well-structured programme of INSET could improve the IT skills of existing staff, avoiding the need to employ more staff.

The action statements that can be funded from next year's budget indicate what can be done towards the realisation of the aims of the IT policy. These are the action statements that should be included in the school's IT policy.

PRESENTATION OF THE IT POLICY

IT policies may be presented in a variety of ways. The proposed approach to arriving at a whole school IT policy described in this chapter may be reflected in the final form of the IT policy. This way of presenting the IT policy clearly separates the long-term aims, the audit of IT resources and the actions to be taken in the next school year. Separate sections can be useful in keeping their content in focus and up to date. The aims provide a relatively static indication of the overall goals that should be taken into account when planning. A separate audit section provides a framework for the administrative work that will need to be done on a day-to-day basis. The action section indicates what should be done in the next school year, providing clear, short-term objectives for day-to-day working. This separation of the aims, audit and action sections may assist clarity in planning, and provide useful working documentation which can be a focus for the day-to-day organisation, administration, and implementation tasks that must be done.

However, presentation of the IT policy with separate sections for each of the aims, the audit and the actions to be taken, can obscure interconnections between them. Thus, when reading the aims section, it may not be clear what is currently being done to achieve them or what the starting point was. In this case, it may be difficult to evaluate progress without reference to the audit and action sections. Similarly, a separate audit section gives an up-to-date snapshot of the resources currently available but does not indicate why these are made available or what is being done to remedy deficiencies. The action section may provide a concise summary of what is being done but will not provide a useful rationale for doing it or show how the actions now being taken contribute to long-term developments. For these reasons, schools may prefer to present the aims, the audit and the actions to be taken in a more integrated format when compiling the version of the IT policy that will be distributed to governors, parents, staff and inspectors. If the IT policy is presented with the associated elements of the aims, audit and action sections summarised and grouped together, it may be more comprehensible; see the example IT policy below. It is not uncommon for schools to present their IT policies in this way to create a more informal, readable document. Greater detail, and the separation of the aims, audit and action sections of the IT policy are useful for day-to-day planning and management. However, the IT policy may be more comprehensible and meaningful to governors, parents, staff and inspectors if these separate sections are then presented in an integrated, summarised form. More detailed information can be included as appendices.

AN EXAMPLE OF A SCHOOL IT POLICY

The purpose of an IT policy is to provide an overview of what is happening in the school, and provide purpose and direction. The example IT policy shown is a summary policy, which does not incorporate all the detailed planning that underpins it, though some of this could be incorporated as appendices and some possible appendices are shown. The IT policy should be comprehensible to governors and useful to teachers. Consequently, only significant developments are described.

Manor School IT Policy for the school year beginning Sept. XXXX

Mission Statement

The school intends to provide all pupils with opportunities to acquire knowledge, skills and understanding of IT in breadth and in depth, so that they can use IT to support their learning throughout the curriculum, and are well prepared for work, or further study when they leave Manor School.

Management structure

The school wishes to establish an IT Co-ordinating Committee that will be chaired by the Deputy Head (curriculum), and will include the IT Co-ordinator, all IT teachers and technicians, and one representative from each subject department. This committee will have oversight of the whole IT curriculum, and overall responsibility for planning and implementation of IT policy, collectively and as named individuals.

At present, there is an IT Co-ordinator who is responsible for all aspects of the use of IT throughout the school. The IT Co-ordinator chairs the IT group which is regularly attended by teachers of Design Technology, Mathematics and Music but no other subject departments. The IT group meets once or twice a term. Minutes are not taken. This group has very little influence on curriculum co-ordination and development planning. There are no other teachers of IT other than the IT Co-ordinator and no IT technician.

By the end of September, all subject departments will nominate a representative to attend the IT co-ordinating committee. This committee will meet for the first time during October, and thereafter twice each term. The Deputy Head (curriculum) will organise and chair meetings. Minutes will be taken. During the Summer Term and by the end of it, the IT co-ordinating committee will organise the review and update of the IT policy. The Deputy Head (curriculum) will report progress to the Headteacher and governors as required but at least annually.

The curriculum and its organisation

The school aims to deliver the mandatory programmes of study through IT subject studies during a single one hour period per week for all pupils. Pupils' experiences of IT throughout the curriculum will be co-ordinated with their IT subject studies to ensure progression and continuity. The school aims to enter all pupils for GCSE IT (short course) and offer them the opportunity to choose to follow a course leading to the GCSE IT (full course).

Pupils' experiences of IT are not as yet fully co-ordinated across the whole curriculum. Pupils in Key Stages 3 and 4 are timetabled for IT for approximately one period per week for one term per year as part of a Technology carousel that also involves Design Technology and Food Technology. As a result, pupils' experiences of IT are restricted and are often too narrow and superficial. The school cannot be sure that the NC IT PoS are covered. No pupils are entered for GCSE or other external assessment in IT.

From the start of the next school year, it is expected that pupils in Key Stages 3 and 4 will be timetabled for at least one period of IT subject studies per week, and that pupils at the start of year 10 will begin a programme of study leading to GCSE IT (short course) assessment at the end of year 11. These pupils will be taught by IT specialists who will take responsibility for all aspects of the development of their pupils' IT capability.

A plan for the co-ordination of IT subject studies and the use of IT throughout the curriculum will be needed by the start of the next school year. To begin with, a curriculum audit will be completed by Christmas. The IT Co-ordinator will ensure that the plan is considered by the whole staff, approved by the IT Co-ordinating committee and completed by Easter. This will be distributed to Heads of Department in the week following the Easter holidays for inclusion in their curriculum plans for the following school year. The Deputy Head (curriculum) will ensure that any necessary adjustments to the organisation of the timetable are made. It should be possible to implement the plan within the level of IT staffing and resources anticipated at the start of the next school year.

Assessment, recording and reporting

The school will report pupils' progress and attainment in IT to parents once each year in accordance with the whole school policy on assessment, recording and reporting, and in such a manner that statutory requirements are met. Teachers will assess and record pupils' progress and attainment in each NC sub-theme in their IT subject classes. Pupils' progress and attainment in subjects other than IT will be assessed and recorded by their teachers who will inform their IT teacher. This will be integrated with assessments made in IT subject classes and a centralised record of pupils' progress and attainment will be assembled by the IT Co-ordinator. The IT Co-ordinator will moderate all assessments, establishing consistent standards throughout the school based on a portfolio of examples of pupils' work at different levels of attainment.

At present, the above system is in place except that the integration of the assessments made in IT subject classes with those made in other subjects is poor, and there is no satisfactory system of internal moderation. As Heads of Departments present their new curriculum plans for the next school year, the Deputy Head (curriculum) will ensure that these include appropriate proposals for assessment, recording and reporting. Centralised recording and reporting will need extending in the next school year to incorporate these assessments and those done by the new IT specialist teachers. The IT

Co-ordinator will ensure this is done, and that pupils' reports include a summary of their progress and attainment in IT. Proposals for instituting a practical system of internal moderation will be included in the next IT policy.

IT resources: hardware and software

The school intends to provide two IT rooms with fifteen computers in each and six clusters of five computers located in the library, the year 12 and 13 common room, the Design Technology base room, the Business Studies resources area, the Humanities block and the Music studio. All computers will be networked, and will be able to access wordprocessing, graphics, DTP, spreadsheet and database software. Where software specific to particular subjects is required, this will be chosen by the teachers concerned in consultation with the IT Co-ordinator. As far as is possible and desirable, a standardised menu will be used giving all pupils and teachers access to all software.

The school has one IT room containing fifteen Archimedes computers. These are not networked. There is a cluster of ten networked IBM compatible computers and a fileserver in the Business Studies resources area. There is one BBC computer in the library and three in the Science Department. Access to software is variable. User interfaces may be radically different and pupils may encounter a range of software that does the same tasks but is operated in very different ways.

Some fifteen IBM compatible computers will be purchased. These will be installed in a new IT room close to the library. Only five of the ten IBM compatible computers in the Business Studies resources area will be moved to the Design Technology base room. All the IBM compatible computers will be connected by the same network. The existing fileserver will be moved from the Business Studies resources area to the new IT room. Some fifteen additional licences will be purchased for the software currently in use. A tape streamer and six tape cartridges will be purchased to back up the hard disk on the fileserver. A further three IBM compatible computers will be purchased and installed in a new staff IT room. Planning, development, and implementation will be the responsibility of the IT Co-ordinator who will make a written progress report to the Deputy Head (curriculum) at the end of each term. These developments should be completed by the start of the next school year.

IT resources: security, disaster recovery and the Data Protection Act

The school aims to protect hardware, software and data by:

- placing grilles over the windows of IT rooms where these are on the ground floor;

- extending the schools' burglar alarm system into IT rooms and surrounding corridors;
- attaching all computers to walls or desks using steel cables;
- locking all rooms containing IT hardware when this is not in use;
- restricting access to networked software by giving teachers and pupils their own individual user identification numbers and passwords;
- allowing users to change their passwords when they wish;
- performing an automatic virus check each time a user logs on to the network;
- installing network cabling so that it is inaccessible;
- backing up all fileservers each week, using the ancestral system;
- correcting hardware and software faults as they arise, and carrying out preventative maintenance once each year during the school holidays;
- establishing mutual support arrangements with a local business or another school so that in the event of widespread and serious damage to IT systems, mission critical software can still be run;
- meeting the statutory requirements of the Data Protection Act.

At present, the above arrangements have been implemented but not always comprehensively, for example, some but not all computer equipment is secured to walls or desks. A system of user identification numbers and passwords is in use but this does not include all teachers and pupils. Backups of the file-server are taken once per term using the ancestral system. This cannot be done weekly as it is time-consuming, and the network must be disabled while it is done. Arrangements for meeting the requirements of the Data Protection Act are *ad hoc* and inconsistently implemented.

The IT Co-ordinator will identify hardware which is not secured to walls or desks, and produce a prioritised list for immediate action. The IT Co-ordinator will devise a comprehensive system of individual user identification numbers and passwords, and ensure that access cannot be gained to networked IT resources without using these. The new tape streamer must be capable of operating in background mode so that backups can be taken weekly without disabling the network.

In the next school year, responsibility for security, disaster recovery and compliance with the Data Protection Act will be delegated to the new IT teachers.

Equal Opportunities

In IT, in addition to implementing the whole school policy for Equal Opportunities, it will be ensured that pupils' access to IT resources is supervised and monitored. At present, there is no unsupervised access as pupils can only use IT resources during timetabled classes. It is intended that a computer club will be run after school each day beginning at the start of the next school year. This will be organised by the new IT teachers. It will be supervised by a rota of teachers who will register daily attendance. These registers will be used to monitor pupils' access. If some groups are found to be under-represented, the reasons for this will be investigated by the IT Co-ordinating Committee, and appropriate corrective action will be determined by them case by case.

Staffing and INSET

The school intends to ensure that all teachers have the skills, knowledge and understanding to enable them to use IT where necessary in their professional activities, and to support pupils who use IT to learn.

The school has one specialist IT teacher, the IT Co-ordinator. Some 20 per cent of the staff can use a wordprocessor with around half of these having a good in-depth knowledge of IT and the skills to use a wider range of IT software which is not always related to their subject. The school intends to employ one additional IT teacher from the start of the next school year and to redeploy an existing member of staff to teach IT. As the focus of development in the next school year is the IT curriculum, INSET for staff will prioritise those activities that support this. This will be based on a support group comprising the three IT subject teachers and other teachers who plan to use IT in their subjects. INSET for those not immediately concerned with teaching IT will be planned for the following school year.

Funding

Proposed expenditure this school year:

15 IBM compatible computers, and associated hardware and software for curriculum use	£21,000
3 IBM compatible computers, and associated hardware and software for the new staff IT room	£4,000
Additional security measures	£1,500

These purchases will be organised by the IT Co-ordinator. Orders must be approved by the Deputy Head (curriculum) and Deputy Head (finance) before they are issued.

Appendices

1 Summary and detailed curriculum audit (when available).
2 Summary and detailed hardware inventory.
3 Summary and detailed software inventory.
4 Security audit.

5 Arrangements for disaster recovery.
6 Job description for the IT Co-ordinator.
7 Job descriptions for the new IT teachers.

SUMMARY

This chapter recommends developing a whole school IT policy by determining the aims of the school, conducting a thorough and detailed audit, then deciding what action will be taken within the next school year.

If possible, an effective management structure should be put in place before the development process begins. For example, a school might establish an IT Co-ordinating Group with the responsibility for co-ordinating IT throughout the school. This could be chaired by a member of the SMT. The IT Co-ordinator, IT Manager and a representative from each subject department could be invited to attend. The subject representatives will have responsibility for the implementation of the school's IT policy within their departments.

The IT policy may be presented with separate sections for the aims, the audit and the action. This can help focus the planning and review process, and assist with day-to-day organisation and administration. However, an IT Policy may be more meaningful if it is then presented in an integrated manner, with the related sections of the aims, the audit and the action adjacent to each other. An example of an IT policy is included at the end of the chapter.

5

HARDWARE

This chapter reviews the practical considerations that should be taken into account when acquiring and managing IT hardware. Sufficient technical jargon is included but this is kept to a minimum. Some suggestions are made regarding what can be done to avoid or overcome the loss of essential IT resources.

THE HARDWARE THAT SHOULD BE AVAILABLE AND ITS CHARACTERISTICS

The hardware that schools should provide so that pupils may have satisfactory experiences of IT is not concisely listed in the NC or the various non-statutory guidance. Similarly, most GCSE syllabuses do not list the hardware needed, though some are relatively specific: for example, the SEG GCSE IT syllabus. However, what is required can be deduced. A careful reading of all the relevant literature indicates the hardware that should be available.

In order to fulfil the Programmes of Study for IT, and meet the requirements of GCSE IT syllabuses by the end of KS4, pupils should have the knowledge and understanding to make use of a wide range of hardware including:

- computers, and their component parts, including a monitor, mouse, processor, keyboard, floppy disk drive and hard disk;
- CD-ROM drives;
- printers;
- scanners;
- sensors, including those for temperature, pressure, light, and sound;
- actuators, including motors, heaters, lights, and fans;

In addition, the following hardware would be useful in extending the breadth and depth of pupils' experiences:

- LANs, and WANs, including hardware for Internet access;
- models to demonstrate computer control of washing machines, cranes, robots, greenhouses, or traffic lights;

- Teletext televisions with remote control units;
- programmable tape recorders, and video equipment;
- computer-controlled sewing machines or lathes;
- computers with midi capability for control of synthesisers and drum machines;
- graphical calculators;
- OMR readers, and bar code readers.

THE FUNCTION OF THE COMPONENT PARTS OF A PERSONAL COMPUTER AND THE CONSEQUENT IMPLICATIONS FOR SCHOOLS

A full appreciation of the practical implications of using IT hardware in schools depends on an understanding of the functional characteristics of the component parts of a modern Personal Computer (PC). These functional characteristics are common across all types of computer commonly used in schools, for example, those manufactured by Apple, Acorn and Research Machines. What follows is a description of the functional characteristics of the component parts of a PC. It is pitched at an appropriate level for Senior Managers and other users who are concerned more with what computers do than the minutiae of how they work. Some implications for administrative and curriculum IT systems are reviewed.

A modern PC system will usually include these component parts:

- a monitor or screen
- a keyboard
- a mouse or tracker ball
- a floppy disk drive
- a hard disk drive
- a CD-ROM drive
- memory (RAM and ROM)
- a processor
- a printer connection
- connections to other peripherals, e.g. Optical Mark Readers
- a network connection.

PCs are available as desk top computers (see Figure 5.1) or portable computers (see Figure 5.2). A portable computer will contain all of the above component parts in one compact case that is slightly smaller in size than the average briefcase. The screen folds up in the same way a briefcase is opened. A portable computer is likely to have a built-in tracker ball whereas a desk top computer will have a mouse. A portable computer can be powered by batteries or from the mains, whereas a desk top computer is only mains powered.

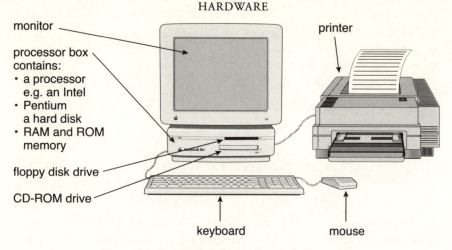

Figure 5.1 A typical desk top Personal Computer

The disadvantages of a portable computer are as follows:

- it will have a screen of a significantly lower quality than a desk top computer that is otherwise of the same price and specification;
- it is not as expandable, that is, only a very restricted number of component parts can be added after manufacture;
- the batteries may need recharging every four or five hours when it is in use.

The advantage of a portable computer is, simply, that it is very portable whereas a desk top computer is not. However, the function of the component parts is the same in both a desk top computer and a portable computer.

Portable computers are also known as 'laptops'. Smaller portable computers are called 'palmtops'. Palmtops do not have a full range of component parts. They do not usually include a mouse or tracker ball, a floppy disk drive, a hard disk drive, a CD-ROM drive, and connection to a printer or a network. They will usually have a small LCD screen and a very compact keyboard which may not have the standard QWERTY layout. However, it is often possible to transfer data to a desk top computer for further processing and storage.

Current research (NCET, 1993c) indicates that pupils and teachers prefer using portable computers because:

- they are more accessible;
- they can be continuously available at home and at school;
- they can become a personal learning environment tailored to each pupil's needs.

The use of portable computers in the classroom is currently increasing. However, not all schools are committed to purchasing them. Teachers wishing

Figure 5.2 A portable computer

to purchase portable computers for use in the classroom will find the booklet *Choosing and Using Portable Computers*, published by NCET in 1992, of interest. The remainder of this chapter relates to desk top computers unless there is specific reference to portable computers.

The monitor used with a desk top computer is usually a separate item but may be part of a unit containing, in addition to the monitor, a floppy disk drive, a hard disk drive, memory and a processor. An example of this is the Apple Classic series. Where the monitor is a separate component, it is not unusual to have a floppy disk drive, a hard disk drive, memory and a processor built into a combined unit that is often called a 'processor box' as for example, in IBM compatible computers. Similarly, the keyboard of a desk top computer is usually a separate component but may be built into a unit also containing a floppy disk drive, memory and a processor, as for example, in Atari ST computers. Any grouping of component parts is possible. The groupings available depend on manufacturers' designs and the current preferences of purchasers.

Monitors with high resolution colour screens display more detail, in colour, than low resolution or monochrome monitors but they are more expensive. The size of a standard monitor screen is usually comparable to that of a 14" television screen but larger screens are available – for example, A4 or double A4 screens. A standard, high resolution, colour monitor is a suitable output device for general use throughout the curriculum and for most administrative uses. Large screens can be useful for specific applications – for example, professional quality Desk Top Publishing in the school office or magnified screen displays for partially sighted pupils.

A standard keyboard is suitable for most uses in school. However, if there is a need for high volumes of numeric input, a numeric keypad may be useful (see Figure 5.3). The numbers on a standard keyboard are usually

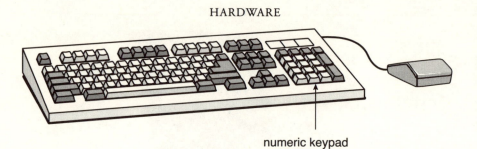

numeric keypad

Figure 5.3 A keyboard with built-in numeric keypad

in a line just above the alphabetic character keys and this makes typing in numbers relatively slow. A numeric keypad is sometimes built into a keyboard on the right-hand side in a 4 × 3 matrix of numbers with an extra large zero key. Consequently, it is faster to type in a high volume of numbers using a numeric key pad. It is worth ensuring that a keyboard with a numeric key pad is available for administrative work, especially for data input in the school office. A numeric key pad is not necessary for curriculum use.

The standard keyboard is not suitable for use by all pupils. Alternative keyboards are available for pupils who have difficulty operating the keys – for example, pupils who are partially sighted or who have poor co-ordination. Flat keyboards are available with a touch sensitive membrane in place of the keys, as, for example, the 'Concept' keyboard. Plastic overlays are placed over the keyboard. These show the keyboard divided up to represent only a few keys of different sizes, possibly only two large keys with simple meanings, such as, 'yes' and 'no'. Used in conjunction with specialist software, these keyboards can help pupils with some forms of disability to use IT and they can also help pupils with learning difficulties by narrowing the range of possible responses. Schools should seriously consider making some of these keyboards available for use by those pupils who may benefit from them.

A mouse is an essential input device if software with a Graphic User Interface (GUI) is to be used. Archimedes, Atari ST and Apple computers, for example, are very difficult to use at all without a mouse. Software for IBM compatible computers is increasingly mouse-operated. Many users find software with a mouse-operated GUI easier to use than more traditional keyboard-controlled software. Computers intended for use across the curriculum should be purchased with a mouse as pupils will almost certainly find mouse-controlled software easier to operate.

Floppy disks and hard disks are types of backing storage. Backing storage is used to store information when the computer is switched off. Floppy disks and hard disks are both magnetic, non-volatile backing storage. Information

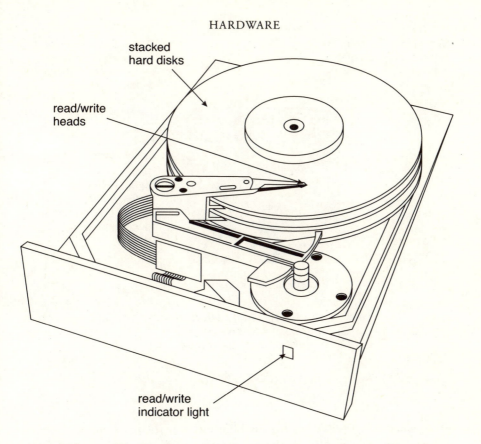

stacked
hard disks

read/write
heads

read/write
indicator light

Figure 5.4 A hard disk drive that would be built into a processor box

can be both written to and read from them. A hard disk (see Figure 5.4) is usually, although not always, supplied as a sealed unit permanently fixed into the computer. This is often already installed when the computer is purchased. Floppy disks (see Figure 5.5) can be put into and removed from the floppy disk drive. Hard disks have a higher storage capacity than individual floppy disks but, as floppy disks are removable, more of them can be used. When software and other files are stored (or saved) on disk they are not lost when the computer is switched off. Software can be stored on either a floppy disk or a hard disk but it will load, and possibly run, faster if it is saved on a hard disk. All the software and data files stored on a hard disk are usually available to all users. Consequently, in order to keep data files private and confidential, it may be preferable to store software on the hard disk and data files on floppy disks. If necessary, the floppy disks with the data files stored on them can be locked away when not in use. Data files on floppy disk can be used on any computer with suitable software available and a floppy disk

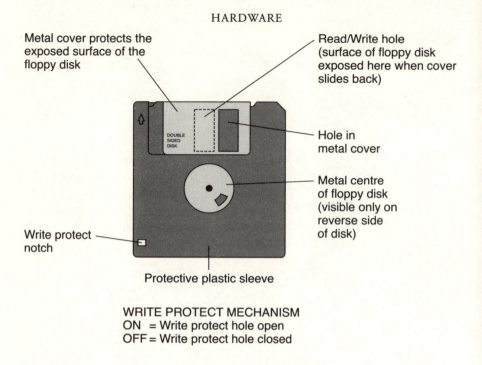

Metal cover protects the exposed surface of the floppy disk

Read/Write hole (surface of floppy disk exposed here when cover slides back)

DOUBLE SIDED DISK

Hole in metal cover

Metal centre of floppy disk (visible only on reverse side of disk)

Write protect notch

Protective plastic sleeve

WRITE PROTECT MECHANISM
ON = Write protect hole open
OFF = Write protect hole closed

Figure 5.5 A 3½" floppy disk

drive, whereas hard disks are usually built into a particular computer. A cost-effective way of providing sufficient, suitable, disk storage is to purchase a hard disk large enough to store all the software to be used, and to use floppy disks to save all the data files generated when using the software. Alternatives are removable hard disks and opto-magnetic floppy disks which are removable and high capacity but relatively expensive.

Computers attached to a network (network stations) do not need to have either a floppy disk drive or a hard disk drive. Software can be stored on a networked hard disk in the network fileserver and loaded into a network station via the network. Data files generated when using the software could be saved on the same network hard disk as the software. However, there are some disadvantages:

● saving data files on a network hard disk is wasteful of expensive, shared storage capacity;
● it may be slow to access software, and load and save data files;
● file management problems may be exacerbated.

Consequently, it is better to purchase network stations with a floppy disk drive. In this case shared software can be stored on the network hard disk in the fileserver, and loaded and run over the network, and data files can be stored on the users' own floppy disks. If network stations also have a hard disk, some software will run faster and network traffic may be reduced, thus improving the performance of the entire network.

Computers to be used for administration should be purchased with both a floppy disk drive and a hard disk drive regardless of whether they are to be connected to a network or not. Computers to be used throughout the curriculum should also have both a floppy disk drive and a hard disk drive unless they are to be connected to a network. In this case, only a floppy disk drive is essential although a hard disk is useful. The school should provide sufficient storage capacity on hard disk for the software that pupils will use. Pupils should be encouraged to provide their own floppy disks to store the data files they generate. They should take responsibility for the care of their floppy disks as they do for school exercise books, text books and other personal learning resources.

CD-ROM is a form of audio CD adapted to store information for computers. CD-ROMs are comparable to floppy disks in that they are portable, however, they can store much more information, and computers can read the information from them much faster. The high storage capacity, fast access speed and portability of CD-ROM make this technology suitable for database applications where there is a need to access very high volumes of text, and for multimedia applications which include sound, pictures, video and text. A major disadvantage of CD-ROM technology is that it is not usually possible to write information to a CD-ROM more than once. Creating CD-ROMs is possible but expensive (Steadman, *et al.*, 1992). This effectively restricts the use of CD-ROM in schools to the storage of reference materials. CD-ROM drives will be most useful when located in areas accessible to pupils, such as the library, or when networked so that the information on them is available throughout the school. CD-ROM technology is a good platform for the development of the variety of attractive and useful applications, such as multimedia, that need to access high volumes of information quickly.

RAM and ROM memory is the area inside the computer where software and data files are stored while they are being used. This memory takes the physical form of microchips. Read Only Memory (ROM) is non-volatile and the information stored on it can only be read. Generally, ROM is installed before a computer is purchased and is used to store software that will always be needed by the computer. For example, in Archimedes computers the Operating System is stored in ROM. It is sometimes necessary to change the ROM, for example, to upgrade the Operating System, but this should only be necessary very infrequently.

Random Access Memory (RAM) is volatile and information can be read from it and written to it. When software is loaded into the computer, for example, from a hard disk, it is stored in RAM memory. When data files are generated, they are stored in RAM and must be saved on a non-volatile media, for example, a floppy disk, before the computer is switched off, as the contents of RAM are cleared at this time. Some RAM memory is installed before a computer is purchased. Its presence and function will be largely taken for granted until it becomes too small to run the required software or store the data files being used. This may happen because software is upgraded. New versions of software often require more RAM memory when they are loaded into the computer and run. They may run but run more slowly. As data files become larger, they may also use up RAM memory so that either the data files must be managed differently or more RAM memory must be made available. It is not uncommon for more RAM memory to be needed when a computer is two or three years old. RAM memory is relatively cheap and its installation is usually straightforward; installing more RAM memory can prolong the useful life of a computer.

The processor is the heart of the computer and its physical form is a microchip. There are a small number of processor manufacturers, such as Intel and Motorola, who produce the variety of different processors that are used by computer manufacturers when they assemble their products. Commonly used processors are the Intel Pentium, used in some IBM compatibles, and the Motorola 68040, used in some Apple computers. The processor is installed before the computer is purchased and it is not normally necessary to change it. Some computers are manufactured in such a manner that it is possible to upgrade the processor. However, it is likely that when the processor needs upgrading other components of the computer will also need upgrading. Consequently, it may be less expensive to buy a new computer than to upgrade an existing machine. The processor is an important factor in determining the speed of operation of the computer and the amount of memory the computer can use. These factors, in turn, influence the length of the useful life of a computer. When purchasing a computer, the fastest processor that can be afforded should be purchased.

Information stored on computers may only be accessed using a computer. Consequently, there is often a need to print some or all of the information stored. Indeed, computers are frequently used to prepare information for printing. Printers commonly used in schools may be classified as shown in Table 5.1.

A good quality black and white laser printer is adequate for management and administration in schools. Colour laser printers can be very expensive to buy and run, and often do not produce printout of a sufficiently high quality to enable schools to dispense with the services of a good commercial printer. For curriculum use, several dot matrix printers will be needed. If standalone computers are being used, it is preferable to share one printer between several computers using a printer sharer as this is more economical than buying a printer for each computer. If the computers are networked, two dot matrix printers for each cluster of network stations should be adequate. Printing will be queued by the fileserver and printed as soon as a

Table 5.1 The types of printer commonly used in schools

Type of printer	Mechanism	Type of printing	Characteristics
Dot matrix printer	Impact printer with ribbon	Black and white printing	Slow printing Low quality printout
Ink jet printer	Non-impact dot matrix printer using ink jet technology	Black and white printing and colour printing	Slow printing Good quality printout
Laser printer	Electrostatic drum	Black and white printing and colour printing	Fast printing High quality printout

printer is available. Black and white dot matrix printers are usually adequate for most of the work pupils will do as high quality printout is generally too expensive for regular use throughout the curriculum. However, where pupils' work is being prepared for external assessment, access to ink jet or laser printing facilities is worth considering. Where colour is an important element in the use of the computer, for example, in art or textile design, it is desirable to have a colour printer available. A colour ink jet printer will probably be adequate.

Optical Mark Readers (OMRs) are a specialised input device that will read marks on paper. The marks on the paper are made in a particular position depending on their meaning, so that the computer is able to work out what each mark means, for example, the form filled in by a customer buying a National Lottery ticket is an OMR form. The ticket is inserted into the Optical Mark Reader where the marks on the form (representing numbers) made by the customer are read into the computer which subsequently prints the chosen numbers on the receipt. This technology can be used to automate the marking of multiple choice test papers, the registration of pupils' attendance at school, and the generation of school reports. It can save considerable time and effort in comparison with that required to enter the same data via the keyboard. If possible, OMR and other Direct Data Entry peripherals, such as swipe card readers, should be used to automate routine tasks, reducing the time and effort needed for data entry.

Standalone computers, or more accurately, computers being used in standalone mode, are not in communication with other computers. Either they are not connected to other computers or they may be connected but not in communication with them. Standalone computers only make use of the hardware immediately accessible to them, and the software that can be accessed using this hardware. Standalone computers can be attached to networks of other computers either by connection through a modem to the telephone network or by connection to a Local Area Network (LAN).

A Modem (MODulator/DEModulator) converts signals from the computer to signals that can be transmitted over the telephone system and vice versa. A standalone computer can communicate with another computer if each computer has a modem and these are linked via the telephone network. Suitable communications software is also needed. Using a modem and the telephone network, computers can be attached to large national and international networks, for example, the Internet. These networks give users access to a wide range of services and information. However, connection to such networks can be expensive. There is usually an annual subscription, and telephone charges must be paid at local rates. However, there is a wealth of information available once schools are connected. Connection to the Internet makes available national and global electronic mail (e-mail) and access to the World Wide Web (WWW). The WWW has an astonishingly diverse range of information stored at an enormous number of sites throughout the world. One example is the British government's public access information service; its WWW address is: http://www.open.gov.uk. This multimedia database gives users access to a range of British and European governmental information, including OFSTED reports! It is but one example of the information accessible on the WWW. Much of the information is produced by multinational companies, universities, and research and special interest groups, giving pupils access to the most up-to-date information and opinion. Some WWW sites deal specifically with pupils' information needs. Connection to the Internet, perhaps via a subscription to BT's Campus 2000, Demon, Compulink or some other service provider, is worth considering for both curriculum and administration activities.

Standalone computers can also be attached to networks of other computers by connection to a Local Area Network (LAN). A LAN is a system of hardware, software and cabling which enables network stations attached to it to communicate with one another and share resources. A network station is a computer with the additional hardware and software to enable it to be attached to and communicate across the network. A LAN will have at least one fileserver. A fileserver is a dedicated computer that manages access to the shared software and other files stored on its hard disk, and the distribution of them across the network to network stations. There may also be a printer server, that is, a computer that manages access to the shared printers on the network. In many smaller LANs of the type found in schools, it is usual for one computer to act as both the fileserver and the printer server. The hard disk on the fileserver and the network printers are common examples of shared network resources. CD-ROM drives can also be shared across networks.

Schools often choose to install LANs instead of standalone computers. An alternative to buying twenty standalone computers for an IT room is to buy a network of twenty computers. Comparisons between these alternatives are difficult to evaluate as each has its advantages and disadvantages. Standalone computers may be more expensive as each may require a higher level of provision of local resources; they may need a hard disk and a printer each. Access to software may also be more difficult on standalone computers as it will be either distributed on floppy disks or installed on local hard disks. If software is distributed on floppy disks, teachers will need to organise at least one floppy disk per computer per piece of software. Computers with hard disks are more expensive than computers without hard disks. The software installed on the hard disk of each standalone computer has to be separately maintained. Its installation may be insecure as it may be easily accessible and could be corrupted by pupils. If every computer used has to be separately maintained, this task can become an overwhelming, time-consuming and expensive burden. When new standalone computers are purchased, each computer must be set up separately and the maintenance burden is correspondingly increased.

In contrast, where a LAN is in use, only one copy of each piece of software is installed on the fileserver and this is distributed to each network station on request. The software installation on the fileserver cannot be corrupted by pupils. Pupils' access to software can be managed, for a pupil or group of pupils, by modifying the menus of software available to them. Consequently, the specific menus of software to which groups of pupils are given access are more likely to be developed to meet their particular curricular needs. When the LAN is extended by adding new network stations to it, all the menus and software are immediately available on the new network stations without extensive, additional set-up or maintenance overheads.

A LAN of twenty computers in one IT room may be connected to a school-wide LAN. All the network stations attached to a school-wide LAN can be given access to the same menus of software whether they are situated in centralised IT rooms, or distributed throughout the school in, for example, the library or the Year 13 common room.

To summarise, it is usually better to buy a network of twenty computers on a LAN because:

- LANs can be easier to manage than large numbers of standalone computers;
- all software can be available at all network stations on the LAN;
- LANs can be used to distribute standardised menus of software throughout the school;
- LANs provide the possibility of managing the menus of software available in order to meet the curricular needs of specific groups of pupils more effectively;
- the cost of installing a LAN is roughly comparable with the cost of purchasing a similar number of standalone computers;
- the total cost, including staffing, of maintaining a LAN is likely to be much less than the total cost of maintaining a similar number of standalone computers.

A REVIEW OF THE ACTUAL PROVISION OF HARDWARE IN SECONDARY SCHOOLS

On average, in 1994, there were ten pupils per computer in secondary schools (DfE, 1995c), and in 1992, thirteen pupils per computer (DfE, 1993a). The average number of pupils per computer has been decreasing steadily since computers were first introduced into schools. In 1994, the average secondary school had eighty-five computers (in 1992, fifty-eight); spent £4,600 (£3,100) on IT equipment for use in administration; and £19,350 (£12,350) for IT equipment to be used throughout the curriculum. This gives an average spending per pupil per year of £29 in 1994 (£21 in 1992), that is, an annual increase in spending on IT of 19 per cent per pupil. Total spending on IT by all secondary schools amounted to £86.9 million in 1994 (£59.5 million in 1992), that is, an increase in total spending of 23 per cent per annum. In 1995, the education sector spent more on hardware than any other market sector, including business services, construction and central government (Green-Armytage, 1996).

In 1994, 94 per cent (in 1992, 88 per cent) of the funding for IT in secondary schools came from public funds. Capitation allowances provided around 62 per cent (52 per cent) of total funding; TVEI or TSI provided 22 per cent (24 per cent); LEAs and central government provided 10 per cent (12 per cent); and PTA or other sources provided 3 per cent (13 per cent).

The type of computer to be used in schools is not specified in the NC. Schools are left to make their own choices and traditionally, most schools have chosen to buy equipment supplied by either Acorn Computers, who manufacture the Archimedes computer, or Research Machines, who sell IBM compatible computers. Both manufacturers make considerable efforts to ensure that their hardware is suitable for use in schools. In 1994, 41 per cent (in 1992, 52.7 per cent) of the computers in use in secondary schools were manufactured by Acorn Computers. Of these, 21 per cent (17.7 per cent) were the more recent Archimedes model. Research Machines manufactured only 29 per cent (27.3 per cent) of the computers in use, but 27 per cent (24.1 per cent) were the more recent Nimbus models, most of which are IBM compatible. In 1996, the top suppliers in the education market were Research Machines (£74m), Apple (£39.5m), Compaq (£22m) and Acorn (£21m) (Green-Armytage, 1996). These figures suggest that the historical dominance of Acorn Computers is being challenged by the proliferation of IBM compatible computers, particularly those supplied by Research Machines. Acorn computers do not sell in large volumes outside the schools market whereas IBM compatible computers are the most widely used in FE and HE, and commerce and industry.

In 1994, secondary schools permanently located 35 per cent (in 1992, 45 per cent) of their computers in specialist IT rooms, with 43 per cent (35 per cent) in subject departments. The remainder were situated in the school library or freely available for use throughout the school. Some 75 per cent (70 per cent) of secondary school departments made use of IT, with 20 per cent (17 per cent) making substantial use of it. Some 94 per cent (86 per cent) of pupils had hands-on experience of IT during the school year and 62 per cent of all children have used a computer by the time they are 10 years old (Acey, 1993). In recent years, schools have moved away from curriculum models where IT is delivered entirely as a specialist subject, towards those where IT is used throughout the curriculum. It might be expected that this change in approach would lead to more hardware being distributed throughout the school, with correspondingly less hardware located in IT rooms. The above statistics indicate that this has happened, though not extensively.

HARDWARE PURCHASE

Hardware is expensive: the purchase of IT hardware requires major capital expenditure by schools. However, it is generally considered that IT hardware is technically obsolete in three to five years. Developments in IT are so rapid that hardware that is five years old will not do some of the tasks that more up-to-date hardware will do and even similar tasks will be performed differently.

In order to get the maximum benefit from the most up-to-date hardware, at the least cost, schools should plan to do the following:

- Buy hardware as cheaply as possible. Schools should negotiate discounts wherever possible. Do not wait to be offered a discount – ask for one. The list price published is always negotiable. There are many suppliers who want your custom. If your supplier will not offer you an educational discount then make it obvious that you will try elsewhere and do so.
- Buy in bulk. Schools will be able to negotiate even higher discounts when purchasing, for example, twenty computers and the associated peripheral devices.
- Get new computers into use as soon as possible. If it is not possible to negotiate a cash discount on purchases, try to obtain a discount in kind: for example, software or services. This could usefully include installation of the new computers at the school.
- Ensure the school's computers are heavily used. If this use is appropriate and educationally sound, the school and its pupils will obtain maximum benefit and value for money. Computers are technically obsolete in three to five years but they can continue to work for a much longer period, for example, the BBC computers purchased in the early 1980s are still in use in many schools. Whilst it is possible that these older computers are of a more robust build quality, it is much more likely that they have not been

65

heavily used. When they were purchased they provided pupils with a satis-factory experience of IT. It is unlikely that they are still able to do so.

- Ensure that the school's computers are repaired as soon as possible when they develop faults. Schools should have well-established arrangements for maintenance in order to ensure speedy repairs. Maintenance arrangements should cover parts and labour. Repairs should be completed on-site or an equivalent replacement computer provided. Satisfactory arrangements include a maintenance guarantee with the supplying company; a mainte-nance contract with a third party maintenance company, and the employment of a competent IT technician.

- Sell computers after three to five years and replace them with more modern equipment. Computers that are between three to five years old will still command a relatively high resale value. This will always be the best strategy unless older computers can be made use of where their lack of modern functionality is not important. For example, the BBC computers purchased in the early 1980s are still useful for data logging and control activities. Consequently, many schools still use them where these activities take place, that is, in Science and Technology. However, in general, it is not economic to retain older equipment. Eventually, this will have a very low resale value or no resale value at all. Older computers rapidly become outdated and, as a result, provide an unsatisfactory experience of IT for pupils and limit the efficiency of administrative work.

The above recommendations are not usually put into practice in schools. Schools tend to treat hardware purchases as if they are permanent acquisi-tions. They do not generally take into account that IT hardware rapidly becomes obsolete. Consequently, many schools are equipped with increas-ingly large numbers of obsolete computers. It may look as if the school is well equipped when the computers are counted but only a small proportion of the computers available are able to provide pupils with a satisfactory experience of IT.

Consider an average secondary school with 850 pupils in total. If the school is to achieve the 1994 national average pupil : computer ratio, it will need eighty-five computers in the school. This could consist of, for example, three IT rooms, each with twenty computers; four clusters of five computers in open access areas and five computers for use elsewhere. To keep its hard-ware and software up to date, the school will need to replace 20 per cent of it each year. That is, seventeen new computers, and the associated software, will be required each year. This is affordable within the £19,350 spent by the average secondary school in 1994.

It would be prudent to replace all the computers in an IT room at the same time. This might require the purchase of twenty modern computers, the associated peripheral hardware, and software. The software could be stored on a new fileserver which also acts as a printer sharer for two networked printers. The computers could be networked within the IT room and connected to the school network. In 1996, these IT resources could be purchased for around £30,000. If the old IT hardware and software that has been replaced is sold, this could raise £3,000. The funding gap of £7,650 (= £30,000 – £19,350 – £3,000) is the annual increase in spending on IT resources that is required to change an average secondary school from a repository of obsolete hardware to a school with the very latest IT resources. Spending at this level per annum would allow the average secondary school to replace all its IT resources and purchase additional specialist equipment (e.g. scanners and CD-ROM stacks) every five years.

Leasing is an alternative to purchasing and it spreads costs over several years. For example, instead of a lump sum payment of £30,000 in the first year, a school could pay £7,594 per annum for five years (Research Machines, 1995). Initially, this looks very attractive as the advantages are:

- the equipment is installed immediately without high initial costs;
- payments are spread over five years;
- expenditure is known in advance.

However, there are some disadvantages as well:

- a lease costs more in the long run, in the example given above it costs £7,970 more (5 × £7,594 – £30,000);
- at the end of the lease the school does not own the equipment, which will be taken away if no further payments are made;
- if the school has planned to replace all its IT resources every five years then leasing is more expensive year on year. In the example, leasing would cost £39,850 per annum (5 × £7,970) whereas purchasing would cost only £30,000.

Set-up costs also need to be taken into account: for example, the alterations that may be needed to premises; INSET training for teachers; and other associated changes that may be necessary before new IT resources can be deployed effectively. However, a substantial part of these set-up costs may only be needed when schools are equipped for the first time. Once electric wiring and sockets are installed in IT rooms they do not need renewing every five years.

Schools should implement plans to keep their hardware, software and other IT resources up to date. That some do not do so may be more related to a lack of institutional awareness and effective planning than a lack of resources. The provision of up-to-date hardware and software is central to providing pupils with a satisfactory experience of IT.

HARDWARE CARE AND MAINTENANCE

Schools should organise their IT resources so that they are accessible and secure. Rooms where IT is to be used will need organising so that hardware can be safely and conveniently used. At least two sockets will be needed for a computer and a printer. As many as thirty electrical sockets may be needed in an IT room. This is rather more than is normally provided in a school classroom. Provision of additional electrical sockets may also be needed elsewhere where IT resources are to be used.

In IT rooms, it may be necessary to provide additional benches for the computers as well as desks for pupils. Pupils may work on the computers some of the time but they will need to work away from the computers at other times. In most classrooms, desk space is provided only for pupils. This implies that IT rooms should be larger than most other classrooms. The benches provided for the computers should have more depth than is usual as computers often do not fit on benches or desks of a standard depth. These benches will need some arrangement to contain the cables connecting the computers and their peripheral devices. For safety reasons, these should not be accessible to pupils.

Computers are easily damaged by food and drink and therefore preventative measures should be taken. Do not let pupils eat or drink when using computers. Few pupils intend to pour their drinks over the printer or squash their sandwiches into the keyboard, but these, and other, unfortunate events do happen when pupils are allowed to eat and drink while using the computers.

Dust can seriously damage computer equipment. If dust penetrates the hard disk unit, a head crash may occur, destroying the hard disk and all the data on it. This could be a very expensive accident. Consequently, if building or repair work has to be carried out in IT resource areas, computers should be removed or covered to protect them from dust. Chalk dust can also be harmful. Whiteboards should be used in IT rooms, otherwise, blackboards should be placed as far as possible from computer equipment.

Damp or other ingress of water can affect all electrical equipment. Computers are particularly vulnerable to the damage caused by damp. This may cause shorting in electrical circuits as there are many exposed connections inside all hardware devices. It is particularly important not to locate computers in rooms with leaking roofs, walls, windows or other problems with damp. Similarly, computers, floppy disks and cabling should not be placed where they will overheat due to exposure to the sun or the school's central heating system as this could result in permanent damage.

Computers can be affected by smoke from a fire. If they are exposed to smoke, before the computers are used again, all exterior surfaces should be wiped and the read/write heads in the floppy disk drives should be cleaned. In computer rooms, there is a risk of electrical fire because of the high concentration of vulnerable electrical cables and other equipment. There is also a fire risk due to the large quantities of waste paper generated by printers which is often strewn carelessly around the floor. A tidier regime may be indicated. Local fire officers should be consulted regarding the appropriate provision of fire extinguishers for electrical fires and the other types of fire that may occur in a computer room.

Data stored on magnetic disks or transmitted via network cables can be corrupted by exposure to electro-magnetic fields. Do not locate disk units or network cables near mains electrical cables. Floppy disks should not be left unshielded on televisions or monitors.

Hardware is often damaged when it is being moved. It is better to locate IT hardware in a permanent location so that pupils and staff must go to it if they wish to use it. However, hardware may need to be moved because it is being repaired or permanently relocated, or because it is a shared resource, for example, where one or two computers are shared between different classes. Prior to moving a computer system, the various cables must be disconnected. When the computer is in its new location these cables must be reconnected. Cables are most often lost and the connecting plugs and sockets damaged when computers are disconnected and reassembled. Some hardware devices, e.g. monitors, are heavy and their weight distribution is uneven. This sometimes makes the transport of hardware from one location to another particularly difficult. The use of a trolley is recommended when hardware is being moved as this will protect both the hardware and the personnel moving the hardware. It is particularly important that a trolley is used when computers are regularly moved from classroom to classroom.

Various security measures can protect IT resources from theft and malicious damage. Equipment in ground floor rooms is visible and accessible to thieves, who may enter through the exterior windows or walls. IT rooms should not normally be located in ground floor rooms. If this is unavoidable, the windows of IT rooms should have opaque security laminates and grilles or bars. The walls in some schools are very thin, sometimes comprising only wood panels and plaster board and these are easily penetrated and can be an alternative means of access for thieves. IT equipment placed in rooms on the top storey of a school may be accessible to thieves entering through the roof. Thieves may also enter from inside the school when the school is open but not in use: for example, in the holidays or at the end of the school day. It is surprising how often IT rooms that have been carefully locked by the IT Co-ordinator at the end of the school day, can be found standing open with little supervision much later in the evening. Careful supervision is necessary at all times to deny access to IT resources to those that are not entitled to use them.

Further precautions can be taken to prevent thieves stealing IT resources once they have entered the building. The component parts of computers can be chained together and the processor boxes can be clamped to the benches. PIR sensors connected to the school's burglar alarm system can be located in IT rooms and adjacent corridors. The computers should also be connected to an independent loop alarm system similar to that used in department stores to prevent the theft of electrical goods. This can be left switched on when the school's burglar alarm is inactive. The fileserver may be locked in a secure room within an IT room. Each item of equipment should have the name of the school indelibly etched into its casing.

A comprehensive inventory of all IT resources should be kept. This should identify what the school owns, its value, where it is located and who has responsibility for it. Before calling the police to investigate theft, it would be prudent to discover exactly what is missing, and whether it has been stolen or simply borrowed. It is not unknown for members of staff to move equipment within the school without the knowledge of those responsible for it. Clear guidelines are needed regarding the relocation or loan of IT resources as there will be a considerable number of items of hardware and smaller pieces of equipment whose whereabouts must be carefully controlled. The establishment and maintenance of an up-to-date, comprehensive inventory is the basis of sensible management and control of IT resources within the school. This is also an essential basis for assessing the insurance required and making claims.

Schools should consider insuring all IT resources, including both hardware and software, but especially hardware. Software can often be restored from backup copies. In contrast, the loss of or damage to hardware will have an immediate impact which may affect all curricular and administrative activities. Loss of or damage to one or two items of hardware is less important than wide-scale loss or damage due to, for example, a major theft, fire or flood. Insurance should cover damage to or loss of the bulk of IT resources, and allow for their speedy replacement at current values. The loss of one or two items of equipment is less costly and might be paid for from current income or otherwise accommodated. Schools could consider an insurance excess equivalent to the replacement cost of one or two computers if it is desired to reduce the overall cost of insurance.

HARDWARE DISTRIBUTION

Access to IT resources by staff and pupils is affected by the distribution of hardware throughout the school. Ideally, pupils should have access to IT resources when they need them, but this is rarely achieved in practice. Schools usually choose one or more of the following when distributing hardware:

- the centralisation of hardware in specialised IT rooms;
- the distribution of hardware in small clusters, in easily accessible locations throughout the school;
- the sharing of hardware using trolleys that can be wheeled from one classroom to another;
- the permanent location of one or two computers in some classrooms.

The balance between centralisation and more widespread distribution will vary between schools. If hardware is centralised in two or three computer rooms, it may not be as readily accessible to all classes as when small clusters and individual computers are distributed throughout the school. However, if accessibility is judged by the proportion of the school day that the computers are in use, then it is clear that the centralisation of IT resources leads to better access for most pupils most of the time. Unfortunately, centralisation may sometimes exclude some teachers and some pupils. Some classes may be taught too far away from the IT rooms for their use to be a practical possibility, or they may want access when the IT rooms are fully timetabled. Centralisation that is not accompanied by some distribution invariably leads to access problems.

Schools should make arrangements so that all staff and all pupils have potential access to IT resources. Individual teachers should write their schemes of work and manage their lessons so that all their pupils can access IT resources when they need them. Teachers should plan which pupils are to use IT resources and when they are to make use of them. With centralised IT resources, this can often be done through the timetable, with an additional booking system for periods when IT rooms are not fully timetabled. It is essential that this booking system is published and well known to all teaching staff so that they do not feel excluded from making use of IT resources.

When small numbers of computers are used in the classroom, it is likely that a few pupils will use the computers while most of the class continue with other activities. It is often easier to plan such lessons if pupils work in groups doing a series of different activities, some of which involve using the computers. If different groups of pupils within the class do the activities in different orders, it will be possible to ensure that each group has access to the computers when they are doing related activities. This can take place within a lesson or over a number of lessons. Teachers should ensure that all pupils have the opportunity to and are expected to make use of IT resources.

Another means of providing pupils with ready access to IT resources is to make some of these resources available on an 'open access' basis but this requires careful management. Pupils will need to be supervised when using open access IT resources, with the possible exception of years 12 and 13. Arranging such supervision is difficult and most schools find that it must be done within current staffing. If the school library is appropriately staffed, one possibility is to locate some open access IT resources in the library. These are then available to pupils when the library is open. Clusters of four or five computers can be situated throughout the school in locations where they can be easily observed by teachers in adjoining classrooms. It is particularly worthwhile considering designating areas adjoining IT rooms for open access as in these situations pupils will have access to both IT resources and, possibly, expert help. The provision of such open access facilities is a small step in the direction of making IT resources available to pupils when they need them.

SUMMARY

In 1994, the average secondary school spent £4,600 on IT for administration and £19,350 on IT for the curriculum. Despite this, many schools are equipped with increasingly large numbers of obsolete computers. However, the annual increase in funding required to keep IT resources up to date is relatively small.

On average, secondary schools had eighty-five computers and ten pupils per computer. Some 35 per cent of these were permanently located in IT rooms and 43 per cent in subject departments. Typically schools organise their IT hardware so that it is:

- centralised in several IT rooms;
- distributed in small clusters throughout the school;
- shared between classes using trolleys;
- permanently located in small numbers in some classrooms.

IT resources should be accessible. Ideally, pupils should have access to IT resources when they need it. If all hardware is centralised, it may not be as readily accessible as when there are some small clusters and individual computers distributed throughout the school. Teachers should carefully manage pupils' access to IT resources, especially when they are using small numbers of computers in the classroom.

IT resources should be secure. Some useful general security measures are as follows:

- IT rooms should not be located on the ground floor;
- the windows of IT rooms should screened and barred;
- computers should be chained together and clamped to the benches;
- PIR sensors connected to the school's burglar alarm system should be installed in IT rooms, and an independent alarm system used that can be activated when the school's burglar alarm system is switched off;
- each item of equipment should have the name of the school indelibly etched into its casing;
- preventative measures should be taken to avoid damage to computers by food and drink, dust, damp, heat, fire, smoke and electromagnetic fields.

An inventory of IT resources should be kept to assist with the management of IT resources and in assessing any insurance cover required. Loss of or damage to software or hardware will affect all administrative and curricular activities. Insurance should allow for replacement at current values.

6

SOFTWARE

This chapter reviews some of the practical considerations that should be taken into account when acquiring and managing software. Some suggestions are made regarding what can be done to avoid or overcome the corruption or loss of software.

THE SOFTWARE THAT SHOULD BE AVAILABLE AND ITS CHARACTERISTICS

The software required by schools so that they can provide pupils with a satisfactory experience of IT is not summarised in the NC. However, its characteristics can be deduced from the Programmes of Study (PoS) that pupils must follow, and an understanding of the curriculum contexts in which they must follow them. Many pupils will follow GCSE IT or other external syllabuses during KS4. Once again, these do not always clearly specify which software is required. However, some do, notably the SEG GCSE IT syllabus. A careful reading of the relevant literature indicates the range of general purpose software, and Computer Assisted Learning (CAL) software required.

General purpose software

In order to fulfil the PoS for IT, and meet the requirements of GCSE IT syllabuses, by the end of KS4, pupils should have been taught to use a wide range of general purpose software, including:

- an operating system, incorporating a Graphics User Interface;
- a wordprocessor;
- graphics (paint and draw) software;
- Desk Top Publishing software;
- a spreadsheet with a facility for graph plotting;
- a database;
- data logging software to measure and record events as they happen, at a

distance, over long periods of time, or in inhospitable situations, using sensors;
- a control language, for example, for robotic control;
- a general purpose programming language that allows the creation and modification of procedures and programs, and the use of variables, as in for example, Logo or BASIC;
- software for simulation and modelling;
- on-line information sources – for example, WWW sites;
- communications software, such as e-mail;
- multimedia – for example, on CD-ROM;
- software for manipulating and controlling sound and visual images – for example, for composition in Music;
- Teletext, or an emulator.

CAL software

Pupils should make use of IT throughout the curriculum. Some of their cross-curricular experiences of IT will involve the use of general purpose software in subject specific contexts. In addition, pupils may find CAL software useful in acquiring subject-specific skills, knowledge and understanding. For example, pupils may use software that helps them to do the following:

- learn the terminology of river valleys in Geography;
- construct and manipulate flowcharts in Technology, time lines in History, or population pyramids in Geography;
- apply vector algebra in Mathematics;
- construct wordsearches and crosswords in English.

There is a wide range of CAL software available. Unfortunately, its focus is often narrow, and its scope fragmented. For example, there is a wide range of CAL software for some aspects of mathematics. Pupils can practise their multiplication tables, draw graphs and analyse statistics. However, there have been few serious attempts to provide a well-integrated suite of software covering all the mathematical skills pupils need. Recently, Integrated Learning Systems (ILS) have been introduced that claim to cover all the mathematical components of GCSE or A-level syllabuses. Coverage is better and integration has been improved. Even so, most ILS are not yet entirely comprehensive or fully integrated.

Software selection

A list of the software that pupils should or might make use of is a helpful starting point when purchasing new software or reassessing the adequacy of the existing range of software available in school. Reference to such a list will help schools ensure they have a sufficiently wide range of software available for pupils to use. Some other considerations that will affect the selection of software are reviewed below.

Software should be easy to use. It should be simple for pupils to learn how to operate the software, and easy to operate it, so that the complexity of the software does not prevent them making effective use of IT. IT should help pupils with their learning and it should be an aid to learning not a barrier. As software is improved from one version to the next, developers try to make the software easier for users to understand and operate; in addition, they also attempt to incorporate more functionality. These objectives may conflict as, unfortunately, on occasions, increased functionality leads to increased complexity of operation. Where software is produced mainly for commercial use, schools may find that they do not need the increased functionality that accompanies new versions of software. The latest version of a piece of software is almost always considerably more expensive than a slightly older version and in this case, the purchase of a slightly older version of the software might be more appropriate. Cut-down versions of software are sometimes available. These are often cheaper versions of current software with the less frequently used functions removed. These cut-down versions may be much easier to use than the full version and still incorporate all the functions schools require. Schools should consider purchasing slightly older versions or cut-down versions of current software if these are suitable. For example, Pagemaker Classic is a much less expensive version of the popular Pagemaker DTP software. It has reduced functionality but, even so, is more than adequate for use in the classroom.

Software should allow pupils to progress as they develop. It should provide a differentiated experience of IT for pupils at different levels of ability. Younger pupils and the less able will need access to software that is appropriate to their level of development. Such software should be easy to understand and use, with a much reduced range of functions. The simplest software will provide pupils with easy access to only essential, easy to use functions. As pupils develop, their understanding of the operation of IT software and hardware will grow, so that they can be expected to make greater use of more functions that are increasingly complex to understand and operate, with a wider range of options. It is unlikely that one piece of software of a particular type will allow for progression from the lowest levels of attainment to the highest. Thus, a complete version of an industry standard wordprocessor that gives pupils access to a full range of functions is unlikely to be entirely suitable for the least able. Schools that wish to make such software available to pupils should also consider purchasing a cut-down version of the same software, or another, simpler piece of software that is more suitable for younger or less able pupils. The best software allows pupils to access it at a level appropriate to their abilities. For example, a version of Word for Windows available from Research Machines allows pupils to access it at different levels.

This software has restricted functionality at the lower levels, progressing to a full commercial version of the software at the highest level.

Continuity and transfer of learning should be maximised by the provision of a consistent experience of IT throughout the school. This can be achieved in a variety of ways. One means of providing an entirely consistent experience of IT for all pupils, throughout the school, is by giving them access only to networked computers that present exactly the same user interface. Pupils using such a network more readily acquire expertise in the use of it. Whenever and wherever they use IT resources in school, they use the same IT resources. The knowledge and understanding acquired in IT lessons or elsewhere are directly applicable in other lessons. However, pupils' knowledge of the school's IT network may not equip them to make use of different IT resources elsewhere. Schools themselves often use a variety of different types of IT hardware because of the different requirements of different subjects and the legacy of earlier purchases. Thus, a school-wide IT network may not be satisfactory for Music, where additional facilities and equipment may be needed, such as computers with midi ports for connection to synthesisers and drum machines.

Another way of providing a reasonably consistent experience of IT for all pupils is to ensure that all the computers they operate have similar user interfaces. Ideally, despite differences in the software and hardware being used, the style of operation should be similar. Graphical User Interfaces (GUIs) provide the easiest to operate, most consistent user interface across different types of hardware and software. They are used in a similar manner on different types of computer and provide a similar means of access to like functions. All computers used for IT in schools up to the end of KS4 should have a Graphic User Interface available. Fortunately, all the popular types of modern computer hardware used in schools can be operated using a GUI. Archimedes and Apple computers automatically display a GUI at start-up; IBM compatibles may be customised to display a GUI at start-up, for example, Windows. In some instances, the same software will run on different hardware, for example, Claris Works is available for both Apple computers and IBM compatible computers. This further extends consistency across different hardware platforms.

In practice, most schools will find it difficult to achieve consistency across all the IT resources used by pupils. Schools can realistically aim for most of their IT resources to be based on the same type of hardware and software. This is best done using a network. The use of GUIs where possible will extend reasonable consistency beyond the main type of IT resource. However, there will almost always be some computers, often older computers, that are operated in an inconsistent manner. Whilst this makes pupils' experience of IT in school less consistent and their learning less transferable, it also exposes them to the variety of styles of operation of IT equipment in use in the wider community and at work. This is not entirely undesirable.

Software should be robust and otherwise usable within a school environment. Software that ceases to work effectively without warning for whatever reason is particularly unsuitable for use in schools. What is acceptable in commerce and industry may not be appropriate in schools. When pupils are learning to use software they will make mistakes. User-friendly software that responds to their mistakes by displaying a meaningful message describing their error and suggesting what should be done helps pupils' learning. Software that crashes in response to user errors or displays cryptic, meaningless messages with no obvious indication of what should be done is unhelpful and inhibits learning. It is not unusual to find that software intended for use in commerce and industry is not sufficiently robust, user-friendly or otherwise usable in schools. Classes using a school's network may attempt to load forty or more network stations with the same piece of software at the same time at the start of a lesson. This could happen at the start of every lesson throughout the day in one or more IT rooms. Repeated loading of multiple copies of the same piece of software is less likely in commerce and industry. Consequently, the effects of this behaviour in schools may not have been considered by the software designers. It is not unusual to find that repeated loading of multiple copies of the same software takes an unacceptable length of time relative to the length of a lesson. To protect themselves from such consequences of the different design requirements of software for education and industry, schools should trial software with a full class in a realistic teaching situation to ensure it is suitable before it is purchased.

SOFTWARE LICENSING

When buying software, purchasers may acquire some or all of:

- a copy of the software on a floppy disk or a CD-ROM;
- a manual explaining how to use the software;
- a licence to use the software.

The owners of software restrict its distribution and sale by licensing it. A software licence gives users the rights to run software under the specific conditions and restrictions stated. Users should conform to the conditions and restrictions specified in their licence when they use the associated software. If a user does not possess a licence for the software then the user's use of it is illegal. It is assumed that if software is installed on a hard disk or there is a copy of it on a floppy disk then it is in use. Schools should not use any software that is not licensed to them.

There are three general categories of software with distinctive licensing arrangements. These are commonly known as:

- Licensed software
- Public domain software
- Shareware.

77

Licensed software is sold and purchasers buy the rights to use the software. These rights are typically one or more of the following:

- the right to use the software on a single standalone computer;
- the right to use the software on a specified number of standalone computers;
- the right to distribute the software over a network for use on a specified number of network stations;
- a site licence, giving the right to distribute and use the software on any computer on a site.

The cost of acquiring a software licence is usually at its highest per user when the right to use a single copy of the software is purchased. It is usual for the cost of individual usage to be at its lowest when a site licence is purchased. However, a site licence may be considerably more expensive than the licence for a single user. Consequently, when purchasing software, schools should consider the extent to which the software will be used. Site licences are preferable where the software will be in widespread use throughout the school as a site licence has the advantage that it covers all the computers on the site at the time of purchase and in the future, consequently, no further rights to use the software are needed for any additional hardware that may be purchased. However, the expense of a site licence may not be justified if only very limited use of the software is anticipated.

Public domain software is free software. The owners of the software make it available to anyone who wants to use it, or specific groups of users, at zero purchase cost. It is usually considered acceptable for distributors, such as mail order companies, to charge buyers the cost of distribution. Owners may place any restriction on the use of the software that they wish. Even so, most public domain software carries no restrictions on its use. Schools should use public domain software whenever possible as the cost of acquiring it may be very low. However, although there is some excellent public domain software, much of it is unusable, or unsuitable for schools. Schools wanting to investigate the range of public domain software available should look for suppliers' advertisements in user magazines. Alternatively, the Higher Education National Software Archive (HENSA) at Lancaster University is a useful source of public domain software. It is accessible on the WWW.

Shareware is licensed software that is initially distributed freely in the manner of public domain software. Users may install the software and try it out. However, if they decide to make regular use of the software they must pay a licence fee. Some shareware is free to specific groups of users: for example, the FileExpress shareware database is free to users in education but other users must pay a licence fee. The owners of the software trust users to pay the licence fee. Users sometimes receive improved versions of the software or a manual when the licence fee is paid. If the payment of a licence fee is required, schools should pay for any shareware they use. Where the licence fee is not paid, use of the software is illegal.

SOFTWARE SECURITY

All users need to protect themselves against the loss of software and this is especially so in schools where many users of different status have access to the software. Not all users will make use of the available software in sensible or ethical ways. Loss of software can be caused by theft of the software or damage to it. Software can be stolen by the removal of the floppy disks or hard disks it is stored on, or by users copying it illegally. Damage to software can be caused by physical damage to the media it is stored on, or by the corruption or deletion of all or part of the software whilst it is stored on disk. This may occur as a result of the malfunction of the computer system, or be done inadvertently or maliciously by users.

Damage to software often occurs inadvertently as a result of attempts to improve the working of a computer system. The extreme complexity and interdependence of the software and hardware components of a computer system can lead to malfunctions that, in practice, cannot be explained within the technical and time constraints imposed on most IT technicians in schools. This encourages technical staff to seek solutions by trial and error methods. Inevitably, mistakes occur resulting in damage to software.

The physical precautions taken to prevent hardware theft reviewed in the previous chapter also provide protection against software theft. Software stored on hard disks is protected against theft to the extent that the hardware is protected. Software stored on floppy disk is much more vulnerable and should be locked in a secure cabinet when not in use.

Viruses can cause extensive damage to computer systems. They infect a computer system when they are transferred onto the system from an infected source. Most virus infections are caused by the use of infected floppy disks or the copying of infected software over a network. Viruses can seriously affect the operation of a computer system. For example, the Form virus infects both floppy disks and hard disks, corrupting software and data files. The damaging impact of viruses can be limited by using software that will detect and kill viruses. It should be used on all computers. Hard disks and computer memory should be checked for the presence of viruses at least once each day. This can be done automatically at the start of the day when the computer is switched on, or each time a user logs on to a network. Floppy disks should be checked when they are inserted into a disk drive. Any virus detected should be killed immediately. Infected disks should not be used until the virus has been killed.

Protection against damage to software as a result of corruption or deletion is achieved by restricting the rights users have to manipulate software. The right to use software on a computer system can be restricted by requiring users to enter a personal user identity number and password before they are given access to it. Most users will only be given the right to use software but not to delete it, move it or overwrite it. These precautions help guard against damage to software but they are not infallible; most computer systems can be penetrated by hackers who may cause malicious damage to software.

Whatever the cause of loss of software, the most effective precaution against its permanent loss is to make backup copies. It is essential that schools make regular backup copies of all software and other information stored on hard disks. This must be stressed. Schools that do not make sufficient, regular backup copies expose themselves to the risk of software loss that can be immediately and permanently damaging. Let us suppose that the school prospectus has just been typed into the computer. It has taken several weeks to compile it, drawing information from many sources within and outside of the school. A printed copy is needed immediately for approval by the governors that evening so that it can be professionally printed and distributed to prospective parents the following week. Unfortunately, the hard disk the prospectus is stored on crashes, destroying all the data on it. If regular backup copies have been taken, this is a crisis that can be quickly overcome. Without a backup copy, weeks of work may have to be repeated and the school will appear incompetent as simple preventative measures were not in place. More seriously, the prospectus may not get to parents in time to influence their choice of school. This may affect the school's income for future years.

Backup copies can be made by copying all the data on a hard disk onto any magnetic storage medium. The data on a hard disk can be copied onto a removable hard disk, onto floppy disks, or onto a magnetic tape cartridge using a tape streamer. Copying backup data onto removable hard disks is fast but expensive. Making backup copies onto floppy disks is very slow but they are a very cheap storage medium. The most appropriate backup medium for schools is magnetic tape cartridges. Data can be copied to these much faster than to floppy disks and they are very much less expensive than removable hard disks. However, if backup copies are to be made of only the data files on a hard disk, then these may be quickly copied to floppy disk using a backup utility, such as Fastback. When software is lost, it can be quickly restored to its original condition by copying it back to the hard disk from the backup medium.

Backup copies should be organised using the ancestral system with its multi-layered structure. A typical, three-layered system for making backup copies of all the software and data stored on a hard disk would be structured as shown in Table 6.1. The magnetic tapes would continue to be used in rotation following on in the order tape (C), tape (A), tape (B), tape (C), tape (A) and so on. If software loss occurs, the software can be restored from the most recent backup copy. If the software on this tape is found to be damaged, then it can be restored from the next most recent backup copy,

Table 6.1 A system for making backup copies

Time	Task
End of first period	Copy all the data on the hard disk onto magnetic tape (A) using a tape streamer.
End of second period	Copy all the data on the hard disk onto magnetic Tape (B) using a tape streamer.
End of third period	Copy all the data on the hard disk onto magnetic Tape (C) using a tape streamer.
End of fourth period	Copy all the data on the hard disk onto magnetic tape (A) using a tape streamer.
End of fifth period	Copy all the data on the hard disk onto magnetic Tape (B) using a tape streamer.

and so on. The most recent backup copy should be stored on site in a secure but accessible location; the next most recent copy should be stored in a secure, fireproof safe in another accessible location; the oldest copy should be stored in a secure, fireproof safe off site. This three-layered system is adequate protection for most purposes.

Clearly, protection can be increased by using more magnetic tapes to create more layers. Protection can also be increased by shortening the period of time between backup copies. It is probably sufficient for curriculum software to have a backup copy made at the end of each week, using three layers of backup copies. In the school office, it may be advisable to use five magnetic tapes, one for each working day. This simplifies the organisation, and provides a high degree of protection against software loss. These tapes could be stored on site in an accessible fireproof safe. A further five tapes from the previous week could be stored in a fireproof safe off site. The two sets of five tapes could be swapped at weekends. This system would provide a high level of backup protection.

Unfortunately, even the most extensive levels of backup protection will not entirely protect users from the consequences of virus infection. If a virus is found and removed after it has destroyed vital data files, it may be possible to restore these from a backup copy. However, if virus checks are not done thoroughly and frequently, it is possible that backup copies will also have been infected by the virus. The longer it takes to detect and kill a virus, the more layers of backup copies will be infected.

SUMMARY

Schools need a variety of software to provide pupils with a satisfactory experience of IT. Pupils entered for GCSE IT should be able to use a GUI; a wordprocessor; graphics software; DTP software; a spreadsheet; a database;

data logging software; a control language; a general purpose programming language; software for simulation and modelling; software for manipulating sound and visual images; on-line information sources; CD-ROM; communications software, including e-mail; multimedia; and teletext. Pupils may also use IT for Computer Assisted Learning in a range of subjects.

A list of the software that pupils should be able to use is a helpful starting point when assessing software provision. Other considerations also affect the selection of software. Software should be easy to use; it should allow pupils to progress as they develop; and it should provide a differentiated experience of IT for pupils at different levels of ability. Continuity and transfer of learning should be maximised by the provision of a consistent experience of IT. Software should be robust and otherwise usable in a school environment.

Schools should conform to the conditions specified in their software licences. These licences are usually bought with the software. Site licences are preferable where the software will be in use throughout the school. Schools should use public domain software or shareware if it is suitable as the cost of acquiring it is often very low. Schools should not use software that is not licensed to them.

Schools need to protect themselves against software loss or damage. Some protection is achieved by requiring users to enter a user identification number and a password before they can use IT resources, and by restricting what they are permitted to do. Viruses also cause extensive damage to software. They should be regularly detected and killed. Whatever the cause of software loss or damage, the most effective precaution against permanent damage or loss is to make regular backup copies.

7

HEALTH AND SAFETY

An environment that is good for computers is usually good for people. A clean, dust-free, dry, warm, well-ventilated environment is good for IT equipment and good for pupils and teachers. However, there are a number of health problems that have been associated with using computers. Very often the association is speculative not proven. Most health problems occur when users make regular and intensive use of computers. Some may occur in schools but most will not. However, it is prudent to be aware of the possible impact of using computers on teachers' and pupils' health as existing health problems may be exacerbated by relatively low usage.

The extensive use of a monitor screen may cause headaches and eye strain, and induce photosensitive (flicker-induced) epilepsy (HSE, 1990). Headaches and eye strain may be caused by a poor quality monitor display and intensive computer usage over a long period of time. A poor quality monitor display may be due to the use of old equipment; purchasing a new monitor of inferior quality; or locating the monitor in a position where there is too much light falling on the screen. A good quality monitor should present a stable, flicker-free screen image. Reading the screen should be nearly as comfortable as reading a book. Old monitors that are unsatisfactory should be replaced. Insist on testing new monitors with a variety of text-based and graphics software before purchase so that the stability of the screen display can be assessed.

Excessive screen static is particularly associated with headaches. To test for excessive screen static, after the monitor has been switched on for fifteen minutes or more, touch the screen with your finger tips and if you receive a static shock, the screen is unsuitable for continuous use. Monitors should be located so that they face away from windows and bright electric lights. Otherwise, these will be reflected on the screen, making it difficult to read.

Headaches and eye strain caused by intensive computer usage over a long period of time are not usually a problem for pupils as they are unlikely to use computers at school for long periods of time without interruption. Those pupils who regularly use home computers, and office staff and teachers who make extensive use of IT throughout the school day, could be affected. Headaches and eye strain can be reduced by taking regular breaks. A break of ten minutes in every hour spent away from the computer can help reduce these symptoms and may also improve concentration.

Photosensitive epilepsy will not be caused by using a monitor but it may be induced in people who already suffer from it. Photosensitive epilepsy is very rare. Pupils will be affected by looking at a monitor screen to the same extent that they are affected by watching television. Schools should identify pupils likely to be at risk. Some schools ask all parents during the initial information gathering exercise undertaken when pupils start at the school whether their child has photosensitive epilepsy. This is to be recommended. If pupils are found to be susceptible, their doctor should be consulted so that the extent of the risk and its effects on a particular child can be assessed. If necessary, pupils with this condition should be withdrawn from lessons where problems are likely to arise. However, adverse reactions are not entirely predictable. Some sufferers find that they can use monitors without provoking an attack.

It is sometimes suggested that other possible consequences of the excessive use of monitors are reduced fertility, a higher likelihood of pregnant women having a miscarriage, and harm to the unborn child. However, there is little hard evidence that this is the case (HSE, 1990). The radiation emitted by monitors is normally very much less than that from natural sources such as the sun or other people. It is well below the levels considered harmful by responsible expert bodies such as the National Radiological Board.

Rooms where computers are used often have unusually high concentrations of electrical equipment, wiring, plugs and sockets and these increase the risk of electrical shock and fire. To reduce this risk, IT equipment should be checked by an electrician or a suitably trained member of staff every two to four years (HSE, 1994). The impact on pupils or staff of an electrical shock can be minimised by the use of circuit breakers. Circuit breakers or Residual Current Devices (RCDs) are tripped by a 30 mA leakage to earth. They can be purchased for use on an individual socket or built into the mains electrical circuit in a computer room when it is installed. When an electrical shock is experienced, current flows to earth and the circuit breaker is tripped, turning off the electric current. The use of circuit breakers is an important safety feature when IT equipment is in use. The Electricity at Work Regulations, 1989, are a useful guide to what are considered to be safe standards in the work place. Schools should seek to achieve comparable standards.

Static electricity can also cause electric shock. The static shock from a monitor screen is usually relatively mild. A more severe shock can be experienced in some instances by touching the prongs on an electrical plug just after it has been removed from a socket. This can be painful and should be avoided.

Computers and their associated peripherals generate heat. Pupils generate heat. An IT room with fifteen computers, being used by thirty pupils can become too hot and stuffy very quickly indeed. Consequently, it is important that there is adequate ventilation, preferably fan assisted.

The legislation governing the use of monitors and other computer equipment at work is extensive and detailed (Council of the European Communities, 1990). Some recommendations are as follows:

- characters on the screen should be large enough to read, and clearly defined;
- the screen image should be stable, with adjustable brightness and contrast;
- screens should easily tilt and swivel;
- there should be no reflective glare from artificial or natural light;
- keyboards should be easy to use with clear and contrasting symbols;
- there should be adequate space for hand support;
- the user's chair should be comfortable and stable, with positional adjustments;
- footrests should be available, if required;
- there should be adequate space to allow users to change posture and position;
- the level of noise should not interfere with thought or conversation;
- there should be a minimum of radiation from the computer equipment being used.

These recommendations refer to the use of computer equipment at work. However, they also indicate the standards considered to be sufficient to ensure health and safety when using computer equipment elsewhere. Schools are advised to take these recommendations into account when considering the health and safety of pupils using computer equipment.

SUMMARY

A number of health risks have been associated with using computers. The use of a monitor screen may cause headaches and eye strain, and induce photosensitive (flicker-induced) epilepsy. Headaches and eye strain can be reduced by taking regular breaks, and positioning monitors where there is no reflected light on the screen. Photosensitive epilepsy may be induced in those who already suffer from it. Schools should identify pupils likely to be at risk and consult their doctors.

There is an increased risk of electrical shock. Shock from static electricity may be experienced by touching inferior quality or old monitor screens, and from the prongs of electric plugs. Circuit breakers should be used to minimise the impact of electrical shock from the mains supply. IT hardware and other electrical equipment should be checked by a suitably trained member of staff every two to four years.

Speculation regarding other health risks remains unproven. However, schools are advised to take into account health and safety regulations governing the work place as these may indicate sensible precautionary measures.

8

EQUAL OPPORTUNITIES

Professional and moral imperatives demand that every teacher should ensure that all pupils have opportunities to develop their full potential. Local Education Authorities and schools will have equal opportunities policies. It is the responsibility of individual teachers to put these policies into practice, so that all pupils are able to develop their IT skills, knowledge and understanding, and have access to IT resources that support their individual learning needs. In this chapter, there are sections on equal opportunities issues in relation to gender, as there is concern that girls may not have sufficient opportunities to develop their IT capability; and in relation to Special Educational Needs (SEN), because IT can be especially helpful in supporting the needs of pupils with disabilities.

In passing, it is worth noting that, in general, if it is possible to identify groups of pupils who are underachieving, there may be opportunities to improve their attainment significantly. By focusing on improving the standards of attainment of specific groups of underachieving pupils, overall standards, measured by test scores and other statistics, may be improved more easily.

GENDER

When computers were introduced into schools in the early 1980s, responsibility for deploying them was often given to Mathematics teachers. Consequently, the interests of Mathematics teachers influenced the development of the IT curriculum and the content of external examination syllabuses, for example, that of GCSE Computer Studies. The attitudes and stereotypes that pupils held in relation to Mathematics often became associated with Computer Studies. At this time, Computer Studies was not a mandatory subject: pupils had to choose to do it. It was not uncommon to have Computer Studies classes with only one or two girls and twenty-eight boys. Many teachers felt that more pupils, especially girls, would choose to study GCSE Computer Studies if the syllabus content was less mathematical and the subject was less associated with Mathematics.

The NC Technology orders (1990) severed this close association between Mathematics and IT. Unfortunately, they created a similar, but stronger association with Design Technology (DT). In the 1990 Technology orders ATs 1 to 4 refer to Design Technology and AT5 refers to IT capability. This association can be expected to have discouraged those pupils who had problems with DT from studying IT. Very often these pupils were girls.

Culley (1986) recommends that, in order to encourage more girls to study IT, it should not be closely linked with other subjects. In particular, it should not be closely linked with subjects that are known to have existing problems of a similar kind with equal opportunities. It is perhaps unfortunate that IT was initially linked with Mathematics and then with Design Technology! However, the NC IT orders (DfE, 1995a) have now established IT as a separate subject in its own right, so it is to be hoped that it will now no longer acquire equal opportunities problems by association with other subjects.

Teachers almost always have high professional standards, and care about their pupils and their schools. They are committed to the development of the full potential of all their pupils. Most teachers do not actively discriminate between pupils or groups of pupils and it is unusual to find teachers who are knowingly sexist, or otherwise prejudiced. Discrimination or prejudice is most likely to be brought into the school and the classroom by pupils themselves.

The use of IT is generally perceived by pupils as interesting in itself and as a valuable preparation for future employment. However, in most schools, IT resources are scarce resources. These circumstances can and do generate intense competition between pupils for the use of IT resources, and this competition may aggravate existing personal and social rivalries. In the classroom, this may be manifest as sporadic squabbles between pupils over the use of IT resources or more systematic discrimination between different social groups. Personal and social prejudices that are generally evident in relationships in the wider community may find an expression in this competition between pupils in schools.

Monitoring

The research into gender bias in IT has almost universally shown that the bias is in favour of boys and to the disadvantage of girls (Culley, 1986; Grundy, 1996; NCET, 1994b and 1996). However, where boys and girls are given the same opportunities and encouragement to make use of IT resources, they will do so to a similar extent (Grundy, 1996). Persistent imbalances in usage should therefore be viewed with concern.

Without adequate up-to-date information it is not possible to determine the extent of current problems or to assess the effectiveness of steps taken to improve the situation. In tackling inequality and discrimination, accurate, quantitative information is essential (Culley, 1986). This is useful in identifying what ameliorative action needs to be taken. Whilst the information that will be needed will vary from school to school, the indicators of gender bias described below are a good starting-point (adapted from Milner, 1989; Culley, 1986).

Some indicators of gender bias are as follows:

- Where there is a choice, pupils will segregate themselves by their selection of IT and related subjects. For example, when making subject choices for the start of year 10, boys will choose to study IT whereas girls will choose subjects such as History.
- Boys generally achieve better results than girls in IT and related subjects in school assessments and in external examinations such as GCSE.
- In class, when boys and girls are asked to use the computers, more boys than girls will usually operate the computers. If there are mixed groups using the computers, in most groups, a boy is operating the computer.
- When boys and girls have a choice whether to use computers or not, more boys than girls will choose to do so. For example, pupils turning up after school for the IT club are nearly all boys.
- Boys are more assertive over the use of IT resources. There may be frequent instances of boys bullying girls in order to get access to the computers.
- Boys compete more for access to IT resources. For example, if pupils have to queue for the lunch-time IT club to open, the pupils at the front of the queue are usually boys. Boys will often skip lunch to be first in the queue.
- Teachers tend to allocate some tasks to boys rather than girls and vice versa. It is usually boys who are asked to dismantle, move and reassemble computers.
- When the teacher asks the class an IT-orientated question, more boys than girls respond.
- Women and girls are under-represented in text books and other materials used in the classroom and elsewhere in the school. Careers literature reinforces traditional stereotypes, showing men in control of computers and related technology, with women in a supporting role.
- When IT is employed as a cross-curricular skill, it is mainly used in subjects which are also known to have problems with gender bias, for example, in Science and Design Technology.
- There is a general assumption that computers are for boys.

It is important that information is collected regularly. In the case of GCSE and other examination statistics, this will be done annually. Most of the other indicators can be recorded as it is thought necessary. For example, the number of boys and girls turning up for the IT club at lunch times could be counted every day to begin with and, later, the frequency of data collection could be reduced. The same information could be recorded on a weekly basis, perhaps on a different day each week. This would avoid possible bias due to conflicting activities on some days of the week. Analysis of gender bias in text books, careers guidance booklets, and other materials might be done before purchasing or distributing new materials. The collection of information that can only be obtained through classroom observation could be done as part of the teacher appraisal process.

Access to IT resources

It may be thought that in order to achieve equality of access it is sufficient simply to give all pupils the same chances to make use of IT resources. However, this is not necessarily so. If pupils' access to IT resources is not carefully supervised, then the discriminatory behaviour of some pupils will exclude others. For example, if access to the lunch-time IT club is on a 'first come, first served' basis, then it is likely that one group will tend to dominate; most probably these will be the stronger boys. The dominant group may arrive first, gain access and monopolise all the IT resources, thus blocking the access of other groups. Even where initial access to the IT rooms is controlled, if supervision is not maintained, the stronger boys will tend to evict other pupils. In order to ensure equal access and, hence, equal opportunities, it is necessary to supervise very carefully all access to IT resources and the continuing use of these resources (Culley, 1986).

A strategy often employed as a means of moving towards equal opportunities for all is that of positive discrimination. The intention is to redress known discrimination by making more resources available to the disadvantaged group. In schools, positive discrimination might lead to IT resources being made available for use only by girls, or only by girls at certain times. For example, girls could be given exclusive access to specific IT resources at a particular time each day or each week. As IT resources are not only hardware and software but also the teacher's time and attention, in coeducational schools it might be considered necessary to establish girls only classes or groups of girls who usually work together in mixed classes.

There can be disadvantages when positive discrimination is adopted in coeducational secondary schools. Making specific IT resources available only to girls, or to girls at particular times, may lead to resentment on the part of boys. Some of this resentment is unreasonable in that it has its origins in the assumption that computers are mainly for boys, or that they should be allocated by some rule of competition taken for granted and manipulated by the boys: for example, 'first come, first served'. However, if girls do not make full use of the IT resources reserved for them, positive discrimination cannot be effective in promoting their learning, and boys will resent not being allowed access to equipment that is apparently available to be used. A better alternative is to give girls first priority usage of some IT resources at all times. This gives girls access to IT resources at all times but does not prevent the use of these resources by boys at other times. This strategy may reduce the resentment felt by some boys.

In addition, single sex groups are especially noticeable in mixed schools. This is particularly true of girls-only classes. As a result, the girls in these classes are likely to be subjected to increased levels of personal abuse and bullying. This is regrettable and should be firmly resisted by teachers. However, it may be kinder to the girls involved to avoid their potential harassment by improving their access to IT resources in other ways. A better alternative is to establish girls-only groups in mixed classes only when they are needed and to abandon them at other times.

When positive discrimination strategies are used, it is essential to have overt rules defining the circumstances when particular groups of pupils are given priority use of IT resources. This reduces conflict by setting clear guidelines that all pupils must follow. Overt rules can be a useful focus for discussion with pupils about the reasonableness of the rules within the general context of equal opportunities. This promotes all pupils' awareness of others' needs and provides opportunities for them to express their sensitivity towards them in particular circumstances.

The discriminatory attitudes that pupils bring with them to school tend to find their expression where there is a lack of effective supervision. Continuous supervision of pupils following clearly defined and overt rules will help ensure that all groups of pupils can gain access to IT resources when it is appropriate for them to do so.

Role models

It is generally thought that boys respond best to adult male role models and that girls respond most to adult female role models. If this is the case, then it provides an explanation of how gender stereotypical behaviour is perpetuated in schools. Put simplistically, we might expect pupils to show more interest in and be most influenced by those lessons where they are taught by a teacher of the same sex. As some subjects are traditionally taught mainly by male or female teachers, these subjects are correspondingly more popular with boys or girls. Pupils thus make choices that confirm traditional stereotypes.

Strategies to encourage the equal development of all pupils in all areas of the curriculum have sometimes involved attempts to manipulate pupils' choices and attitudes by providing male or female role models in specific subjects, such as IT, where boys or girls are under-represented. As many IT teachers are male, in order to provide encouragement for girls to develop IT skills, a female teacher may be appointed to teach IT. The appointment of a female IT teacher clearly demonstrates that women can be expected to have IT skills and this may encourage girls to study IT. However, there are several factors that may influence the outcome of this strategy. It is especially important that the teachers appointed as role models do not undermine the roles they have been ascribed. If a female teacher appointed to provide a role model for girls is not seen to be competent, this further emphasises a supposed lack of technical ability in IT on the part of women and girls.

It is also important that teachers believe that all pupils have the potential to acquire technical skills and knowledge, otherwise they will tend to discourage some groups of pupils and encourage other groups, perhaps unknowingly. Men and women often have complementary role scripts, that is, men who believe that women in general cannot or should not acquire technical or other skills may be reinforced in their beliefs by women who hold the same prejudice. A woman with beliefs that are prejudicial to the development of girls cannot be a good role model for them in this respect. A man who believes that girls can and should learn technical skills is more likely to facilitate their development.

Competence and empathy with pupils are important factors in establishing the effectiveness of a teacher. A teacher who does not believe that some pupils can or should learn certain skills is unlikely to be an effective teacher of those skills. A competent, effective female teacher who believes that all pupils can and should learn IT skills is probably the best role model for girls. However, a male teacher who is competent and effective, with similar beliefs, may also be effective in encouraging girls to study IT.

The selection of teachers as role models is further complicated by the covert nature of sexist prejudice. Adults with discriminatory attitudes are often unaware that they are prejudiced. The common belief that 'a woman's place is in the home' is almost entirely due to the historical subdivision of domestic labour and child rearing, and the importance of the relatively greater physical strength of many males in a traditional economy dominated by manual labour. However, whilst these historical conditions are on the whole no longer evident, the social beliefs and prejudices which they gave rise to have persisted. These tend to be transmitted through socialisation in the family and elsewhere. As a result, both children and adults may express these attitudes in their speech and behaviour without previous reflection on their validity. Consequently, it can be expected that some teachers will unconsciously communicate discriminatory attitudes and behaviour. In addition, when discriminatory beliefs are conscious, if they are held to be true, they are likely to be concealed in a professional setting in education.

To summarise, perceived competency and supportive attitudes towards the development of all learners are especially important for teachers of IT. A female teacher is probably the best role model for girls and a male teacher is probably the best role model for boys, so it is appropriate to ensure that both male and female teachers have responsibility for delivering IT. However, competency and a belief that all pupils can develop their IT capability are more important than the gender of the teacher.

Case Study

The case study that follows is an entirely subjective account of the experiences of a single teacher in one school. Nevertheless, it has some relevance to all schools as it describes a conscious implementation of recommendations derived from research and an evaluation of their consequences.

IT at Manor High School

My name is Alan. Before I was appointed as Head of Mathematics, Computing and IT at Manor High School, I had had some fifteen years' experience as a secondary teacher. I was trained as a Mathematics teacher and for many years taught Mathematics. As computers came into schools in the late 1970s and early 1980s, I was asked to develop courses in computer programming. In due course, this early interest grew and I became involved in setting up computer awareness courses. Eventually, I was appointed to Head of IT and set up IT skills courses in wordprocessing, databases, spreadsheets, graphics, DTP, and robotics. I also encouraged colleagues to use IT to support learning in all the subjects of the curriculum.

When I started work at Manor High School, I was surprised to find that all the optional lessons in IT and computing that I taught were to classes that were either all boys or very nearly all boys. There was a well-established IT club every lunch time and this was almost always attended only by boys. It was not unusual for pupils to ask to use the computers before and after school. Again these pupils were almost always boys. It was clear to me that most boys enjoyed an extensive experience of IT and computing whereas girls did not. This situation surprised me because it was so extreme. At other schools I had taught in, boys had tended to be more interested than girls in IT and computing but, as this was not so marked as at Manor High School, I had not been concerned.

I was at first puzzled as to how to react to what I observed. Was it a problem? Since the boys dominated in subjects that all pupils could choose to do, and in the IT club which was open to all pupils, was I wrong to identify this as a problem? Clearly a lack of IT skills would be a disadvantage to the girls but as they had chosen this, was I right to interfere? As I often taught in one of the rooms in which the IT club was held, I began to do my lesson preparation and marking in this room at lunch times. I noticed that occasionally girls did come into the IT club, often with some wordprocessing to do for their English coursework. These girls were generally unsuccessful in getting the use

92

of a computer throughout lunch time because either the computers were all in use when they arrived, or they left when more boys arrived wanting to use the computers. I concluded that it was possible that the girls did want access to the computers but that something about the existing situation was discouraging them.

I had recently completed an MEd degree, in the course of which I had read Culley's research report (Culley, 1986). It seemed well founded and relevant. I decided that what I was observing at Manor High School was a situation in which it was possible that there was a relatively high level of sexist bias. I decided to try out Culley's recommendations. Culley had proposed a series of measures to counter sexist bias which I adapted to the situation at Manor High School and attempted to put into effect.

One of the recommendations is that gender differences in participation and performance should be monitored. This seemed largely irrelevant to begin with as it was obvious to me that the use of IT resources was dominated by the boys. However, I did start to record the numbers of boys and girls choosing to study courses in IT and computing and attending the lunch-time IT club so that I would be able to quantify improvements, if any, as they happened. To begin with, I noticed very little difference from week to week. However, as we started to make changes, the statistics showed a small improvement and this encouraged me to persevere. Over a period of about four years the situation changed remarkably and I was able to record this.

A close look at the subjects that pupils could choose from in Year 9 for study in Key Stage 4 showed that these option groups encouraged boys to choose to study IT courses and discouraged girls. For example, one choice was between IT, History and French. Most boys chose IT whereas the girls chose History or French. I pressed for a realignment of these choices so that the choice was between History, IT and Motor Vehicle Studies. Whilst this was not ideal, it was successful in encouraging more girls to choose IT. The gender balance in IT classes improved as a result.

Culley suggested that girls are more receptive to IT and computing when they study it in single sex groups and/or are taught by a female teacher. With increased numbers of girls studying IT, we were able to start a girls only class in Year 10. There was also a female teacher who agreed to teach the class. Unfortunately, this was not successful in terms of promoting the girls' achievements as measured by examination success. The standards achieved by the girls in school assessments became progressively lower and lower throughout the year. It seemed to me that, in part, this happened because of the attitude of the female teacher. She was lacking in confidence in her own use of IT, and did not inspire or enthuse the girls. In Year 11, another teacher taught the all girls class. In contrast, he was competent and confident, and motivated and encouraged the girls. As a result, standards of attainment rose. This experience emphasised to me the importance of the teacher's attitudes. The gender of these teachers was only of secondary importance. Their competence and attitudes had a much more immediate effect on the girls' motivation and their standards of achievement.

This class of girls was very noticeable to other pupils. It is unusual to see a class of only girls in a mixed school. The confidence that the girls gained because they weren't in competition with the boys in the classroom was undermined by their unease with this unusual situation. Other pupils who noticed it sometimes teased them. There was considerable verbal abuse and some bullying. Consequently, we did not repeat these arrangements again. However, I had some all girls groups in my mixed classes from time to time. Sometimes I would ask some of the girls to work in groups with girls only but usually pupils decided whom they would work with. Some girls in mixed groups worked effectively with the boys but others let them dominate all the time. Getting these girls to work in single sex groups gave them a chance to participate and gain confidence.

I noticed that if I asked the whole class a question on IT, only the more confident pupils would respond. The girls often sat passively. As I would ask one of the pupils who had their hand up, it was more often than not, one of the boys. To encourage the girls to participate more, I picked out specific pupils, making sure that I chose a roughly equal number of boys and girls to answer the questions. Again, this encouraged the girls to join in and they began to ask questions and volunteer answers more readily.

The two IT rooms at Manor High School were also Mathematics rooms when I was appointed. I was based in one of these rooms for most of my teaching. In some ways, this was excellent for teaching Mathematics. My classes had much better access to IT resources during Mathematics lessons than most other classes. However, there were some considerable disadvantages. I was forever being pestered by individual pupils from other classes wanting to use the IT resources while I was teaching. On many occasions, I was asked to swap rooms with other teachers so they could use the IT resources in my base room. Similarly, I was regularly timetabled out of my base room so IT could be taught in it. The rooms I was swapped into, or was timetabled into, were not usually well equipped for teaching Mathematics.

Initially, the school had not given much thought to the location of IT resources. As computers arrived in the school for the first time, they had been set up in the two Mathematics rooms. These rooms were very inhospitable. They badly needed redecoration and new furniture. There were no curtains or blinds on the large windows, all of which were south facing. The light shining in through the windows was sometimes so bright it was impossible to read the computer screens. The roof in one room leaked when it rained. The computers had to be dragged away from the walls to avoid the damp. These rooms were cold and uncomfortable in winter and too hot in summer. The rooms were hardly suitable for teaching Mathematics. They were certainly not the place to locate expensive computer hardware or any type of electrical equipment. The lunch-time IT club was held in one of these rooms. The pupils attending the IT club were obviously keen enough on computing to ignore the uncomfortable surroundings. As I said before, these pupils were mainly boys.

The rooms shared by Mathematics and IT were refurbished two years after my arrival at Manor High School. Fortunately, at the same time, it was also possible to relocate the IT resources to rooms in a different part of the school, separating Mathematics and IT. The new IT rooms were very smart and well equipped. They were warm comfortable rooms. It was immediately obvious that pupils were choosing to spend their lunch times in the new IT rooms even if they were not especially enthusiastic about IT and computing! Girls started to come to the lunch-time IT club in large numbers. If there were no computers available, they would sit in groups talking or doing homework until they could get onto a computer. Although the boys still dominated, the girls started to make much greater use of the computers at lunch times.

Because of the much greater number of pupils attending the lunch-time IT club, we were obliged to supervise them more closely. We opened the club about fifteen minutes after the end of morning classes. Pupils arriving early had to queue outside. Some boys started to eat their sandwiches in the queue or skip lunch completely in order to be first into the IT rooms. Eventually these boys came to monopolise the lunch-time IT club once again.

As I was now convinced that the girls were interested but were being squeezed out, my initial reaction was to make the IT club available to the girls only on one lunch time each week. This was excellent for the girls who turned up but unfortunately they did not turn up in sufficient numbers to use all the computers. The boys noticed this and were resentful. They were only just prepared to accept that it could be reasonable to be excluded so that the girls could have their fair share of access to the computers, and were not at all happy to see computers stand idle when they could be using them. I was also unhappy with this situation. Not only were computers not in use when they could be but I was continually pestered by the boys to let them use them.

When matters had not improved after a few weeks we changed our strategy. We designated several computers which would always be available to girls. However, we did not ban the boys from using these computers, we simply gave the girls priority of use of them at any time. This meant that a boy could use one of these computers, if they were not all in use, but if a girl arrived wanting to use one, she could take it over from the boy. We realised that this strategy would need careful supervision until it was well established and possibly even after that. We had to indicate which computers were to be available on first priority to the girls, so we put colourful stickers on these computers. We wrote the simple rules regulating pupils' access to the IT club on several large posters. We stuck these posters on the wall by the computers and outside the IT club in the corridor where pupils queued to enter. These rules became well known and pupils would often refer to them when arguing with each other. They would also challenge my judgement when it did not appear to conform to the rules for one reason or another. The boys were keen to know why these rules had been made and the purpose of them. This led to useful discussions about the reasons for giving girls priority and the rules themselves. Giving the girls priority on some computers, making the rules well known to everyone, and explaining the reasons for them were successful in establishing an atmosphere where all pupils felt welcome to use IT resources.

At about this time the English Department became very interested in using Desk Top Publishing to produce the school magazine. A mixed group of pupils worked on the magazine in class and at lunch times. They were very interested in the magazine and in using Desk Top Publishing for good quality presentation. Having a mixed group of highly motivated pupils in the IT club every day had the effect of encouraging other pupils to become involved, especially the girls. Very soon a second group started to produce another school magazine in competition. The involvement of the English Department, and the focus on a task which was of interest to pupils even if they were not keen on IT, were important factors in broadening the appeal of IT.

These are some of the strategies we tried. They helped us widen the appeal of IT at Manor High School. Once we were aware of the problem in IT, we tried to tackle it. This awareness of what was happening turned out to be most important as not everything we tried worked. Not all the strategies we read about and tried out worked for us in our school. However, some of the strategies we used were successful and access to IT has improved for all our pupils but especially for the girls.

SUMMARY: GENDER

IT should not be too closely associated with any other subject. The establishment of IT as a separate NC subject should help prevent pupils being discouraged from developing IT skills because of their difficulties with or dislike of another subject.

School timetables should be constructed so that they do not encourage pupils to make selections that reinforce social and cultural stereotypes. Careers advice, text books, videos and other materials shown in schools should not confirm traditional stereotypes.

A female teacher will be the best role model for girls if she encourages all aspects of their development and is perceived as being competent. If this is not the case, then it may well be that a competent male teacher with positive attitudes towards the development of girls could encourage them to study IT to a greater extent. A school's IT staff should be a mix of male and female teachers so that both boys and girls have appropriate role models.

Positive discrimination can be effective but should be implemented with care as it can give rise to counter-productive resentment and hostility. Overt rules governing pupils' access to IT, and careful supervision, are essential means of ensuring that disadvantaged groups feel sufficiently safe to take advantage of the resources reserved for their use. These overt rules may act as a useful focus for discussion of the underlying issues.

Single sex classes in mixed schools may encourage girls and help them become more confident. This is a high-risk strategy as bullying and verbal abuse may be directed at girls in such classes. Transitory, single sex groups within the classroom will attract less attention. This strategy is preferable to the more rigid option of the all girls class which may have to be set up for an entire school year.

The standard of the environment in the classroom is important in attracting girls. Observation of the importance of environment is not a new consideration (Stebbins, 1976). It is interesting, though perhaps not surprising, to note the encouraging effects of a pleasant and comfortable environment. It would seem that girls may be particularly influenced by an improved environment.

The variety of influencing factors noted in this chapter indicates the complexity of the nature of gender discrimination in IT. This is, however, only one of the most obvious categories of discrimination evident in schools. To counteract inequality, discrimination and stereotyping in schools, teachers must be constantly vigilant, well informed and imaginative in devising and applying ameliorative strategies. Reliable information about the extent of gender discrimination is an essential prerequisite for tackling it.

SPECIAL EDUCATIONAL NEEDS (SEN)

Some 20 per cent of children will have some SEN requirements during their school career (DfEE, 1995). Within its published code of practice the DfEE suggests that schools should consider whether IT can help meet pupils' needs. Helping pupils with SEN is a specialised role within schools, and using IT to do this is only a part of this highly demanding task.

IT can help ensure that pupils' disabilities do not prevent them from learning. IT can support pupils with SEN in their learning in similar ways to those in which all pupils' learning needs are supported but adjusted to their own individual needs and abilities. IT can motivate by providing highly differentiated learning programmes, incremental success, and apparently infinite patience. Pupils with poor concentration can be prompted or stimulated using sound or images following predefined or random schedules so that their attention is returned to the task in hand. In addition, pupils with specific disabilities can use IT to help overcome them (NCET, 1996b; Research Machines, 1996).

Some of the ways in which IT can contribute to helping pupils with SEN are briefly described below.

Pupils who have difficulties acquiring basic literacy and numeracy skills:

- may have their learning needs assessed using diagnostic software;
- can draft and redraft their work using IT, for example, using a word-processor;
- can concentrate on the content of their written work rather than the act of writing it, knowing that the product of their work will be neatly printed;
- can use CAL programs to practise basic numeracy and literacy skills;
- can access and manipulate information through images and sound text, speech and pictures;
- can listen to the computer 'speaking' their work as they read it on the screen, or read 'talking books';
- can use touch screens to operate the computer, or keyboard overlays with pictures that correspond to images on the screen.

Pupils with speech and language difficulties, including dyslexia:

- may have their learning needs assessed using diagnostic software;
- can use a talking wordprocessor to speak;
- can use a spelling checker to identify and correct incorrect words;
- can use grammar checkers to identify and correct incorrect phrases, and words with similar pronunciations but different meanings;
- can use a computer-based thesaurus to select different words with similar meanings;
- can improve their language capability using in combination speech recognition software, spelling and grammar checkers, and speech synthesis;
- can communicate over long distances using e-mail.

Pupils with emotional and behavioural difficulties:

- receive consistent, non-judgemental feedback;
- can interact with others using IT to neutralise negative responses and prejudice;
- can practice decision-making using adventure games.

Pupils with physical disabilities, for example, very poor movement or co-ordination:

- can use IT for writing and drawing using keyboard guards and overlays, and touch screens;
- can select words and sentences using a switch, helping them communicate with others;
- can use word predictors to suggest the next word or phrase;
- can concentrate on the content of their work rather than the act of writing knowing that the product of their work will be neatly printed;
- can play computer games that help improve hand–eye co-ordination;
- may find a slow key repeat speed helpful;
- may find non-standard keyboards useful, for example, miniature and ergonomic keyboards, or keyboards with enlarged keys;
- may find alternatives to mouse controls useful, for example, switches instead of buttons; a drag latch instead of keeping a mouse button depressed; head-operated controls; and voice control systems;
- can use IT to control their environment, for example, to answer the door using CCTV to see who has called and a control switch to admit them;
- can use virtual reality systems to practise dangerous tasks before attempting them, for example, pouring hot water into a cup;
- can use virtual reality systems to extend their experience and understanding of the wider social context by 'visiting' supermarkets, shops, towns and cities.

Visually impaired pupils:

- can enlarge text and images on-screen, and quickly reverse the process. Similarly, teachers can prepare worksheets using enlarged fonts;
- can re-size the mouse pointer, and set trails and direction indicators to help locate it;
- can adjust screen colours, brightness and contrast to suit their own needs;
- can use speech synthesis to keep track of what is being written;
- can articulate text by entering it in a wordprocessor that can 'read' it using speech synthesis software. This can be done as a word is entered, or the whole document can be read back;
- can use a Braille keyboard and a Braille printer. Similarly, teachers can output their worksheets in Braille;
- can use keyboard overlays with embossed images and textures to learn the feel of different materials.

Pupils with impaired hearing:

- can use IT for talking, by typing words into a speaking wordprocessor;
- can communicate quickly over long distances using e-mail instead of a telephone;
- can use video conferencing to communicate over long distances by signing.

Pupils with profound and multiple learning difficulties:

- can use combinations of the software and hardware listed above to support their individual needs.

Although the above list is grouped into broad categories of need with some suggestions as to how IT may be helpful to pupils with these disabilities, it may be more useful to first consider what IT can do for an individual pupil. Particular IT resources may be useful to pupils with a wide range of SEN.

Pupils with SEN should participate in mainstream lessons with other pupils. However, some pupils may find it difficult to acknowledge their SEN in these circumstances. Where special hardware adaptation is needed to help them use IT, this potential reluctance should be taken into account. If possible, standard computer equipment should be customised to meet their needs. It may be possible to re-program a standard keyboard rather than installing a specialist keyboard and using overlays. Where pupils have their own specialist hardware or software, this should be quickly and easily run from a standard classroom computer.

Some pupils with SEN find portable computers useful. These can be set up with appropriate software and any special hardware. They can accompany and support pupils throughout the school day and at home. It is worth considering purchasing an additional printer to be used at home. In addition, a modem and e-mail software at home can help pupils establish and sustain social relationships. If a suitable portable computer is not available, a specially adapted desk top computer can be more portable if it is installed on a trolley that can be moved from room to room. Some pupils will need help in moving their IT equipment. Others may need physical adaptations to wheelchairs to facilitate both using and moving their IT equipment.

Schools should consider organising training for all those who may be called on to support pupils with SEN when they are using IT. Parents and teachers will need to be familiar with what is possible so that they can be of assistance when necessary.

Where schools have set up IT hardware and software to support the particular needs of a pupil with SEN, this may be useful to that pupil on leaving school. It may be helpful if schools are able to offer such pupils the possibility of acquiring the IT equipment they have been using at school so that they can make use of it in the longer term. This may be especially useful where pupils are moving on to FE or HE. Access to IT resources and the ability to use them effectively may improve employment prospects for pupils with SEN.

SUMMARY: SEN

IT can support pupils with SEN in their learning, and motivate them by providing highly differentiated learning programmes. It can be helpful to pupils who have difficulties with basic literacy and numeracy skills: for example, they can use CAL programs to practise basic numeracy and literacy skills. Pupils with speech and language difficulties, including dyslexia, can improve their language capability using speech recognition software, spelling and grammar checkers, and speech synthesis. Pupils with emotional and behavioural difficulties can receive consistent, non-judgemental feedback, and interact with others using IT to neutralise negative responses and prejudice. Those with physical disabilities can use alternatives to mouse controls. Switches can be used instead of buttons, and a drag latch instead of keeping a mouse button depressed. Virtual reality systems can be used to extend their experience and understanding of the wider social context by 'visiting' super-markets, shops, towns and cities. Visually impaired pupils can enlarge text and images on-screen, and quickly reverse the process. Similarly, teachers can prepare worksheets using enlarged fonts. Pupils with impaired hearing can communicate over long distances using e-mail instead of a telephone, or use video conferencing to communicate by signing. Pupils with profound and multiple learning difficulties can use combinations of the software and hardware listed above to support their individual needs.

Some pupils may find it difficult to acknowledge their SEN in mainstream classes. Where possible, standard computer equipment should be customised to meet their needs, and their own specialist hardware or software should be quickly and easily run from it. Some pupils with SEN find portable computers useful. These can accompany pupils throughout the school day and at home. It is worth considering purchasing an additional printer, a modem and e-mail software for use at home. This can help pupils establish and sustain social relationships. Schools should consider organising training for all those who may be called on to support pupils with SEN when they are using IT.

Where schools have set up IT hardware and software to support the particular needs of pupils with SEN, this may be useful to the pupils when they leave school. The ability to use IT resources effectively may improve education and employment prospects for pupils with SEN.

9

TRAINING ACTIVITIES

This chapter looks at some activities that support the development of teachers' and trainee teachers' IT skills, and their knowledge and understanding of how IT is managed and used in secondary schools. The acquisition of IT skills is essentially an active process. Learners must be actively engaged otherwise they will not acquire skills. They may need access to reference manuals, learning guides, help sheets, tutorial exercises, and on-line help, and advice from an expert practitioner. The acquisition of IT skills is often a time-consuming process so that learners must find sufficient time to devote to learning. However, the most important aspects of IT skills acquisition are the involvement and motivation of the learner.

Trainee teachers are relatively well provided for. They are usually on full time courses where they have some development time allocated, and may have access to expert help from lecturers with specialist IT skills. Their motivation is high as they are focused on passing the relevant sections of their BEd or PGCE course. IT skills are a major part of one of the competencies trainee teachers are expected to gain.

Teachers in schools are in an altogether different situation as the learning of new IT skills has to be done in addition to their normal work load. As this can be unrealistically high, learning new IT skills can have a very low priority. Schools should encourage teachers to develop their IT skills, and take steps to improve their motivation. There should be a whole school IT policy in place that clearly demonstrates that the school values IT and this should also be evident in the operational practice of the school. IT should be used in administration and throughout the curriculum so that teachers can see that time invested in learning IT skills is not wasted. Using IT can lead to real gains in teachers' personal productivity, in that less time is spent on administration, information is available more easily and the quality of presentation is enhanced. If teachers can see that what is done can be done more thoroughly and effectively using IT, then they will be more inclined to spend time developing their IT skills.

Teachers will need access to appropriate learning resources. It is advisable to reserve some IT resources for staff use only. These should be placed in a location close to the staff room that is inaccessible to pupils. This makes it more likely that teachers will be able to gain access to IT resources when they have the time to learn, and gives them privacy in which to make the mistakes that inevitably accompany learning. Not all staff are comfortable displaying their lack of knowledge to pupils who are often regarded as being more naturally skilled at using IT. It is therefore worth considering the establishment of one or more staff IT rooms. The existence of a staff IT room, equipped with suitable hardware, software and learning resources, demonstrates the school's commitment, provides staff with open access to IT resources and gives them the opportunity to learn in privacy. The staff IT room can become the focus for staff training in IT skills. It should contain reference manuals, learning guides, help sheets and tutorial exercises for the software used in the school. Teachers using the staff IT room will help each other acquire skills. If the IT Co-ordinator and the IT Technician are based in the staff IT room, teachers will have opportunities for informal training from skilled practitioners.

Whilst the establishment of a staff IT room demonstrates the school's commitment and can give staff adequate access to learning resources, it does not provide them with the time to learn. Some staff will be more enthusiastic than others, devoting much of their own time to learning and using IT. Special events, such as residential weekends, or training courses held at the end of the school day, can be helpful in encouraging teachers to spend time learning IT skills. However, it is unreasonable to expect that all staff will be able to set aside sufficient time in this way. Schools are unlikely to be able to give teachers a great deal of time to develop their IT skills during directed time but limited provision can help motivate staff. For example, an occasional INSET day devoted to IT skills training can have a significant impact on motivation.

The development of IT skills will be accompanied by increased knowledge and understanding of the technical operations of IT software and hardware. However, whilst improvements in teachers' personal familiarity with IT does increase the likelihood that they will use IT in the classroom, it does not in itself improve their ability to make use of IT successfully in their teaching, nor does it help them understand the place of IT within the whole curriculum. This is also true of trainee teachers. The acquisition of personal IT skills is only the beginning; it is also necessary to learn how to organise IT within the classroom, how to teach and assess it, and the place of IT within the whole curriculum and the school. The remainder of this chapter looks at learning activities which help participants develop an understanding of aspects of the management and use of IT in schools.

The learning activities described are complete in themselves. They can be used independently or in the sequence they appear but they all require participants to become actively engaged in tasks with some immediate goal or outcome. This provides a focus for each learning activity and serves to motivate and involve participants. Participants are not required to have extensive knowledge of any aspect of IT; only a basic understanding of IT skills is assumed. It is taken for granted that participants will have some familiarity with the English secondary school system and the NC. If not, then the essential background knowledge required can be provided as a part of the resources used within each activity.

The activities described should not be viewed as a complete course covering all aspects of how IT is used and managed in schools. Such a course would be accompanied by a variety of lectures, seminars and workshops which would supplement the sharing of insights that the activities seek to encourage. However, these activities could form the foundation of an intensive introductory experience. They are presented as, hopefully, a source of useful ideas and inspiration. They may be useful to lecturers, school-based ITT mentors, IT Co-ordinators in schools and others who are organising courses of initial teacher training or in-service training, perhaps for the first time. All the activities have been successfully trialed by the author.

Overall, the training activities described below will encourage participants to develop:

- an understanding of the dynamics of whole school planning for IT;
- an understanding of the cross-curricular nature of IT;
- an appreciation of the uses of IT in a range of subjects;
- an awareness of the range of Computer Aided Learning software available;
- an ability to evaluate software and CD-ROMs etc. for use in the classroom;
- an appreciation of the funding needed to provide sufficient hardware;
- an awareness of the different types of hardware used in schools;
- an awareness of the roles and responsibilities of those teachers who play a significant part in managing IT in schools;
- an appreciation of how equal opportunities issues influence the use of IT in schools;
- an awareness of the variety of uses of IT in schools, and the diversity of different ways in which schools manage and use it.

The training activities described are:

1 The 'IT across the curriculum' game.
2 The 'Where is IT?' activity.
3 The 'Evaluation of Computer Aided Learning software' activity.
4 The 'Whole school planning for the provision of hardware' role play.
5 The 'Roles and responsibilities' game.
6 The discussion of 'Equal Opportunities issues in relation to Gender'.
7 The 'Sharing of personal experiences of IT in schools'.

1. THE 'IT ACROSS THE CURRICULUM' GAME

The IT across the curriculum game helps participants to develop an under-standing of the cross-curricular nature of IT and to appreciate its uses in all subjects of the curriculum. It is best organised in groups of five participants with a good mix of subject expertise amongst them. The game will last a minimum of three-quarters of an hour but can last much longer. The Curriculum Board (see Figure 9.1) is a grid with years 7 to 11 across the top and most of the NC subjects down the side. If desired, these could be changed to show, for example, Key Stage 3, Key Stage 4 and Post-16 along the top, and different subjects down the side, depending on the context in which the game is played and the aims of the organiser. Trainee teachers may find it helpful to have their specialist subject included even though it may not be central to the NC, as in the case of Business Studies. The Activity cards (see Figure 9.2) could also be changed to take into account participants' subject backgrounds, or par-ticular concerns, such as the use of IT in Music. It may also be desirable to adjust the rules to achieve particular training objectives. Rules 6 and 7 ensure a good distribution of activities throughout the curriculum. However, they do rule out one possible outcome of the game, that is, the identification of those subjects which could be given extensive responsibilities for the development of pupils' IT capability. Suitably adjusted to the context in which it is to be played, the 'IT across the curriculum' game is a useful training activity. Stripped of its rules, it is also a good framework for planning the IT curriculum.

The resources needed to play the game are:

- the Curriculum Board (see Figure 9.1);
- the Activity cards (see Figure 9.2);
- the NC programmes of study for IT at KS3 and KS4;
- relevant external assessment syllabuses for IT.

The rules of the game are:

1 The game is played in groups of five players.
2 Deal out the Activity cards equally, discarding the remainder.
3 Starting at the dealer's left, in turn, each player places an Activity card on the Curriculum Board.
4 When an Activity card has been placed by a player, the group decides whether it has been placed in an appropriate cell on the Curriculum Board.
5 If the Activity card has not been placed in an appropriate cell on the Curriculum Board, the Activity card is returned to the player who placed it. Otherwise, the Activity card remains on the Curriculum Board and the game moves on to the next player.
6 If an Activity card is placed on an IT cell, the player misses a turn.
7 If an Activity card is placed on a cell that already has an Activity card on it, the player misses a turn.
8 The winner is the player to discard all their Activity cards first.

Year 7	Year 8	Year 9	Year 10	Year 11	
					English
					Maths
					Science
					Information Technology
					Design Technology
					PE
					Modern Languages
					Business Studies
					Music
					RE
					Other

Figure 9.1 The Curriculum Board

Set up a database of the names and addresses of pupils in their class.	Use a wordprocessor to write a letter to a friend.	Control a turtle using a simple control language.	Describe how hospitals and GPs use IT to handle medical records.	Use a spreadsheet to work out percentage discounts on a range of goods.	Use search conditions with AND, OR and NOT operators to search a database.
Measure and record the temperature every hour for one month.	Format a floppy disk.	Send personalised letters to sponsors of the football team.	Use different fonts, sizes and styles of text.	Use clip art to illustrate an advert for a sports shop.	Describe the function of a supermarket stock control system that uses bar codes.
Model the growth of bacteria using a spreadsheet.	Delete a file on a floppy disk.	Use a spelling checker to help eliminate spelling mistakes.	Scan a photograph of themselves and include it in their c.v.	Discuss problems associated with the storing of personal data on a computer.	Guide a Valiant turtle around an obstacle.
Analyse survey data from questionnaires using a database.	Draft and edit an article for the school newspaper using a wordprocessor.	Set up a spreadsheet to work out the cost of making a bicycle.	Explain how feedback is used in a computer-controlled central heating system.	Generate pie diagrams, bar charts and line graphs using a spreadsheet.	Describe how to use an ATM or a cashpoint.
Explain how an automatic door works.	Extract a list of books on horses from a library database.	Discuss the social, economic, ethical and moral issues related to software piracy.	Copy a file onto a floppy disk from another floppy disk or a hard disk.	Design a questionnaire so that it is easy to input the data collected into a computer.	Use a database to sort a list of names into alphabetical order.
Write a logo procedure to draw a square on the screen.	Describe how a robot can be made to follow a dark line on the floor.	Design a questionnaire about people's attitudes to a new supermarket.	Draw a wallpaper design with a repeated pattern.	Using IT, compose a piece of music and print the score.	Use a simple control language to operate a computer-controlled robotic arm.
Using IT, modify a recorded piece of music so that it is played on different 'instruments'	Design a company logo, business card and headed note paper.	Get information from a database and import it into a wordprocessed essay.	Use teletext, e.g. Ceefax, and explain how it is transmitted and accessed.	Draw a picture and print it.	Recognise that poor quality data may give inaccurate results.
Explain the advantages and disadvantages of electronic mail.	Write an article about a dance, and design tickets and posters advertising it.	Use IT to keep a record of the books they have read and their opinions of them.	Reorganise blocks of text to improve the sense of a report about the youth club.	Write an illustrated book to help young children learn to read.	Record a piece of music and play it through a synthesiser at a concert.
Compare the use of a card index file with the use of a database.	Scan part of a magazine article and include it in a wordprocessed essay.	Save a file on a floppy disk and load it at a later date.	Set up a printer so that it is ready to be used.	Investigate how height is related to strength and speed.	Extract a list of books on cars by authors beginning with 'H' from a library catalogue.
Analyse census data and parish records on a database.	Lay out a page of text and graphics for the school newspaper using DTP software.	Set up a viewdata system giving information about the day's events.	Scan a picture and modify it using graphics software.	Explore how to control inflation using a computer-based model of the economy.	Manage a petrol refinery using a computer-based simulation.

Figure 9.2 Activity cards for the 'IT across the curriculum' game

2. THE 'WHERE IS IT?' ACTIVITY

The 'Where is IT?' activity is also helpful in encouraging an appreciation of the cross-curricular nature of IT and an understanding of its uses in all subjects of the curriculum. This activity is a useful follow-up to the 'IT across the curriculum' game.

In the 'Where is IT?' activity, participants are asked to think of an activity for pupils that could take place in each subject at each key stage and to estimate the extent that the subject could be expected to contribute to the development of pupils' IT Capability as a whole. The 'Where is IT?' activity may be expected to last only fifteen to twenty minutes and, consequently, could be used as an extension activity for those groups that quickly complete the 'IT across the curriculum' game. It could also be used at the start of a later training session to remind participants of the insights they had when playing the 'IT across the curriculum' game during a previous session, before moving on to other activities.

The 'IT across the curriculum' game and the 'Where is IT?' activity prepare participants to discuss issues such as:

- Should IT be taught, used and assessed in all subjects, or should responsibility for delivering different aspects of IT be concentrated in only a few subjects?
- If it is decided to deliver IT Capability through only a few subjects which subjects should be involved?
- Which curriculum model should be used for the delivery of IT skills and knowledge?

In consequence, more focused versions of these questions appear on the bottom of the 'Where is IT?' activity sheet, so that participants may move seamlessly into a discussion of these issues.

The resources needed for this activity are:

- the 'Where is IT?' activity sheet (see Figure 9.3);
- the NC programmes of study for IT at KS3 and KS4;
- relevant external assessment syllabuses for IT.

In this activity participants are asked to:

- Describe a possible classroom activity for pupils, at each of Key Stages 3 and 4, which involves the use of IT within the given subject.
- Rate each subject, at each of Key Stages 3 and 4, on its potential contribution to the overall development of pupils' IT Capability, using the rating scale on the 'Where is IT?' activity sheet (Figure 9.3).
- Discuss the merits of teaching, using and assessing IT across the curriculum.
- Choose an appropriate curriculum model for the delivery of IT.

3. THE 'EVALUATION OF COMPUTER AIDED LEARNING SOFTWARE' ACTIVITY

It is important that trainee teachers and teachers are able to evaluate software, particularly Computer Aided Learning (CAL) software. Most software vendors will provide an assessment of the capabilities of their products as a part of their

You are asked to do the following:

- Describe a possible classroom activity for pupils, at each of Key Stages 3 and 4, that involves the use of IT within the given subject.
- Rate each subject, at each of Key Stages 3 and 4, on its potential contribution to the development of pupils' IT Capability, using this rating scale:

1 = There is no opportunity for this subject to contribute to the development of IT Capability in this Key Stage.
2 = There are opportunities to use IT in this subject in this Key Stage.
3 = This subject should be given specific responsibilities for some aspects of the delivery of IT Capability in this Key Stage.

Key Stage 3		Key Stage 4		
Example activity for pupils	Rating	Example activity for pupils		
				En
				Ma
				Sc
				IT
				DT
				PE
				ML
				BSt
				Mu
				RE
				Other

- Should IT be taught, used and assessed in all subjects, or should only a few subjects have the responsibility for delivering aspects of IT Capability?
- If your school had decided to deliver IT in only three subjects, which subjects would you choose?
- Which curriculum model would you prefer for the delivery of IT?

Figure 9.3 The 'Where is IT?' activity sheet

109

advertising. However, they have a tendency to emphasise what is good about the software they sell, omitting to mention its drawbacks, which may be considerable. Purchasers should ensure that the software they are buying satisfies their needs. This can be difficult even for specialists but it is particularly difficult for non-specialists. Very often it does not become clear what the deficiencies are until the software has been used for some time. Some vendors will demonstrate their software to you on-site or send demonstration disks for evaluation. Whilst this is helpful, again, deficiencies may not be immediately evident as they will tend to be disguised. It is advisable to speak to existing users before purchasing any software. Unfortunately, contact with existing users may be through the software vendor. Consequently, these contacts may not provide entirely impartial references. *Caveat emptor!*

The ability to evaluate software is an essential prerequisite to deploying it effectively in the classroom. However, there is often little time to develop this ability beforehand. Trainee teachers and teachers also need some awareness of the range and type of CAL software available for use. Combining the need to develop software evaluation skills with the need for some awareness of the CAL software available gives rise to a useful, if intense, training activity. Participants are provided with one of the various schema for evaluating software (see Figure 9.4) and are asked to take a critical look at a range of CAL software. They should be encouraged to adapt the schema they have been given, developing their own perspectives on the efficiency and usefulness of the CAL software. They should be asked to describe how the software could be useful in helping pupils learn and whether it could be used in the classroom, given suitable IT facilities.

There are many different categories of CAL software but there is no generally agreed, detailed taxonomy. In order to simplify this activity, only three broad categories of CAL are referred to. These are drill and practice, programmed learning, and simulation and modelling. Other categories could be included to suit the needs of participants.

The CAL software to be evaluated could be adjusted to meet different circumstances. It could be tailored to meet the subject backgrounds of the participants. As a part of an awareness-raising exercise on the importance of numeracy across the curriculum, a selection of software could be evaluated that could be used to develop pupils' number skills.

Participants could be given the CAL software in the form it would arrive in school when first purchased. They will then need to install or load the software, and run it, before its suitability for use with pupils in the classroom can be evaluated. This will give participants an immediate appreciation of the quality and appropriateness of documentation provided with software, and experience of the problems encountered in getting software to work satisfactorily.

The resources needed to evaluate the CAL software are:

- a range of CAL software;
- a schema for evaluating software (see Figure 9.4).

You are asked to do the following:

• Use the software, exploring its full range of operation.
• Evaluate the software for use in the classroom using the schema below.
• Evaluate the schema itself and propose improvements.

In the classroom:	
Could be useful in these subjects:	Ma/En/Sc/IT/DT/PE/ML/BSt/Mu/Re other:
Suitable for:	individual use/groups/presentations to the whole: class/other:
Related classroom activities:	
Other learning resources needed:	
The software:	
Name:	
Description of content:	
Type of software:	drill and practice/programmed learning/ simulation and modelling/ other:
Special software features:	e.g. MS Windows
Reliability of software:	
Address of vendor:	
The hardware:	
Can be used with these computers:	Apple/Acorn/IBM compatible/RM Nimbus/ other:
Special hardware features required	e.g. mouse-operated, needs a printer

Circle a number to rate the software on its usefulness in the classroom:

Clear objectives	1	2	3	4	5	No clear objectives
Achievable objectives	1	2	3	4	5	Unachievable objectives
Appropriate subject content	1	2	3	4	5	Irrelevant subject content
Appropriate use of graphics	1	2	3	4	5	No graphics
Appropriate use of colour	1	2	3	4	5	No colour
Appropriate use of sound	1	2	3	4	5	No sound
Easy to use	1	2	3	4	5	Unusable
Clear instructions on screen	1	2	3	4	5	No instructions on screen
Well written on-line help and other documentation	1	2	3	4	5	No on-line help or other documentation
Useful pupils' worksheets provided	1	2	3	4	5	No pupils' worksheets provided

Other good features:	
Other bad features:	

Figure 9.4 An example of a schema for evaluating CAL software

111

In this activity participants are asked to do the following:

- Use the software, exploring its entire range of operation.
- Evaluate the software for use in the classroom using a given schema.
- Critically evaluate the schema provided, developing their own criteria for the evaluation of CAL software.

4. THE 'WHOLE SCHOOL PLANNING FOR THE PROVISION OF HARDWARE' ROLE PLAY

It is important that teachers understand the dynamics of whole school planning for the provision of IT resources, and have an appreciation of the level of funding required. The possession of personal IT skills does not necessarily equip teachers with an understanding of the political and social processes that determine the distribution of IT resources in schools. IT resources are desirable and expensive. Those who control them have responsibility for a relatively high proportion of a school's expenditure on learning resources. Inevitably, IT resources are associated with high status amongst pupils, parents, governors and colleagues, and their possessors may be viewed as relatively rich and powerful. Perhaps this overstates the argument. However, it is certainly true that unless teachers forcefully present well-informed arguments to support the acquisition of the quantity and type of IT resources they need, then they will be given what is available whether it is suitable or not. For example, the use of IT in Music is often very limited in secondary schools, due to a lack of access to suitable IT resources, yet the potential to make effective use of IT in Music is greater than in many other subjects. Clearly, there may be many reasons why Music departments do not have sufficient access to IT resources. However, if Music teachers had a greater understanding of what is required, and what must be done to acquire it, then it is likely that more Music departments would be more extensively and appropriately equipped.

The way in which IT resources are allocated to subject departments and distributed throughout the school is closely linked to the curriculum model adopted for the delivery of IT Capability. IT resources include staffing, time, rooms, and consumables, in addition to hardware and software. All these will be deployed to support the curriculum model adopted. In order to reduce its complexity and make it more manageable within a reasonable period of time, this role play exercise focuses on the acquisition and allocation of hardware. Some consideration of an appropriate curriculum model is encouraged, as an implicit model will inevitably emerge as the role play progresses.

This role play helps participants explore their own needs in relation to those of colleagues in other subjects. It is based on participants role-playing a meeting of Heads of Department and others engaged in planning expenditure on hardware for a secondary school. It is best conducted with groups of five or six participants. So that they will have some knowledge of current hardware and its costs, participants should either research these beforehand or be given a summary by the organiser. If possible, the subject specialisms of the participants should match the subject backgrounds of the roles. The roles given to participants and the support materials provided could be adjusted to model particular circumstances or reflect local needs.

The initial focus of the role play is the planning of the reorganisation and improvement of IT hardware provision in a secondary school and this has to be done within realistic financial constraints. One participant should be given the role of Deputy Head (Resources) with the task of organising the meeting of the IT Committee. During the meeting, participants are asked to produce a report recording the outcomes of their deliberations. The meeting of the IT Committee should last around half an hour. This can be presented as the length of time that would be available to a committee meeting in the lunch time at school. Participants are also asked to present their plan to the 'Board of Governors' shortly after the end of the meeting. This simulates the situation where a plan is discussed at lunch time prior to presentation to governors the same evening, by a teacher who has a full timetable during the afternoon, and other responsibilities at the end of the school day. Teachers are often under pressure to meet tight deadlines and must be able to make decisions quickly. The requirement to report to the 'Board of Governors' provides a focus, and some impetus, for the role play exercise.

Each group is asked to make a presentation to the 'Board of Governors'. This may last around ten minutes per group. While each group presents its solution to the 'Board of Governors', the other groups role-play the governors. Discussion of each group's plan should be encouraged and this can be made more interesting by giving individuals the roles of particularly well-informed, vociferous or 'luddite' governors, and encouraging some groups to be particularly outspoken or argumentative. Surprisingly, otherwise shy individuals often appear to relish playing the role of vociferous and argumentative governors! Giving participants these roles can make potentially dull presentations much more lively and interesting. However, if individuals or groups are given provocative roles without the knowledge of other participants, it is advisable to explain what was being done when the role play is finished. Otherwise, some participants may continue to feel resentment to others after the role play is over, and there is a risk of personal acrimony between them. 'Letting the cat out of the bag' can diffuse possible tensions.

At the end of the role play, these points might be discussed:

- The need to participate in decision-making processes in order to ensure an acceptable distribution of IT resources.
- The need for long-term planning for the acquisition of IT resources.
- Attitudes in schools towards obsolescence of capital resources and their renewal.

- The ethical implications of funding IT resources while more basic needs are not met. That is, should schools buy IT resources or mend holes in the roofs of school buildings?

Manor High School is an 11 to 18 co-educational comprehensive school, housed in a single two-storey building on a compact site. There are forty classrooms and a library. There are about 1,000 pupils.

The full range of GCSE courses is available and some vocational courses. The number of pupils studying post-16 is increasing as GNVQ has just been introduced to complement the full range of A and A/S levels.

Information Technology resources at Manor High School

At present Manor High School has these hardware resources:

- 25 Amstrad PCWs in a Business Studies room;
- 15 standalone BBC Masters and 2 dot matrix printers in a room shared by Maths and Science;
- A network of 20 RM Nimbus (IBM compatibles) in an IT room with 1 networked dot matrix printer;
- 2 Archimedes computers in Design Technology;
- 1 Archimedes computer shared by Art and Music.

These hardware resources are to be extended in the near future. Development funding will come from capitation and from various grants from external sources. The following funding is currently available:

- £4,000 for new equipment for Design Technology;
- £4,000 for developing the use of IT in Business Studies;
- £2,000 for developing data logging in Science;
- £2,000 for developing Music technology;
- £2,000 for resources for teaching Mathematics;
- £60,000 to develop open learning and IT throughout the school. This money is available spread over two years.

Figure 9.5 Excerpts from the Manor High School Staff Handbook

The resources needed are:

- a sheet summarising current hardware costs (to be taken from current hardware advertisements);
- excerpts from the Manor High School Staff Handbook (see Figure 9.5);
- the Deputy Head's survey (see Figure 9.6);
- the Role Play scenario: a meeting of the IT Committee (see Figure 9.7);
- appropriate resources to help with group presentations, e.g. overhead projector transparencies and pens.

The Deputy Head (Resources) has surveyed the school's staff regarding their preferences for IT hardware and talked to a local IT advisor. Only 40% of the staff returned the completed survey.

The Deputy Head has summarised the survey results, as follows:

- The Business Studies staff would like IBM compatible computers as they are more often used in business;
- The Music teacher would like several Apple computers with midi
- The art teacher would like Apple computers;
- The Science teacher wants hardware and software for data logging;
- The Design Technology teacher wants more Archimedes computers because of the wide range of easy-to-use design software;
- Maths finds sharing computers with Science very inconvenient. Maths want access to at least twenty computers on a network with some CAL programs for learning maths.
- Several teachers have suggested that there should be a computer in every classroom;
- The IT department need access to computers for all lessons. The IT
- Co-ordinator wants to centralise resources in a suite of three adjacent IT rooms, each containing fifteen IBM compatible computers on a single network. The IT Co-ordinator would like a high quality laser printer in each room, in addition to a networked dot matrix printer;
- Some teachers would like open access IT resources to be available to all pupils but have worries about supervision;
- The librarian is constantly approached by pupils wanting access to wordprocessing and database software. The librarian would like to computerise the library and give pupils access to on-line databases, teletext, CD-ROM and the Internet;
- Some teachers would welcome more access to IT resources but they do not feel that they should have the responsibility for teaching and assessing IT;
- Post-16 need an open access IT area for use by pupils on GNVQ, A/S and A level courses;
- The IT technician wants the school to sell all the existing computers and standardise on one type of computer. The IT technician prefers Apple computers;
- The IT adviser says the school should adopt a curriculum model where all IT is taught, used and assessed across the curriculum. The IT Co-ordinator should be redeployed and the computers in the centralised IT rooms distributed to other subjects

Figure 9.6 The Deputy Head's survey

There is to be a meeting of the IT Committee to decide on a school development plan for extending hardware provision. How this is done will to some extent depend on the curriculum model adopted.

You are to role play one of those present at this meeting. You have available to you the results of the Deputy Head's survey. The meeting should produce a costed plan for the acquisition and deployment of IT hardware.

Below are some of those who might be present at the meeting:

Chairperson: Deputy Head (Resources)
HoD English
HoD Maths
HoD Science
HoD Design Technology
IT Co-ordinator
HoD Music
HoD ML
HoD RE
HoD Business Studies
Librarian

The Deputy Head (Resources) should introduce the participants and ensure that business is conducted equitably.

The preferences of teaching and support staff should be taken into account (see the Deputy Head's survey).

Your plan should attempt to resolve conflicts between the need for consistent, school-wide provision of IT hardware resources and the need for specific computers for specialist subjects.

The plan should be costed and all decisions justified. Estimated costs could be used.

The plan should be presented in a concise form on a single A4 sheet.

One of those present at this meeting of the IT committee should be prepared to report its conclusions to a meeting of the Board of Governors. You should all expect to be present at this meeting which will take place shortly after the meeting of the IT committee.

Figure 9.7 Role-play scenario: a meeting of the IT Committee

116

In this activity participants are asked to do the following:

- Role-play teachers attending a meeting of the school's IT committee. One participant takes the role of the Deputy Head (Resources).
- Represent the interests of their subject and resolve conflicts between competing perspectives.
- Decide on a costed plan for the development of hardware resources throughout the school.
- Present their plan to the school's Board of Governors.
- Role-play governors on the school's Board of Governors.

5.   THE 'ROLES AND RESPONSIBILITIES' GAME

Because IT is a cross-curricular skill and a subject in its own right, it is a somewhat unusual component of the NC. In addition, the management of the hardware, software and other resources needed to support IT provision is complex, and requires technical skills and abilities beyond those normally required of a classroom teacher. Many teachers, technicians and others could be involved in delivering the IT curriculum and they will need to know that their efforts provide coverage of the NC. Unnecessary duplication of pupils' experiences and teachers' efforts should also be avoided, if at all possible. The Roles and Responsibilities game can be used to help participants develop an understanding of how IT is currently organised in their school or to explore how IT should be organised, depending on the instructions given. The game is best organised in groups of five participants with a good mix of subject expertise amongst them.

The Roles and Responsibilities board (see Figure 9.8) has on it the titles of Deputy Head, School Secretary, IT Co-ordinator, IT Technician, Head of Subject Department, Subject Teacher, School Librarian and Other. Clearly, these could be extended, elaborated or reduced depending on the current position in the school or future proposals. They have been chosen because most teachers and trainee teachers will easily differentiate between them. The title of IT Manager has been omitted because most participants are likely to confuse the roles and responsibilities of the IT Manager and the IT Co-ordinator. The Activity cards (see Figure 9.9) can also be edited to take into account particular concerns, such as who should have responsibility for organising a programme of work for the IT Technician. Suitably adjusted to the context in which it is to be played, the Roles and Responsibilities game is a useful training activity. Stripped of its rules, it is also a good framework for drawing up a job description for the IT Co-ordinator and identifying the IT-related responsibilities of all teachers.

The resources needed to play the game are:

- the Roles and Responsibilities board (see Figure 9.8);
- the Activity cards (see Figure 9.9).

The rules of the game are:

1 The game is played in groups of 4 or 5 players.
2 Deal out the Activity cards equally, discarding the remainder.
3 Starting at the dealer's left, in turn, each player places an Activity card on the Roles and Responsibilities Board in the same box as one of the job titles.
4 When an Activity card has been placed by a player, the group decides whether it has been placed in an appropriate place on the Roles and Responsibilities Board. If the Activity card has not been placed in an appropriate place on the Roles and Responsibilities Board, the Activity card is returned to the player who placed it. Otherwise, the Activity card remains on the Roles and Responsibilities Board and the game moves on the next player.
5 Cards which could be placed in all the boxes (except 'Other') are bonus cards. When placing them players can claim another turn.
6 The winner is the player to discard all their cards first.

Deputy Head	School Secretary
IT Co-ordinator	IT Technician
Head of Subject Department	Subject Teacher
School Librarian	Other

Figure 9.8 The Roles and Responsibilities Board

Put bar codes on all the books in library.	Circulate details of an important exhibition of IT resources for schools.	Set up a database to record pupils' personal details.	Purchase software and hardware for SEN teaching.	Prevent pupils from hacking into the school's network.	Use IT to design the school timetable for the following year.
Help English teachers learn to use Desk Top Publishing software.	Use the administration computer system to order Science equipment.	Set up a CD-ROM system for use in the library.	Help pupils revise for their GCSE Maths exams using CAL software.	Co-ordinate the school's IT policy with departmental development plans.	Write a computer program to analyse the school's GCSE examination results.
Advise on the adequacy of the school's hardware and software resources.	Design a questionnaire to collect personal information from pupils.	Move IT equipment from one classroom to another.	Arrange for a display of pupils' work using IT, at the school's open evening.	Advise the HoD Maths on the use of spreadsheets software in Maths.	Send out personalised letters to parents advertising a treasure hunt.
Convene a meeting of the school's IT committee.	Recommend a home computer to a pupil.	Provide support in the classroom for a Geography teacher using statistics software.	Inspect computer equipment for electronic safety.	Conduct an audit of IT activities throughout the curriculum.	Scan pupil's photographs so that they can be added to the school's pupil database.
Use IT software to timetable a parents' evening.	Advise Science teachers on the use of data logging software.	Use a database to keep records of all the books in the school library.	Write a five-year plan for developing the school's IT resources.	Chair the school's IT Committee.	Put a new user on the school's IT network.
Produce the school prospectus using Desk Top Publishing software.	Change users' passwords every month.	Run INSET activities on aspects of using IT in the classroom.	Set up user identification numbers and passwords for staff and pupils.	Show pupils how to write a program to control a robot.	Enter details of today's activities on the computer display in the foyer.
Connect IT hardware to a synthesiser for the Music teacher.	Inform the Head Teacher of the latest changes in the IT NC.	Install network cabling throughout the school.	Survey teaching staff to find out the IT skills training they need.	Help a teacher decide on a personal development plan for IT skills.	Use Electronic Mail to contact a school in France.
Maintain an inventory of software and hardware resources.	Introduce pupils to the technical knowledge needed to use a computer.	Write the school's IT policy.	Use a spreadsheet for modelling the English department's budget.	Be aware of different models of the IT Curriculum in schools.	Format a floppy disk.
Use a wordprocessor.	Set up equipment to record data on pupils' health and analyse it.	Help pupils use a computer-based model of the economy.	Use a database to organise Maths classes into sets.	Plan the layout of IT rooms in a new building to be built next term.	Use the Internet to access the Spacelink database at NASA.
Find faults in hardware and repair them.	Bid for funding to extend the school's IT resources.	Clamp all the hardware to benches.	Demonstrate CAL software for Modern Languages to French teachers.	Set up hardware and software for an Art teacher to use.	Teach pupils how to use Desk Top Publishing software.
Install software on the school's IT network.	Repair printer cables.	Ensure all computers are connected to the school's burglar alarm system.	Make new teachers aware of the school's IT resources.	Show Business Studies teachers how to access share prices on teletext.	Decide on the location of IT hardware throughout the school.

Figure 9.9 Activity cards for the 'Roles and Responsibilities' game

119

6. THE DISCUSSION OF 'EQUAL OPPORTUNITIES ISSUES IN RELATION TO GENDER'

The aim of this training exercise is to encourage participants to develop a greater understanding of the equal opportunities issues in relation to gender that arise when IT is used in schools. They are asked to discuss these issues, drawing on their own experiences of IT in schools. Equal opportunities issues still arouse strong emotional feelings in many people. If asked to discuss the equal opportunities issues that arise when IT is used in schools, some participants will not do so, preferring to chat about other, safer topics; some passionately air their prejudices, taking little cognisance of others' views and experiences. For these reasons, it is important that equal opportunities issues are discussed in a carefully structured way so that participants are restrained from over-indulging their personal prejudices, yet are exposed to others' views. It is hoped that this will encourage participants to reflect on their own opinions, modify their prejudices and develop a more balanced perspective.

In this exercise, participants are asked to choose between statements describing different perspectives on equal opportunities issues in relation to gender (see Figure 9.10). Discussions take place in groups of four or five participants. The groups should be of mixed gender if possible which helps ensure that different perspectives are represented in each group. Hopefully, because discussion takes place in small groups, participants will feel able to express their views openly. If participants are unable to choose one of the two statements given, they should write a statement which reflects their own views.

The requirement to choose between statements representing different perspectives will stimulate discussion. Participants should be asked to come to a decision on all the alternatives given within 45 minutes. The pressure on participants to discuss all the statements within a relatively short time should ensure that the discussion has some pace, minimising the impact of strong personal prejudices on the group, yet allowing everyone to be exposed to differing points of view. Hopefully, polarisation will be avoided and participants will move towards perspectives that can accommodate others' viewpoints.

The resources needed to conduct this discussion are:

● the gender discussion sheet (see Figure 9.10).

In this activity participants are asked to do the following:

● Discuss the issues raised by each of the pairs of statements given.
● Decide which of the given statements represents the views of the majority of the group, or, if neither statement is representative, to write a different statement which is.

You should discuss the issues raised by each of the pairs of statements below. You should decide which statement best represents the views of your group or, if neither does, write a short statement that does represent your opinions.

1. Girls are usually very interested in IT.

   or Computers are 'toys for the boys'.

2. Boys are always better at using IT.

   or Ability with IT is not related to gender.

3. Boys always dominate in mixed groups and classes.

   or Single sex classes and groups are better for girls.

4. Boys always dominate in mixed schools.

   or Single sex schools are better for girls.

5. Female teachers are always the best role models for girls.

   or Teachers' attitudes and competence are more important than their gender.

6. Girls are discouraged from using IT in schools.

   or Girls fail to take advantage of the opportunites offered to them.

7. Schools should discriminate positively in favour of girls.

   or Schools should offer the same opportunities to both boys and girls.

8. Monitoring Equal Opportunities is the best way ensure fairness.

   or Monitoring Equal Opportunities is inherently sexist.

9. Schools and LEAs should have Equal Opportunities policies and enforce them.

   or Equal Opportunities policies interfere with the right of the individual to freedom of thought and speech.

Figure 9.10 The gender discussion sheet

7. THE 'SHARING OF PERSONAL EXPERIENCES OF IT IN SCHOOLS' ACTIVITY

It may seem somewhat trite to observe that teachers' and trainee teachers' collective experiences of schools are broader and more varied than those of an individual teacher or trainee teacher. However, it is undoubtedly true. Individual trainee teachers usually have little experience of what is happening in schools in general. They tend to assume that the one or two schools in which they are placed during their training course are typical of all schools but it is unlikely that they are. Similarly, individual teachers often spend a large proportion of their professional careers in two or three schools. As a result, teachers may also have a narrow view of what is happening in schools in general. Moreover, the organisation of individual schools often isolates teachers and trainee teachers within their subject departments and within their classrooms. It is not unusual for them to be unaware of what is happening elsewhere in the school in which they teach, and this is particularly true of the use of IT in schools. However, in order to understand the strengths and weaknesses of the ways in which IT is used within their own school, it is important that teachers, trainee teachers and others are aware of the variety of different approaches to organising IT provision in schools and the diversity of provision.

This exercise seeks to broaden participants' experience, building on their current experience by sharing it with others and listening to others' descriptions of what they have encountered. It also illustrates another means of structuring discussion between participants so that a useful exchange of views takes place within a short time. Initially, participants are asked to divide into groups that have a similar type of hardware mix in their schools. For example, participants might join a group for those schools that use mainly Apple hardware, mainly IBM compatible hardware or mainly Archimedes hardware. They are then asked to pair up with someone from one of the other groups. Each member of the pair is given an interview prompt sheet (see Figure 9.11) and asked to interview the other. After a short time, these pairs are then asked to join another pair. Each member of the group of four then describes the experience of IT of the person they have just interviewed. This encourages participants to share their different experiences and, almost inevitably, leads to a useful exchange of views and opinions.

If a balance of different hardware types is not available, another approach is to ask participants to interview those with experience of the same type of IT hardware. This pair then joins another with similar backgrounds. These groups of four should be able to clearly identify the common features of their experience and could be asked to describe these in a short presentation to all the participants. During these presentations, the similarities and differences between participants' experiences will become evident.

This exercise could usefully be done at the start of a course or as the first session in a series. It is a good 'ice breaker' as it encourages participants to get to know each other. However, it can be a useful exercise at any stage of a course. A brief glance at the interview prompt sheet shows that there is a wide range of issues to be discussed. My personal preference is to place this exercise towards the end of a course when participants have had opportunities to reflect on their own experiences of IT. This can make the sharing of experiences richer and more informed.

You are asked to interview a colleague about their experiences of IT in secondary schools. You should be able to describe their experience and discuss any significant issues, conflicts, contradictions, and good or bad ideas that are mentioned.

The following indicates some of the information you might record:

Hardware:

- What type of computers were used? Model? Features? Costs?
- Who supplied them? Repairs them?
- Where were the computers located? Why?
- Were all the IT rooms suitable? Accessible? To everyone?
- Were all the computers compatible?
- How was printing organised? When could it be done?
- When did pupils have access to the hardware?
- What restrictions were placed on pupils' use of the hardware? Why?
- Was there enough hardware?

Software:

- What type of software was available?
- Name all the software that was available and indicate its type.
- Why was that particular software available?
- Who was allowed to use the software? Where? When?
- What restrictions were placed on access by pupils? By staff? By others?
- Was all the software easy to use? Was a GUI used?
- Were the files generated by one piece of software compatible with other software?
- Was the software integrated or were different pieces of software used?
- How did the software provide for progression, continuity and differentiation of learning?
- How was the software distributed? On floppy disk? Over a network?

Supervision and control of IT resources:

- Who was responsible for computer resources?
- Who controlled the use of IT resources? Why? In what ways? For staff? For pupils? For others?
- Who else was associated with IT provision in the school? What did they do?
- How did you find out what IT resources were available for your use?
- Who was allowed to use the IT resources? When? Where?
- Was technical help available? From whom? When? Where? For staff? For pupils? For others?
- How were technicians trained? What qualifications did they have?
- What organisational structures are used to manage IT?

contd...

Figure 9.11 An interview prompt sheet for the 'sharing of personal experience of IT in schools' activity

Teachers' attitudes and experiences:

- Were all the teachers enthusiastic about IT? Technophobic?
- Which teachers used IT in teaching their subjects? Where? When? To which pupils?
- What teaching styles were used when teaching IT?
- Was there an induction programme in IT for trainee teachers and other teachers new to the school?
- What provision did the school make for training teaching staff in IT? When? Where?
- Were there IT resources reserved for staff use? Were these sufficient?

Pupils' attitudes and experiences:

- Were pupils well motivated in IT? Boys? Girls?
- Were pupils well behaved in IT? Boys? Girls?
- Did pupils believe IT is relevant and useful? Why?
- Did all pupils have equal access to IT? During timetabled lessons? Outside timetabled lessons?
- Did pupils' experiences of IT meet the statutory requirements of the NC?

Applications:

- What applications were studied? Why? By which pupils? In which subjects?
- What IT coursework projects were done? Why? By which pupils? In which subjects?

IT policy and the curriculum:

- Did the school have an IT policy?
- Was the policy agreed? By whom? How?
- Do you have a copy of the IT policy? Why not?
- Have you read the IT policy? Why not?
- Was all the policy written or is some of it informal?
- Was the policy part of a school booklet? Which?
- Was IT taught as a subject? Across the curriculum? Using a hybrid combination of these?
- How did the IT policy affect the delivery of IT?
- In your opinion, was IT used appropriately?
- How were assessments of pupils' IT Capability recorded and reported?

Administration:

- Was IT used for school administration? Departmental administration? Individual teachers' administration? What else?
- Were senior management enthusiastic about the use of IT for administration? Office staff? Year Heads? Subject HoDs? Teachers?
- Did the use of IT for administration decrease or increase work loads?

contd...

Figure 9.11

124

The good and the bad:

- What experiences of IT were particularly successful? Disastrous?
- Identify any issues, conflicts or contradictions, and good or bad ideas that you are aware of.

Figure 9.11

The resources needed to conduct this discussion are:

- the interview prompt sheet (see Figure 9.11).
- overhead projector, transparencies and pens.

In this activity participants are asked to do the following:

- Interview each other, in pairs, regarding their experiences of IT in schools.
- In groups of four, describe the experiences of the person they have interviewed.
- Give a short presentation to all participants on the common features of their experiences of IT in schools and the differences.

SUMMARY

This chapter contains suggestions for activities that could be a part of a training programme that aims to raise participants' awareness of the issues that arise when IT is used in secondary schools. They are all attempts to structure participants' discussions so that they share their experiences and encounter new ideas. The activities include games, role-play scenarios and check lists.

These training activities are a few examples of the variety of those possible. Readers are invited to use them as they are or to adapt them to suit their own circumstances. The structure of most of the activities is generic and can be adapted to accommodate quite different focal topics. For example, the discussion of 'Equal Opportunities issues in relation to gender' is based on a discussion sheet that presents alternative, polarised views. Groups of participants are asked to choose one alternative or write a sentence summarising their own opinion. This technique for stimulating and directing discussion can easily be applied to almost any topic. Readers may have noticed that 'IT across the cirriculum' and the 'Roles and Responsibilities' game show the same structure. All of the activities in this chapter have been trialed by the author with some success.

10

IT IN SCHOOL
ADMINISTRATION AND
MANAGEMENT

Management Information Systems can help save money and time in schools .... Increased knowledge about the school's finances meant that money could be spent for the improvement of the school and the betterment of pupils' education.

(NCET, 1995b)

Many school administration and management tasks can be performed more efficiently and effectively using IT. This chapter reviews what can be done, and the advantages and disadvantages of using IT to do it. A list of software suppliers, and brief reviews of some of the software available are given in Appendix 2, p. 159. The requirements of the Data Protection Act (1984) are reviewed in relation to the responsibilities of schools.

SOME SCHOOL ADMINISTRATION AND
MANAGEMENT TASKS THAT CAN
BE DONE USING IT

Most administration and management tasks can be facilitated using IT. Some schools may wish to purchase a comprehensive Management Information System (MIS) which performs a wide range of tasks. Other schools will buy individual items of applications software in response to particular needs. A wide range of tasks can be done using IT, some of which are listed below. Not all software will do all these tasks and some software will do other tasks. However, when considering the purchase of new software or evaluating it, the following may be a helpful indication of what it is realistic and possible to expect:

- Information about pupils can be stored. This may be simply the type of information that is routinely kept about pupils, for example, pupils' names, addresses, next of kin, form group, emergency contacts, and doctor's name. Keeping this information on a computer instead of on paper should facilitate access to it, and the production of a variety of useful reports such as form lists, class lists, lists of pupils taking school meals, and lists of

126

pupils living in specific areas. Many of these would be too time-consuming to produce and keep up to date without the use of IT.

- Records of attendance can be kept and analysed. Pupils' attendance can be recorded in registration or in other periods during the day. Systems that allow immediate input of attendance data to the computer system can produce a report showing which pupils are absent immediately after registration. Reports can be printed showing patterns of absence for individual pupils, a group of pupils, a particular class or a year group. Statistical analyses and tables can be generated, including Form 7. If attendance is recorded during each period, the location of a particular pupil can be output on demand and pupils' whereabouts can be tracked. Letters to parents can be generated, informing them of their child's absences from school, and this information can be summarised for the relevant members of staff and Educational Welfare Officers. Attendance data can be input using a variety of methods, including OMR, swipe cards, or portable computers with communications links. Schools using such systems often report dramatic drops in absenteeism. For example, Brentford School for Girls recorded a 31 per cent drop in absenteeism (Frost, 1994).

- Records of Achievement, and other curriculum-related records of pupils' attainment and progress, can be assembled. This could include the recording, analysis and reporting of pupils' progress in relation to the NC. There may be provision for appropriate pupil inputs, for example, pupils might input their own curriculum vitae for inclusion in their Records of Achievement. Teachers should be able to input the results of their pupils' assessments, and comments for their pupils' school reports, using OMR forms or other convenient input methods. Such software often makes use of a statement bank, that is, a database of statements about pupils' progress that teachers can edit and include in their reports. School reports to parents should be automatically generated. Reports can be printed analysing the progress of particular pupils, classes, year groups or the whole school. Examination entries to GCSE and other examination boards can be compiled and submitted, and the results analysed and printed in suitable formats for reporting to Governors, parents, the press, subject departments within the school, class teachers, or individual pupils. Software of this type often becomes the focus for the organisational activity that is needed to assemble Records of Achievement, school reports, and examination entries for every pupil in the school. It can be expected to indicate omissions and discrepancies and to help in other ways with the administration of these tasks.

- The planning, administration and record-keeping tasks associated with organising pupils' work experience placements can be facilitated. Standard letters to parents and employers, and progress reports, can be easily generated. Reports can be printed immediately or fed into software for producing Records of Achievement, and school reports.

- Expert systems and databases can be used to inform many aspects of schools' forward planning. For example, a database containing all the Programmes of Study in the NC can help with curriculum planning; a database of courses in Further and Higher Education can give faster access to a wider range of information, improving teachers' advice to those considering such courses, and helping pupils with the difficult choices they have to make; a suitable expert system may help with the application of educational law.

- Personnel records can be kept for all staff. The information collected can be related to payroll, financial forecasting of a school's staff costs, audits of teachers' skills and knowledge, the planning of staff development, and whole school development planning.

- Appraisal and staff development can be organised, and records kept and analysed and these can be co-ordinated with staff job descriptions, staff responsibilities, and INSET records. The construction of individual staff action plans can be assisted and co-ordinated with whole school development and resource planning.

- The school timetable can be constructed using IT. Timetabling software can automatically allocate teachers, rooms and other resources to classes, and clashes and shortfalls will be identified. Such software can usually be adjusted manually at any stage in the process. Acceptable parts of the timetable can be preserved while the software attempts to produce a more acceptable timetable for the remainder. Often, several possible timetables can be generated. A variety of reports can be printed, including time-tables for individual pupils and teachers, classes, year groups and the whole school, in various formats. The actual curriculum of the school can be derived from the timetable showing the time spent on NC subjects and other identifiable activities for each pupil, a class, a year group, and the whole school. This analysis of the actual curriculum can be used to set up structures for assembling Records of Achievement and pupils' school reports. Timetabling software can also help with the timetabling of parents evenings, careers evenings, school examinations and other school events of this type.

- The staffing resources needed to cover for the absence of teachers and other employees can be automatically identified. Cover for absent teachers can be arranged using those teachers who are not teaching when a substitute teacher is required. This can be done so that the additional workload is spread fairly among the available staff. Records of teachers' absence and the extent of teachers' deployment as substitutes can be kept and analysed. Past absences can be used to forecast probable future requirements. Details of the supply staff used by the school and their current availability can be recorded, so that those with the appropriate expertise to cover a teacher's absence can be selected.

- Finance and budgeting software can be expected to help with cost control and the monitoring of spending against budgets. Budgets can be allocated to cost centres, such as departments. The software should produce analyses contrasting spending against budget, possibly showing actual cash flow per period against profiles of projected outgoings for the school and for cost centres. The software should help maintain records of purchases and sales, printing the appropriate documentation, such as orders and invoices. Heads of Department or other authorised staff can be given access to the software, allowing them to set up orders and monitor progress with deliveries. In setting up the orders, there should be access to a database of supplier and catalogue details with these being automatically entered as orders are prepared. A wide variety of standard reports should be available. It should be possible for users to edit these or generate their own reports in the format they require. Standard reports should include audit trails, historical expense analysis, and trial balance. A well-established system will provide a sound basis for forecasting, planning and analysis, including 'what if' modelling.

- An inventory of all resources, assets and equipment can be maintained. A variety of standard reports should be available, such as a list of equipment stored at a given location, or the current values of specific categories of equipment, such as printers, or other computer hardware.

- The inspection and maintenance of premises and estates can be organised. Tenders and contracts can be monitored and reviewed, giving the full costs of these and other identifiable processes or events.

- Library automation software can be used to organise the borrowing of books and other resources from the school library or other resource centres within the school. Catalogue information can be entered using the keyboard, or from a variety of other sources, for example, Whitaker's Book Bank. Issues, reservations, renewals and returns can be recorded via the keyboard or using a bar code reader. The catalogue can be searched by author, publisher, or keyword. A variety of reports can be produced, including overdue lists and resource use analysis. The bar codes to be used to identify books and borrowers can be printed when required. The library information system should be capable of distribution over a network so that it can be searched at On-line Public Access Computers (OPACs) within the library and staff can have private access for administration and research.

- Sports days can be organised. Results can be recorded and analysed, showing comparisons with school, national and international records for each event.

With suitable hardware, it should be possible to do this on the sports field while the events are taking place. Printed reports should show outstanding individual performances, class, year, house and school achievements. Other software can be used to help keep records of specific sporting events, such as cricket matches.

- Campus messaging systems help schools communicate with their staff and pupils. Such systems may distribute both public and private messages. Public information will be broadcast to a number of televisions or monitors placed at convenient locations throughout the school. Screens of text and graphical information, probably in a teletext style format, will be displayed for a set length of time in rotation. It should be possible to change, at any time, the information displayed, the length of time it is displayed and the order of rotation of the different screens to be displayed. Private messages can be distributed where there is individual access. For example, where a swipe card registration system is in use, on registration, a message can be displayed for the specific pupil who has just registered. The message can be displayed on an LCD screen built into the swipe card reader or an adjacent monitor. The physical arrangements for accessing the hardware determine the degree of privacy given to staff or pupils registering.

When schools turn to IT to assist with administration and management tasks, they often overlook software that they may already own because its full potential is not realised. It is tempting to buy new applications software that appears to offer an immediate solution to pressing problems because the software is promoted as being a complete and instantaneous solution to that problem. However, it may well be that a school already owns software that could be equally useful. Many schools have found that some administration and management tasks can be done effectively using general purpose software, that is, wordprocessing, graphics, Desk Top Publishing, database, and spreadsheet software. For example:

- A wordprocessor can be used to send personalised letters to parents.
- Graphics and Desk Top Publishing software can be used to produce Governors' reports, or the school prospectus, with a high standard of presentation.
- Database software can be used to keep pupil and personnel records.
- Spreadsheet software can be used to keep day-to-day financial records, to do the payroll and to perform a variety of financial forecasts.

This general purpose software is frequently bundled with purchases of new hardware or may be already owned because it is used in the curriculum of the school. It is an error to assume that software acquired for curriculum use is unsuitable for administrative applications. Some curriculum software is of the highest quality and may be the same as that used in commerce and industry.

Applications software often makes use of this general purpose IT software to perform some of the tasks done. However, whereas applications software is set up to do a specific job when it is purchased, general purpose software must be programmed to do the required tasks. Initially, using general purpose software may be cheaper than buying applications software but time and expertise will be needed to set it up so that it can be used as easily and effectively.

THE ADVANTAGES AND DISADVANTAGES
OF USING IT

The advantages of using IT for school administration and management are most obvious when schools are committed users of comprehensive, integrated Management Information Systems. However, most schools do not change from manual systems to whole school, IT-based MIS systems overnight. Some tasks in a predominantly manual system may be done by individuals working in relative isolation, for example, entering pupils for the GCSE examinations. Often these tasks are computerised before a comprehensive MIS is brought into use. Indeed, it may be necessary to proceed step-by-step in order to build up the necessary skills, resources and confidence to commit the school to more wide-ranging developments. In general, the advantages of using IT-based systems for school administration and management are as follows:

- Routine manual tasks are performed faster. For example, there is faster access to individual pupil records, and staff personnel records.

- Some tasks that could be done manually are now done for the first time, or done more often, as they can be done faster, and with less effort using IT. For example, information on groups of pupils with some shared characteristic could be listed immediately. This could be a list of all those pupils in Year 9 who were absent from registration at the start of Thursday afternoon. The names of these pupils could be printed with their addresses and telephone numbers, so that their absence can be investigated and their parents contacted. Similarly, a list of pupils' attainment levels in Mathematics in Year 10 could be generated. This could be in order of merit so that decisions regarding setting arrangements can be made, or in alphabetical order within sets for easy reference at parents' evenings.

- What is done is extended to include those tasks that are impractical using manual systems. For example, an up-to-date summary of spending in relation to budget could be produced automatically at any time. This might not be practical without considerable prior notice where a manual system is in use.

- Record keeping is more orderly and reliable. Manual records may be lost or misplaced due to poor filing or loans not being returned but this is unlikely to happen with an IT-based system. The need for wider access to a pupil's record may lead to it being printed or distributed throughout the school on a computer network but will not lead to its absence from the file.

- Information can be distributed throughout the school whilst remaining complete and secure. To ensure the completeness of manual files, they are either not distributed or are photocopied for distribution. Typically, there is a loss of security when photocopies are made. IT systems can distribute information across networks throughout the school whilst maintaining integrity and confidentiality.

- Information can be available at the time and place of need. IT can be used to distribute information to where it is required. The speed of extracting relevant information means that the demands made can be focused and re-focused as necessary.

- Mistakes can be minimised by the use of software with self-checking or programmable features. For example, when timetables are constructed there can be automatic checks that rooms are not used by more than one class at a time unless this is intended.

- The cost of performing some administrative tasks may be lower, or the tasks may be done more thoroughly and comprehensively. If newly intro-duced IT-based systems only perform the tasks that the displaced systems did, then fewer administrative staff will be needed as productivity improves. Consequently, running costs will be lower. However, it is a common expe-rience that more administrative staff are needed when new IT-based systems are introduced, due to the demand for the additional information that can be generated by such systems.

- The display of recorded information is consistently uniform and there is less time spent copying across information or re-entering information at the keyboard. It is often a feature of paper-based record-keeping systems that there is considerable copying across of written information from one form to another. The necessity to copy across written information onto standard card filing systems may, however, be replaced by equivalent activ-ities, such as entering information at a keyboard. The use of poorly integrated IT-based systems leads to duplication of effort as it is possible that the same information will be input several times to different pieces of software using the keyboard. If automatic forms of input, for example, OMR, are used, this reduces the need to enter large volumes of data at the keyboard. Well-integrated software should be able to assimilate all the information input from a variety of sources, at different times, making it available in a form that is widely accessible, and displaying it in a uniform format.

- Reports generated by an IT-based system can be more reliable, flexible and focused than those produced by manual systems. Often reports can be produced automatically: for example, a summary analysis of GCSE results for printing in the local papers could be generated from the EDI data returned to the school by the examination boards. Such a summary can be relied on to be accurate. The form of the summary analysis may be altered by the school, or rearranged to focus on some unusual feature, such as the high number of pupils obtaining ten or more grade A* to C passes in their GCSE examinations. More reliable, detailed information and useful summaries help teachers with all aspects of their work. Teaching can be better targeted on individual pupils' needs where whole school, IT-based, profiling systems are used to record and report on pupils' progress. Curriculum design and planning for individual pupils, classes and the whole school are facilitated.

- IT-based systems can serve as a focus for the standardisation of method-ologies throughout the school providing, for example, a unified framework for recording and reporting assessments.

- IT-based systems can be used to model the performance of schools, allowing different strategies to be evaluated before committing actual resources to particular forward plans.

All these advantages may not be evident until a comprehensive, well-integrated MIS is in use. Invariably, the advantages of using IT become clear only after most of the disadvantages have been overcome. The disadvantages in using IT relate almost entirely to the difficulty and expense of setting up an IT-based MIS, using it, maintaining it, and up-grading it. Initially, what needs to be done is determined and, in consequence, what is required in order to do it. This leads to decisions regarding the hardware and software to be used, who will use it and how it will be deployed. The outcomes of these decisions influence what can be done in the short term and in the long term, and give rise to a range of resultant problems:

- IT-based Management Information Systems are expensive to set up. Hardware and software must be purchased and staff must be re-trained or recruited. Some disturbance and expense can be expected due to the need for the installation of additional electrical power circuits and computer network cabling and redecoration in parts of the school.

- Staff may resist the introduction of IT-based methods of working. IT-based systems and manual systems are unlikely to give rise to the same administrative procedures. It is often assumed that an MIS will replace some aspects of the current manual system but otherwise leave the manual system unchanged, but this is unlikely. It may be necessary to change the way some administrative tasks are done in line with the capabilities of the software and hardware. Administrative staff may not welcome changes in their established routines; they may resent the need to learn different ways of doing the same tasks; or they may fear that they will not be able to understand IT and worry that they will be made redundant. As a result, staff may resist the introduction of IT-based methods of working.

- Methods of working may be distorted to fit the requirements of the software used. If the software is not sufficiently flexible so that it can be changed to support current or proposed methods of working then these may have to be adjusted to match the requirements of the software. In extreme cases this is the 'tail wagging the dog' and can lead to severe organisational inefficiencies.

- Bringing new IT-based systems into use can be time-consuming, as it is prudent to continue with both the old system and the new system until it is clear that the new system is working effectively. This duplicates effort but, hopefully, ensures that the new system works effectively before the old way of working is entirely abandoned.

- Hardware may breakdown or be stolen. If it cannot be repaired or replaced, and any lost data recovered almost immediately, then related administrative activities will cease and information will not be available when it is needed. A backlog of work will quickly accumulate. For example, if the hard disk which is used to store all the school's financial records ceases to function, then this information will be immediately unavailable and, possibly, unrecoverable. In the short term at least, access to funds, and the sending of orders and invoices will cease. Such an event could have immediate and long-term consequences for the financial management of the school.

- Software may not do what is required of it. This may happen because the software does not work as it should or because new demands are made for additional facilities that the software is not designed to supply.

- Software from different vendors may not be fully compatible. The greater the number of pieces of software from different producers that are used, the more frequent and intractable are the ensuing compatibility problems. Unfortunately, a whole school MIS, which can be expected to be internally self-compatible, is unlikely to be seen as having sufficiently comprehensive functionality, so that schools may wish to purchase some other items of software. Inevitably, this will lead to problems with compatibility of software and data files.

- What can be done may be restricted because communication between different pieces of software may be difficult or impossible because it runs on different types of hardware. As a result, information accessible through one piece of software may not be available to another. Consequently, some of the information stored may need to be duplicated, thus wasting IT resources and staff time.

- There may not be enough hardware or software of the right type. An advantage of IT-based systems is that they provide access to information when and where it is needed. However, this will not be the case if there are insufficient computers of the right type, too few copies of the software licensed, or access to information across networks is limited.

- IT-based systems restrict where work can be done. If IT resources are to be used to do a task then they must at least be available. This may necessitate opening parts of the school at some time during the school holidays, or allowing staff to take the required resources home. Whatever arrangements are made, they will restrict access to IT resources for some staff, which may affect their willingness to undertake some administrative and other organisational tasks.

- Unauthorised users may be able to access confidential files, resulting in the information stored on the files being changed, copied or otherwise misused. Information stored in electronic form can be altered without leaving any indication that this has been done. It is also more easily copied and distributed.

- The input of information to the MIS software may be time-consuming and, in consequence, expensive, thus outweighing some advantages in using a computer-based system. Many systems demand that information must be entered via the keyboard, but this is likely to be relatively slow compared with data entry using swipe cards, OMR or other methods of Direct Data Entry. However, swipe card systems may be unreliable, and OMR forms may not be accurately completed, causing additional problems.

WHAT TO LOOK FOR WHEN CHOOSING SOFTWARE

If software will not run on the hardware already used for administration and management, it is unlikely to be a satisfactory purchase. Thus, if the school already uses IBM compatible computers and is considering purchasing software that runs on Apple computers, new hardware must be bought, in addition to the software. This could add £1,000 or more to the purchase costs and may lead to compatibility problems. In contrast, software that will run on IBM compatible computers may run on the existing hardware and compatibility problems are less likely.

Careful enquiries should be made regarding the software licensing arrangements. A licensing structure that suits the school's requirements should be available. Licences may be available for a single user; for a fixed number of single users, for example, ten; for a fixed number of networked users; or for a site. It is important to be very clear what the specific licence conditions are as these will affect usage and software costs. For example, the licence conditions stipulated by specific vendors may regard a split site school as two sites so that it may be necessary to purchase two site licences at double the cost; a licence to use the software on IBM compatible computers may not cover its use on Archimedes computers, so that additional licences may need to be bought.

Having purchased the software, it must be installed on a suitable computer and staff must be trained to use it. It is helpful if the software suppliers provide these services as there may be unforeseen difficulties. However, schools may wish to do the installation and training themselves. Even so, prospective purchasers should look for some of these services from software suppliers:

- Installation of the software by the supplier on the school's hardware.
- Initial training in using the software, and in-depth training for advanced users, both in the school and on the suppliers' premises.
- A telephone help line or e-mail help service that can be contacted when difficulties arise as the software is being used.
- Manuals that thoroughly and comprehensively cover all aspects of setting up and using the software. In the manuals, there should be sections giving a detailed specification of the software and hardware, an introductory tutorial, a reference section and a comprehensive index.
- Extensive on-line help built into the software should be available to assist users with problems that arise while they are running the software.
- Support for local user groups, where users can meet, exchange views, and support each other. Very often, one user's current problems will have just been solved by another user. Talking about common problems and sharing solutions to them can save all users time and effort. Independent evaluations of new pieces of software are often available through user groups.

All software purchased should be capable of generating a wide range of standard reports. This will help new users get started more quickly. However, it is also important that software should permit users to edit these reports and set up entirely new reports to meet their own particular needs. In general, software that can be easily adapted to suit schools' requirements should be preferred to software that is relatively inflexible.

Wherever possible, the data files generated should be compatible with all software and hardware currently in use. It should be possible to import or export all data files in formats suitable for use in other software. Thus, timetabling software might generate an analysis of the curriculum of each pupil which can be exported to software used to assemble Records of Achievement. The Record of Achievement software might then generate a list of the subjects each pupil is entered for in the GCSE examinations that can be imported into the software used to communicate the school's entries to the examination boards. In particular, it is important that data files can be exported in formats suitable for importing into any general purpose software used by the school. This is most important as it gives access to the wide range of features offered by such software. For example, most word-processors support mail merge. Consequently, any software that has data files that can be used by a wordprocessor also has access to mail merge. As a result, output from the software can easily be personalised, printed and circulated to large groups of people. In general, new software should be chosen so that it integrates easily with the existing software that it will be used with. Inevitably, there will be a need to transfer files between different pieces of software that perform distinct tasks. Consequently, compatible file types are an essential feature of well-integrated software.

Most software eventually becomes less than satisfactory. It may be that a well-loved program runs on hardware that becomes obsolete. So when the hardware is no longer available, the software cannot be run. It is more likely that software that was once considered satisfactory starts to be seen as lacking some new feature that would be especially useful. Perhaps the needs of the school have changed and the software is not flexible enough to meet the new demands made of it. To avoid this, some vendors publish regular software upgrades. These will improve existing features of the software and add new ones. It is preferable to buy software that will be continuously upgraded rather than software that will not be developed further.

Software should be easy to use, reliable and robust. Menus or simple instructions, giving access to everything that the software can do, should be available on screen. The software should not crash when mistakes are made but provide meaningful error messages and on-line help. Generally, users prefer Graphical User Interfaces, controlled using a mouse and windows, icons, menus and pointers, to more esoteric methods of operation. If staff and, where appropriate, pupils, find software easy to use, reliable and robust, then it is more likely that they will use it, and, as a result, improve the standard and quality of their work. Schools that purchase such software will come to rely on it and trust it. However, schools which buy inappropriate or poorly written software will not like using it and may feel it is a waste of money. *Caveat emptor.*

The software available

The range of software available to schools is listed in Appendix 2 on p. 159. The list is comprehensive but cannot be said to be complete. It is a fairly extensive review of the software currently available to help with the management and administration of schools and the curriculum. Inevitably, this software will be quickly updated by its authors and new software will be published. Even so, the appendix is a useful starting-point for those looking for software to assist with a particular task, or for those who are curious as to what is available.

Most software distributors will supply copious advertising literature on request and many will provide demonstration copies of the software on disk. Demonstration disks allow potential users to evaluate the software before purchasing it. The software on a demonstration disk is provided to give some idea of how the software works when it is fully operational. Do not expect to receive a fully functional copy of the software on a demonstration disk! It is prudent to ask also for the name, address and telephone number of a local user of the software so that you can verify the distributor's claims regarding the functionality of the software. There may be problems with the software or limitations to its functionality that are not clearly explained in the advertising literature.

CURRENT USAGE OF IT

Evidence of the current usage of IT in secondary schools is based on two surveys conducted by the DfE and NCET in 1994. The focus of the DfE and NCET reports is different, but they are consistent in indicating that, in the schools surveyed, IT is widely used to support a variety of administration, organisational and management tasks.

The DfE *Statistical Bulletin 3/95* reports that, in the sample of 371 secondary schools responding to the survey, 86 per cent (82 per cent in 1992) made substantial use of IT for administration. Wordprocessing was used in almost all the schools surveyed, with 98 per cent (95 per cent) using IT for school budgeting and accounts; 90 per cent (84 per cent) for pupil records and assessments; 86 per cent (72 per cent) for statistical returns, such as, Form 7; 75 per cent (64 per cent) for timetabling; 72 per cent (69 per cent) for teachers' records. Expenditure on IT per annum for administration is reported to be £4,600 (£3,100) per school or approximately £6 (£4) per pupil.

The National Council for Educational Technology report, *Using IT for Assessment*, (NCET, 1994h), records that, in the sample of schools surveyed, 60 per cent of teachers use IT for administration and management tasks; and 50 per cent of senior managers and 45 per cent of administrators use IT. IT is used in 74 per cent of schools for academic and pastoral management; in 70 per cent for record keeping; in 60 per cent for assessment, Records of Achievement and reporting; in 45 per cent for monitoring pupils' performance; and in 25 per cent as a support system for the diagnosis of learning needs, and planning learning pathways for individual pupils.

The DfE report describes a slightly more extensive usage of IT in schools than the NCET report. However, both reports support the view that the use of IT in secondary schools is widespread and increasing. IT is used to support all aspects of the administration, organisation and management of schools by an increasing number of administrators, senior managers and teachers.

Popular choices

Of the software listed in the appendix, the most popular would appear to be the Schools Integrated Management System (SIMS). This is an integrated, modularised Management Information System for school administration. Many individual pieces of software recognise the popularity of SIMS and ensure compatibility with it. SIMS themselves claim that 80 per cent of LEAs, 80 per cent of GM schools and 90 per cent of sixth form colleges use SIMS (advert in *Times Educational Supplement*, 17 July 1994). However, the popularity of SIMS does not necessarily mean that it is the most appropriate for the circumstances current in a particular school. It is always prudent to evaluate alternative approaches that might be more suitable, that is, either an alternative comprehensive suite of software, for example, Key Solutions, or software for a particular task, for example, the Alice library management system. In many instances, even enthusiastic SIMS users may wish to use other pieces of software which facilitate specific tasks that SIMS does not support or does less effectively.

THE DATA PROTECTION ACT (1984)

When schools use IT to store information about pupils, teachers, governors and others, their activities may be covered by the Data Protection Act (1984). It may be necessary for schools to register with the regulatory body, that is, the Data Protection Registrar. Those who do not register are committing a criminal offence, as are those who misuse personal information that has been registered.

The Act regulates the use of personal information stored on computer systems. It does not cover information which is held and processed manually. The Act gives individuals the right to know what information is stored about them on computers, and to change it if it is incorrect. It also requires individuals and organisations that store personal information to be open about what is stored and to make use of the information in ethical ways. They must register the personal information they store and its uses, with the Data Protection Registrar. Personal information is about living, identifiable individuals. It is not necessarily particularly sensitive information, though it could be: a pupil's name and address is personal information, as is more confidential information taken from medical records, such as whether a pupil is HIV positive.

The Act allows individuals to have access to the information held about them on a computer system, and gives them some rights to have the information corrected, or deleted, if it is inaccurate. Individuals are entitled to be supplied with a printed copy of any personal information held, within forty days of making a written request. A fee of up to £10 may be charged for providing a printed copy of the stored personal information. If a copy is not provided, individuals may ask the Data Protection Registrar to ensure compliance or apply to the Courts for access to the data. Individuals may seek damages through the Courts from those who misuse their personal information.

With very few exceptions, individuals and organisations that hold personal information on a computer system must register with the Data Protection Registrar. Registration is usually for a period of three years. Those who have legal responsibility for the use of personal information must register its use rather than those who have delegated, day-to-day control over it. An LEA-maintained school cannot register as a data user as it is not a legal entity. In an LEA-maintained school, the LEA, the governing body and the headteacher may all need to register as they each have legal responsibility for particular aspects of the running of the school (The Data Protection Registrar, 1991). Thus, if a computerised registration system is in use, the governing body must register its use with the Data Protection Registrar as it is the governing body which has responsibility for ensuring an attendance register is kept under the Pupils' Registration Regulations (1956). In contrast, the headteacher is responsible under the Education Reform Act (1988) for ensuring that an annual report is prepared for parents showing their child's achievements. If a computerised profiling system or other software is used to prepare these reports, it is the headteacher who must register as the data user. If staff and personnel records are held on a computer in the school on behalf of the LEA, they remain the responsibility of the LEA which must register as the data user.

When a data user registers, a register entry is compiled. The data user must supply the following information for inclusion in the register entry:

- the name and address of the individual or organisation holding the personal information;
- the details of the personal information to be stored;
- what the personal information will be used for;
- where and how the personal information will be obtained;
- the people to whom the personal information will be disclosed.

Once registered, data users must comply with the principles of good practice, which state that information must be:

- obtained lawfully and fairly;
- held and used only for those purposes described in the register entry;
- disclosed only to those people described in the register entry;
- relevant to its registered use;
- adequate in scope for the use to which it will be put but not excessive;
- accurate;
- up to date;
- held no longer than it is needed for its registered use;

- accessible to the individuals whose personal information is stored;
- confidential and secure.

Clearly, pupils and parents have the right to see personal information held about them on a computer system, and to be reassured that the information is used only for its registered purpose. Schools would be well advised to have procedures in place so that those who ask to see their personal information can be easily given access to it. Personal information should also be kept secure and disclosed only to those people who are described in the Data Protection Register entry.

Further information about the Data Protection Act (1984), and schools' responsibilities under the Act, is available from the Data Protection Registrar *Guidance Note 5* (Data Protection Registrar, 1991) and the DfE Circular (DfE, 1991). In addition, many Local Education Authorities have an officer with specific responsibilities for implementing data protection legislation.

The Data Protection Act (1984) only covers information stored on computer files. It does not cover manual records, that is, information written on paper or card index files. However, it is unlikely that manual records will remain excluded from data protection provisions for much longer. The Commission of the European Communities (CEC) has recently published proposals to include manual records in new data protection legislation. Further information is available from the European Commission Office in London.

SUMMARY

In this chapter, the many school administration and management tasks which can be done using IT are reviewed. Very often, these tasks can be performed more efficiently and effectively using IT. The advantages and disadvantages of using IT to do them are outlined and there is some advice given regarding what to look for when choosing software.

There are many different pieces of software that can be of assistance with the administration and management of schools. These can be purchased from a variety of suppliers. The software can be used to manage many aspects of a school's finances and its curriculum. Brief reviews of some of the software available, and a list of suppliers are provided in Appendix 2.

When schools use IT for school administration and management their activities may be covered by the Data Protection Act (1984). The requirements of the Act are reviewed. The Act gives individuals the right to know what information is stored about them on computers, and to change it if it is incorrect. It also requires those who store personal information to be open about what is stored and to make use of the information in ethical ways. They must register the personal information they store and its uses, with the Data Protection Registrar.

APPENDIX 1:
GCSE IT syllabuses

The examination boards in England and Wales that offer GCSE syllabuses in IT for end of Key Stage 4 assessment are as follows:

- City and Guilds of London Institute (C & G)
- Midland Examining Group (MEG)
- National Design and Technology Education Foundation (NDTEF)
- Northern Examinations and Assessment Board (NEAB)
- Royal Society of Arts (RSA)
- Southern Examining Group (SEG)
- University of London Examinations and Assessment Council (London)
- Welsh Joint Education Committee (WJEC)

These examination boards offer syllabuses which cover the IT content of the NC subject orders for IT (DfE, 1995a), and the National Criteria for GCSE IT (SCAA, 1995e). From September 1996, pupils beginning KS4 may take courses leading to certification in the GCSE IT (full course) and the GCSE IT (short course). To obtain copies of these syllabuses contact the subject officer for IT at the relevant examination board. The addresses of the examination boards are given in Appendix 4.

In assessments based on the GCSE IT (full course) and the GCSE IT (short course) pupils are expected to demonstrate their skills, knowledge and understanding of the two themes of IT described in the NC orders for IT (DfE 1995a). These are:

- communicating and handling information;
- controlling, measuring and modelling.

All GCSE IT syllabuses cover these two themes. A GCSE IT (short course) may only cover these two themes, whereas a GCSE IT (full course) may include additional material which extends pupils' experiences of IT.

Assessment is based on a combination of terminal examinations and coursework; 40 per cent of the final assessment is based on terminal examinations, and 60 per cent is based on coursework. An additional 5 per cent is awarded for spelling, punctuation and grammar. Pupils are entered for assessment in one of two tiers determined by their ability. These are the Foundation tier (grades C to G) and the Higher tier (grades A* to D). Pupils entered for a tier can be awarded only the restricted range of grades available in that tier. The terminal examinations are taken at the end of the course, whereas the course-work will be done throughout it, possibly as part of the learning process.

Terminal examinations may consist of several independent questions set in different contexts, or a series of questions linked by a theme. Terminal examinations are externally marked; that is, the examination boards organise the marking, ensuring that this is done accurately and consistently following a detailed marking scheme. The marking scheme is published following the publication of pupils' results.

Coursework is likely to consist of one or more tasks, projects, design assignments, portfolios, coursework collections or case studies that demon-strate pupils' competence in using IT. Pupils may be required to analyse, design, implement, test, document and evaluate IT systems. All pupils may do the same or similar coursework. The coursework is almost always inter-nally marked by the teachers who have supervised pupils doing it. To ensure accuracy of marking and consistency of standards, the coursework is moder-ated within the school and by the examination boards. Moderation methodologies may vary between examination boards. The most common method is postal moderation and this involves each school sending a sample of pupils' coursework to an external moderator for re-assessment. If the moderator is in broad agreement with the school's assessments, these are confirmed. Otherwise the school is asked to re-assess all pupils' coursework to bring the school's standards in line with the moderator's. Alternatively, the external moderator may re-mark all the school's coursework.

An additional 5 per cent may be awarded for Spelling, Punctuation and Grammar (SPaG). The performance criteria for SPaG are given in detail in the GCSE Mandatory Code of Practice (SCAA, 1995d). Pupils with a 'threshold' level of performance will be reasonably accurate, making use of a limited range of specialist terms; those with an 'intermediate' level will usually be accurate, making use of a good range of specialist terms; at the 'Higher' level, pupils will be almost always accurate, and use a wide range of grammatical constructions and specialist terms adeptly and with precision.

The results of assessment are reported as grades from A* to G. Grade A* is the highest grade available. Individuals and schools can appeal against the grades awarded for a modest fee. In addition, a report on the work of a candidate, or a group of candidates, can be obtained and these are often written by the Chief Examiner. Schools should consider asking for a report on the work of a group of candidates. Such a report may help identify specific inadequacies in pupils' knowledge and understanding and this can be helpful in improving course design and the teaching of aspects of the subject. Enquiries should be directed to the school or examination board through which entry for the examination was made.

THE SYLLABUSES

The following is a brief review of the GCSE IT syllabuses available from each examination board.

City and Guilds of London Institute (C & G)

GCSE IT (full course)

The syllabus content is organised into six sections. These are:

- communicating information;
- handling information;
- modelling;
- measurement and control;
- design and development;
- business applications and systems analysis.

Coursework is 60 per cent of the final assessment. It consists of a portfolio that includes:

- at least four short IT tasks;
- a design assignment;
- a case study.

In each short IT task, pupils are required to use IT to solve a simple problem. The problem can be identified by the teacher. A solution to the problem will be possible using a particular range of IT skills or processes. In the design assignment, pupils are expected to solve a more substantial problem that they have identified themselves by constructing an information system. Pupils should analyse, design, develop, evaluate and document the information system so that others can use it. In the case study, pupils undertake a detailed study of an information system that is used in a commercial or industrial environment. Coursework is assessed by matching it against the different Assessment Components given in the syllabus for each section of it.

The method of moderation is agreed between teachers, moderators and the board. Moderation in school must involve at least 10% of each teacher's pupils' work being re-marked by another teacher. It may be followed by postal moderation by the board, a visit to the school by the moderator or an area moderation meeting.

The terminal examinations are 40 per cent of the final assessment. Candidates are entered in one of two tiers:

- Foundation tier; one paper of duration 2 hours; target grades C to G.
- Higher tier; one paper of duration 2.5 hours; target grades A* to D.

145

Each paper has three sections. Section A has general questions; section B has questions on IT in banking; section C has questions on IT in newspapers. The applications that are the focus of sections B and C will be changed regularly. They will be based on a study document available from the board in March, immediately preceding the terminal examinations.

GCSE IT (short course)

The syllabus content is organised into five sections. These are:

- communicating information;
- handling information;
- modelling;
- measurement and control;
- design and development.

Coursework is 60 per cent of the final assessment. It consists of a portfolio that includes:

- at least two short IT tasks;
- a design assignment.

In each short IT task, pupils are required to use IT to solve a simple problem. The problem can be identified by the teacher. A solution to the problem will be possible using a particular range of IT skills or processes. In the design assignment, pupils are expected to solve a more substantial problem that they have identified themselves by constructing an information system. Pupils should analyse, design, develop, evaluate and document the information system so that others can use it. Coursework is assessed by matching it against the different Assessment Components given in the syllabus for each section of it.

The method of moderation is agreed between teachers, moderators and the board. Moderation in school must involve at least 10 per cent of each teacher's pupils' work being re-marked by another teacher. It may be followed by postal moderation by the board, a visit to the school by the moderator or an area moderation meeting.

The terminal examinations are 40 per cent of the final assessment. Candidates are entered in one of two tiers:

- Foundation tier; one paper of duration 1 hour; target grades C to G.
- Higher tier; one paper of duration 1.5 hours; target grades A* to D.

Each paper has two sections. Section A has general questions; section B has questions on IT in banking. The application that is the focus of section B will be changed regularly. It will be based on a study document available from the board in March, immediately preceding the terminal examinations.

Midland Examining Group (MEG)

GCSE IT (full course)

The syllabus content is organised into seven sections. These are:

- communicating information;
- handling;
- measuring;
- control;
- modelling;
- IT systems design;
- effects of using IT.

Coursework is 60 per cent of the final assessment. It consists of from one to three coursework tasks. At least one task must be a solution to a Systems Design problem. These tasks are assessed against two out of the five Minor Assessment criteria given in the syllabus. The Minor Assessment criteria cover the following:

- information handling;
- communicating;
- measuring;
- control;
- modelling.

The tasks are also assessed against the four strands of the Major Assessment criteria. These cover aspects of System Design. Coursework is moderated in school, followed by postal moderation by the board.

The terminal examinations are 40 per cent of the final assessment. Candidates are entered in one of two tiers:

- Foundation tier; two papers each of duration 1 hour; target grades C to G.
- Higher tier; two papers each of duration 1.25 hours; target grades A* to D.

In each tier, the first terminal examination paper covers Information Handling, Communicating, Modelling, Control, Measurement, Systems Design, and Applications and Effects. The second paper focuses on Systems Design, and Applications and Effects.

GCSE IT (short course)

The syllabus content is organised into seven sections. These are:

- communicating information;
- handling;

- measuring;
- control;
- modelling;
- IT systems design;
- effects of using IT.

Coursework is 60 per cent of the final assessment. It consists of one or two coursework tasks. These tasks are assessed against two out of the five Minor Assessment criteria given in the syllabus. The Minor Assessment criteria cover:

- information handling;
- communicating;
- measuring;
- control;
- modelling.

Coursework is moderated in school, followed by postal moderation by the board.

The terminal examinations are 40 per cent of the final assessment. Candidates are entered in one of two tiers:

- Foundation tier; one paper of duration 1 hour; target grades C to G.
- Higher tier; one paper of duration 1.25 hours; target grades A* to D.

In each tier, the terminal examination paper covers Information Handling, Communicating, Modelling, Control, Measurement, Systems Design, and Applications and Effects.

National Design and Technology Education Foundation (NDTEF)

GCSE IT (full course)

The syllabus content is organised into two sections with several subsections. These are:

- development of systems;
- practical activities/systems in society.

Development of systems includes the analysis, design, implementation and testing, evaluation, and documentation of information systems. Practical activities/systems in society includes communicating and handling information; controlling, measuring and modelling; social, moral and ethical aspects; and hardware and software.

Coursework is 60 per cent of the final assessment. It consists of:

- a portfolio;
- a case study.

The portfolio records a major system design and development task that has been chosen by the pupil. It can be supplemented by other coursework. The case study is an investigation of a control system, focusing on its use in manufacturing, production or the service industries. Coursework is moderated in school, followed by postal moderation by the board.

The terminal examination is 40 per cent of the final assessment. Candidates are entered in one of two tiers:

- Foundation tier; one paper of duration 1.5 hours; target grades C to G.
- Higher tier; one paper of duration 2 hours; target grades A* to D.

The terminal examinations are based on a research task issued to schools one year before the examinations.

GCSE IT (short course)

The syllabus content is organised into two sections with several subsections. These are:

- development of systems;
- practical activities/systems in society.

Development of systems includes the analysis, design, implementation and testing, evaluation, and documentation of information systems. Practical activities/systems in society includes communicating and handling information; controlling, measuring and modelling; social, moral and ethical aspects; and hardware and software.

Coursework is 60 per cent of the final assessment. It consists of:

- a portfolio;
- a case study.

The portfolio records a major system design and development task that has been chosen by the pupil. It can be supplemented by other coursework. The case study is an investigation of a control system, focusing on its use in manufacturing, production or the service industries. Coursework is moderated in school, followed by postal moderation by the board.

The terminal examination is 40 per cent of the final assessment. Candidates are entered in one of two tiers:

- Foundation tier; one paper of duration 1 hour; target grades C to G.
- Higher tier; one paper of duration 1.5 hours; target grades A* to D.

The terminal examinations are based on a research task issued to schools one year before the examinations.

Northern Examinations and Assessment Board (NEAB)

GCSE IT (full course)

The syllabus content is organised into two sections each with several subsections. These are:

- tools, techniques and systems;
- information systems in society.

The tools, techniques and systems section includes awareness of the structure of information systems; hardware; software; evaluation of the suitability of information systems; the methods used to gather, store and process data; presenting information; modelling and simulation; and the system life cycle. The information systems in society section includes communications; the Data Protection Act; copyright law and anti-hacking legislation; and the effects on society of the growth of information.

Coursework is 60 per cent of the final assessment. It consists of:

- an assignment;
- a project.

The assignment is set by the board. It is sent to schools at the start of the course. Pupils are required to produce a report that demonstrates their ability to design, implement, test and evaluate solutions to the set assignment using IT. A marking scheme is provided with the set assignment. The project involves pupils producing a report on a solution to a problem. The solution should demonstrate their IT capability. The problem can arise in any curriculum area or from any area of interest to pupils. The project is assessed using the marking criteria given in the syllabus for analysis, design, implementation, testing, and evaluation.

Coursework is usually moderated in school, followed by postal moderation by the board. However, teachers at centres entering pupils for assessment for the first time will be required to attend a standardisation meeting arranged by the board. Teachers who had their marks significantly adjusted in the previous year's examination are also required to attend a standardisation meeting to bring them in line with the moderators' assessments.

The terminal examinations are 40 per cent of the final assessment. Candidates are entered in one of two tiers:

- Foundation tier; two papers each of duration 1.5 hours; target grades C to G.
- Higher tier; two papers each of duration 1.5 hours; target grades A* to D.

GCSE IT (short course)

The syllabus content is organised into two sections each with several subsections. These are:

- tools, techniques and systems;
- information systems in society.

Tools, techniques and systems includes awareness of the structure of information systems; hardware; software; and the methods used to gather, store and process data. The information systems in society section includes communications; the Data Protection Act; and the effects on society of the growth of information.

Coursework is 60 per cent of the final assessment. It consists of an assignment which is set by the board. It is sent to schools at the start of the course. Pupils are required to produce a report that demonstrates their ability to design, implement, test and evaluate solutions to the set assignment using IT. A mark scheme is provided with the set assignment.

Coursework is usually moderated in school, followed by postal moderation by the board. However, teachers at centres entering pupils for assessment for the first time will be required to attend a standardisation meeting arranged by the board. Teachers who had their marks significantly adjusted in the previous year's examination are also required to attend a standardisation meeting to bring them in line with the moderators' assessments.

The terminal examinations are 40 per cent of the final assessment. Candidates are entered in one of two tiers:

- Foundation tier; one paper of duration 1.5 hours; target grades C to G.
- Higher tier; one paper of duration 1.5 hours; target grades A* to D.

Royal Society of Arts (RSA)

GCSE IT (full course)

The syllabus content is not organised into sections but listed as a whole. It includes the applications of IT; problem-solving using IT; the effectiveness and limitations of IT; selecting IT resources appropriate to a particular task; hardware and software; the systems development cycle; methods of data capture; and verification and validation. Assessment of the syllabus content is related to four assessment objectives defined by the RSA. These are:

1. Techniques for communicating and handling information;
2. Techniques for measuring, modelling and controlling;
3. Evaluation and problem solving;
4. Applications and implications of IT.

151

Coursework is 60 per cent of the final assessment. It consists of:

- practical tasks;
- a case study.

The practical tasks include a compulsory task set by RSA. This is set in the context of a particular industry, commerce or community and for 1998, this context is 'the police'. Other practical tasks may be chosen from a list of optional tasks provided by the RSA. Alternatively, these may be agreed between teacher and pupil, and approved by the RSA. In the case study, pupils explore a particular information system within a business or community organisation. They write about its context, how the system handles information, and the technology used. Pupils also evaluate the information system.

Pupils must participate and score in each of the four assessment objectives. Assessment of the coursework done by pupils entered for the Foundation tier is equally weighted between the four assessment objectives. Assessment of coursework done by pupils entered for the Higher tier places a greater weight on assessment objective 3. Coursework is moderated in school, followed by postal moderation by the board.

The terminal examinations are 40 per cent of the final assessment. Candidates are entered in one of two tiers:

- Foundation tier; one paper of duration 1.5 hours; target grades C to G.
- Higher tier; one paper of duration 2.25 hours; target grades A* to D.

The examinations include some questions set in the same context as the compulsory practical coursework task set by the RSA. The examination covers all four assessment objectives.

GCSE IT (short course)

The syllabus content is not organised into sections but listed as a whole. It includes problem solving using IT; the effectiveness and limitations of IT; selecting IT resources appropriate to a particular task; and hardware and software. Assessment of the syllabus content is related to three assessment objectives defined by the RSA. These are:

1. Techniques for communicating and handling information;
2. Techniques for measuring, modelling and controlling;
3. Evaluation and problem solving.

Coursework is 60 per cent of the final assessment and it consists of several practical tasks. The practical tasks include a compulsory task set by the RSA and this is set in the context of a particular industry, commerce or community; for 1998, this context is 'the police'. Other practical tasks may be chosen from a list of optional tasks provided by the RSA. Alternatively, these may be agreed between teacher and pupil, and approved by the RSA.

Pupils must participate and score in each of the three assessment objectives. Assessment of the coursework done by pupils entered for the Foundation tier is equally weighted between the three assessment objectives. Assessment of coursework done by pupils entered for the Higher tier places a greater weight on assessment objective 3. Coursework is moderated in school, followed by postal moderation by the board.

The terminal examinations are 40 per cent of the final assessment. Candidates are entered in one of two tiers:

- Foundation tier; one paper of duration 1 hour; target grades C to G.
- Higher tier; one paper of duration 1.75 hours; target grades A* to D.

The examinations include some questions set in the same context as the compulsory practical coursework task set by the RSA. The examination covers all three assessment objectives.

Southern Examining Group (SEG)

GCSE IT (full course)

The syllabus content is organised into four sections. These can be summarised as:

- skills, knowledge and understanding of the use of IT tools;
- hardware and software;
- using IT to solve problems;
- social, legal, ethical and moral issues.

Coursework is 60 per cent of the final assessment and it consists of two coursework tasks of equal weight. One task is from the IT NC theme of Communicating and Handling Information; the other task is from the theme of Controlling, Measuring and Modelling. Each task consists of the specification, analysis, design, implementation, testing, documentation and evaluation of an IT system. Pupils are assessed on the extent to which they successfully complete each of these stages of the task. Coursework is moderated in school, followed by postal moderation by the board.

The terminal examination is 40 per cent of the final assessment. Candidates are entered in one of two tiers:

- Foundation tier; one paper of duration 1.5 hours; target grades C to G.
- Higher tier; one paper of duration 1.5 hours; target grades A* to D.

Candidates are expected to be familiar with a range of IT hardware, software and applications. The papers include all the material examined in the corresponding IT (short course) paper.

GCSE IT (short course)

The syllabus content is organised into four sections. These can be summarised as:

- skills, knowledge and understanding of the use of IT tools;
- hardware and software;
- using IT to solve problems; ·
- social, legal, ethical and moral issues.

Coursework is 60 per cent of the final assessment and it consists of one coursework task. This task is from either the IT NC theme of Communicating and Handling Information, or from the theme of Controlling, Measuring and Modelling. Each task consists of the specification, analysis, design, implementation, testing, documentation and evaluation of an IT system. Pupils are assessed on the extent to which they successfully complete each of these stages of the task. Coursework is moderated in school, followed by postal moderation by the board.

The terminal examination is 40 per cent of the final assessment. Candidates are entered in one of two tiers:

- Foundation tier; one paper of duration 1 hour; target grades C to G.
- Higher tier; one paper of duration 1 hour; target grades A* to D.

Candidates are expected to be familiar with a range of IT hardware, software and applications.

University of London Examinations and Assessment Council (London)

GCSE IT (full course)

The syllabus content is not organised into sections but specified as fifty-four discrete learning objectives. The production of the coursework collection is the key to the learning approach of the whole syllabus. This is organised under five process headings:

1. Identify
2. Analyse
3. Design
4. Use and/or implement
5. Evaluate.

Coursework is 60 per cent of the final assessment and it consists of a coursework collection. This involves pupils in the solution of four distinct types of problem. These should be small but worthwhile problems. Each involves a range of IT activities and is marked using the different assessment criteria given for each of the five process areas. Two of the distinct types of problem that pupils must do are:

- File Creation and Interrogation;
- Creation and Manipulation of Spreadsheets.

The remaining two types of problem must be chosen from:

- Data Logging and Control;
- Wordprocessing;
- Desk Top Publishing;
- Free Choice 1;
- Free Choice 2.

Any Free Choice task must be different from any other task that is presented for assessment. Tasks may be 'different by software' or 'different within a family of software'.

Coursework is moderated in school, followed by postal moderation by the board. The board reserves the right to visit every centre and to request evidence as necessary in order to complete effective moderation.

The terminal examinations are 40 per cent of the final assessment. Candidates are entered in one of two tiers:

- Foundation tier; one paper of duration 2.5 hours; target grades C to G.
- Higher tier; one paper of duration 2.5 hours; target grades A* to D.

The terminal examination is divided into two sections. Section A examines pupils' knowledge of systems design. The framework for this section is a detailed specification of a design problem available from the board early in year 11. Section B includes structured questions that go beyond those of section A.

GCSE IT (short course)

The syllabus content is not organised into sections but specified as thirty-eight discrete learning objectives. The production of the coursework collection is the key to the learning approach of the whole syllabus. This is organised under five process headings:

1. Identify
2. Analyse
3. Design
4. Use and/or implement
5. Evaluate.

Coursework is 60 per cent of the final assessment and it consists of a coursework collection. This involves pupils in the solution of two distinct types of problem. These should be small but worthwhile problems. Each involves a range of IT activities and is marked using the different assessment criteria

155

given for each of the five process areas. One of the distinct types of problem that pupils must do should be chosen from:

- File Creation and Interrogation;
- Creation and Manipulation of Spreadsheets.

The remaining problem must be chosen from:

- Data Logging and Control;
- Wordprocessing;
- Desk Top Publishing.

Coursework is moderated in school, followed by postal moderation by the board. The board reserves the right to visit every centre and to request evidence as necessary in order to complete effective moderation.

The terminal examinations are 40 per cent of the final assessment. Candidates are entered in one of two tiers:

- Foundation tier; one paper of duration 1.25 hours; target grades C to G.
- Higher tier; one paper of duration 1.25 hours; target grades A* to D.

The terminal examination examines pupils' knowledge of systems design. The framework for this section is a detailed specification of a design problem published each year early in year 11.

Welsh Joint Education Committee (WJEC) or Cyd-Bwyllgor Addysg Cymru (CBAC)

GCSE IT (full course)

The syllabus is divided into three sections, each with several subsections. These are:

- the core;
- IT applications;
- tools, techniques and systems.

The core includes measurement and control, databases, data logging, spreadsheets, wordprocessing and Desk Top Publishing. The IT applications section includes IT in the high street; the electronic office; and the implications of using IT.

Coursework is 60 per cent of the final assessment. It consists of:

- a portfolio;
- a project.

The portfolio is based on any two of the four elements of Communicating Information, Handling Information, Controlling and Measuring, and

Modelling. The project is a report on a solution to a problem which demonstrates a candidate's information systems capability. It is based on the two elements not covered in the portfolio.

Candidates' work for the portfolio is assessed against criteria given in the syllabus that are specific to each element. The project is assessed against criteria for the analysis, design, implementation and testing of an information system. Coursework is moderated in school, followed by postal moderation by the board.

The terminal examinations are 40 per cent of the final assessment. Candidates are entered in one of two tiers:

- Foundation tier; two papers each of duration 1 hour; target grades C to G.
- Higher tier; two papers each of duration 1.5 hours; target grades A* to D.

In each tier, the first terminal examination paper covers the requirements of the Key Stage 4 programmes of study for IT. Candidates are expected to have had experience of software for information retrieval, measurement and control, data logging, spreadsheets, wordprocessing and Desk Top Publishing. The second paper focuses on the extension content. This includes hardware, software, and operating systems.

GCSE IT (short course)

The syllabus is divided into three sections, each with several subsections. These are:

- the core;
- IT applications;
- tools, techniques and systems.

The core includes measurement and control, databases, data logging, spreadsheets, wordprocessing and Desk Top Publishing. The IT applications section includes IT in the high street; the electronic office; and the implications of using IT.

Coursework is 60 per cent of the final assessment and it consists of a portfolio based on any two of the four elements of Communicating Information, Handling Information, Controlling and Measuring, and Modelling. Candidates' work for the portfolio is assessed against criteria given in the syllabus that are specific to each element. Coursework is moderated in school, followed by postal moderation by the board.

The terminal examination is 40 per cent of the final assessment. Candidates are entered in one of two tiers:

- Foundation tier; one paper of duration 1 hour; target grades C to G.
- Higher tier; one paper of duration 1.5 hours; target grades A* to D.

In each tier, the terminal examination paper covers the requirements of the Key Stage 4 programmes of study for IT. Candidates are expected to have had experience of software for information retrieval, measurement and control, data logging, spreadsheets, wordprocessing and Desk Top Publishing.

APPENDIX 2
Software for school administration and management

There are many different pieces of software that can be of assistance with the administration and management of schools. These can be purchased from a variety of suppliers. The software can be used to manage many aspects of a school's finances and its curriculum. Brief reviews of some of the software available and a list of suppliers is given below.

The information given about the software listed has been obtained from the supplier's own literature. No attempt has been made to evaluate the software. The author's approval is not implied nor is any of the software specifically recommended. The author has no financial interests in any of the software or suppliers referred to. If the software is of interest, the distributor should be contacted directly.

The approximate price of most of the software is given to allow readers to gain some impression of potential purchase costs. These prices are the author's own estimates based on the information provided by the software suppliers at the time of writing. They are only approximate and can be expected to change, sometimes dramatically. Prices should be confirmed by contacting the suppliers directly. The software is listed in alphabetical order of the supplier's name.

AVP

School Hill Centre
Chepstow
Gwent
NP6 5PH
Tel: 01291 625439

Library System

The software takes care of the day-to-day running of a school library, handling up to 8,100 books and 2,700 borrowers. Library System deals with the issue and return of books, overdues, reservations, and frequency of borrowing. The typical cost for a secondary school with 1,000 pupils is £115.50 + VAT. The software runs on Archimedes computers.

Profile

The software maintains records of pupils' profile documents. There is a statement bank that can be edited, and individual pupil's statements can be customised. Pupils' profile documents can be compiled over a period of time, and can be reviewed and edited as necessary. Pupils' profiles can be printed, either singly or all at once, or can be exported to a wordprocessor for further formatting and editing. The typical cost for a secondary school with 1,000 pupils is £128.70 + VAT. The software runs on IBM compatible computers.

BLACKPOOL SIXTH FORM COLLEGE

Highfurlong
Blackpool
Lancashire
FY3 7LR
Tel: 01253 394911

Cosmex

The software supports pupil and staff registration using swipe cards and will display a personal or general message as each person registers. The swipe cards have a bar code on them which identifies the pupil or member of staff. Various reports can be printed, including an analysis of absences and poor punctuality. The typical cost for a secondary school with 1,000 pupils is £16,000 + VAT. This includes hardware and some other costs. The software runs on Apple computers.

Hyperview

Hyperview is a campus messaging system which displays news and information on television screens located throughout the institution, using teletext style graphics and text. The typical cost for a secondary school with 1,000 pupils is £10,000 + VAT. This includes hardware and some other costs. The software runs on Apple computers.

Libra

Libra is a library administration system. Borrowers and resources being borrowed are identified using bar codes. Borrowers' bar codes are the same as those used in the Cosmex registration software, so that the swipe cards used for registering attendance can also be used as library membership cards. The software has an educational focus, for example, it automatically takes into account school holidays when books are issued, and can prevent books and other resources being issued to pupils leaving school. The typical cost for a secondary school with 1,000 pupils is £10,000 + VAT. This includes hardware and some other costs. The software runs on Apple computers.

Sesame

This software limits access to secured areas to specified holders of valid Cosmex swipe cards. Access is monitored using a swipe card-operated locking mechanism. The system records who has entered secured areas. Teachers' and pupils' movements can be tracked by the system. The typical cost for a secondary school with 1,000 pupils is £2,000 + VAT. This includes hardware and some other costs. The software runs on Apple computers.

BROMCOM

417 Bromley Rd
Downham
Bromley
Kent
BR1 4PJ
Tel: 0181 461 3737

Radio-ears

The software provides facilities for recording pupils' attendance at registration and post registration, and can be used as a pager to contact teachers, as a messaging system, a bulletin board and a personal organiser.

The Radio-ears system uses light-weight, portable computers with radio transmitters that link them to a central computer. Each teacher is equipped with a portable computer, and several radio transceiver units are located throughout the school. Teachers input registration details to their portable computers in their classrooms. These details are automatically transmitted to the school's central Radio-ears computer in the school office. As a result, the attendance of individual pupils can be monitored quickly and easily from a central location. A variety of reports can be printed, including attendance records for a pupil, and for a class; lists of pupils with poor attendance records; and mandatory DFEE reports. Teachers can be reminded to follow up absentees, and letters to parents can be printed automatically.

The portable computer also has software that enhances teachers' personal productivity. This includes a timetable, a diary, wordprocessing, database, and spreadsheet software.

In an advertisement in the *Times Educational Supplement* (20 January 1995), Bromcom claimed that when the Radio-ears system is 'used as a part of a whole school MIS, it can contribute significantly to improve the effectiveness of a school'. They state that it represents an 'added value of £130,000 p.a. against annual amortisation and running costs of £10,000'.

The typical costs for a secondary school with 1,000 pupils are:

Radio-ears central computer (1 required)	£5,500 + VAT
portable computer (1 per teacher required)	£295 to £495 + VAT each
radio transceiver unit (15 to 20 required)	£125 + VAT each
site licences for e-mail software	£450 + VAT per facility
installation, cabling, and training.	£1,500 + VAT

The software runs on IBM compatible computers.

CAREERSOFT

60 New Rd
Halifax
HX1 2LH
Tel: 01422 330450

Careers Administration

The software is designed to help with the administration of a careers guidance programme. Various lists and standard letters can be printed, including details of appointments for careers interviews, leave of absence slips and letters to parents. The typical cost for a secondary school with 1,000 pupils is £29.50 + VAT for a site licence. The software runs on Archimedes computers.

Careers Information Database

The software is designed to help pupils decide which type of job might suit them, to give pupils some information about what the job entails, and to inform them of useful subjects to study and the qualifications they need to acquire. The database covers all levels of ability but is particularly suitable for pupils with reading difficulties. The typical cost for a secondary school with 1,000 pupils is an annual subscription of £45 + VAT for a combined site and network licence. The software runs on IBM compatible computers and Archimedes computers.

Chec2

The software is designed to help students in years 12 and 13 choose a course of Higher Education. Year 11 pupils are able to explore the suitability of different combinations of A-levels. The database covers 2,200 courses at 450 institutions. The typical cost for a secondary school with 1,000 pupils is an annual subscription of £75 + VAT for a combined site and network licence. The software runs on IBM compatible computers.

Student work experience processor

The software is designed to help pupils produce a coherent report on their work experience. The typical cost for a secondary school with 1,000 pupils is £49 + VAT for a site licence. The software runs on IBM compatible computers and Archimedes computers.

Record of Achievement Processor

The software helps pupils produce and print their Records of Achievement, curriculum vitae, action plans, work experience reports and other personal documents by entering their information in pre-designed sections. The sections can be modified. The typical cost is £45 + (£0.60 per pupil using the software) + VAT. The software runs on IBM compatible computers.

Work experience administration package

The software takes care of the routine administration associated with the organisation of pupils' work experience. Various lists and standard letters can be printed, including a list of all pupils and their work experience placements, an insurance document, a letter to parents, and a confirmation letter to the placement firm. The typical cost for a secondary school with 1,000 pupils is £29.50 + VAT for a site licence. The software runs on Archimedes computers.

COGENT SOFTWARE

30 Norton Way North
Letchworth
Herts
SG6 1BX
Tel: 01462 637017

All the following software has been designed to work with the DRS, CD210 Optical Mark Reader (for supplier details see Appendix 4, p. 209).

Attendance

The software can analyse and report on patterns of absence for individual pupils, and year groups. Summaries of lateness and absenteeism can be created, for example, monthly summaries of attendance for all pupils. Registration data can be entered via the keyboard or using OMR. Using OMR enables lists of absentees to be produced immediately after registration. The typical cost for a secondary school with 1,000 pupils is £250 + VAT for a site licence. The software runs on Archimedes computers.

Curriculum auditing package

The software is designed to help curriculum managers produce a view of the whole school curriculum. Used in conjunction with Cogent's monitoring and reporting package, the curriculum can be audited against assessment objectives. The typical cost for a secondary school with 1,000 pupils is £250 + VAT for a site licence. The software runs on Archimedes computers.

Monitoring and reporting package

The software helps teachers record, report and analyse pupils' achievements. Information can be input using the keyboard or OMR. Various reports can be printed, including reports to parents and Records of Achievement. The typical cost for a secondary school with 1,000 pupils is £450 + VAT for a site licence. The software runs on Archimedes and IBM compatible computers.

Mentor–teacher appraisal

The software helps schools establish a consistent teacher appraisal process, producing reports, personnel specifications and staff audits. A range of core appraisal objectives are supplied. A staff skills audit can be compiled, to assist with development planning, and recruitment activities. Appraisal data collected during classroom observations and interviews can be entered using the keyboard or OMR. The typical cost for a secondary school with 1,000 pupils is £250 + VAT for a site licence. The software runs on Archimedes and IBM compatible computers.

Quicktest

Teachers can use this software to produce multiple choice tests, and mark and analyse the results. Pupils can do the tests on the computer or write their answers on an OMR form. The typical cost for a secondary school with 1,000 pupils is £105 + VAT for a site licence. The software runs on Archimedes computers.

CSL

Computer Systems Ltd
Allan Bank
Circular Rd
Douglas
Isle of Man
IM1 1AY
Tel: 01624 627522

CoNCquest

CoNCquest is a database file containing all the programmes of study for all the subjects of the NC. It helps teachers find the answers to questions, such as, "Where are there references to Japan in the NC?" and "Which Key Stage 3 subjects require an understanding of coordinates?". It then displays or prints a suitable report. The database file is accessed using the Filemaker Pro database. The typical cost for four computers is £500 + VAT (including Filemaker Pro). The software runs on Apple computers and IBM compatible computers.

DOLPHIN COMPUTER SERVICES LTD.

5 Mercain Close
Watermoor
Cirencester
GL7 1LT
Tel: 01285 659291

Mentor

Mentor is a modular suite of software for financial administration. It caters specifically for fee-paying schools. All the modules are fully integrated with the General Ledger module and, where appropriate, with each other. Prices are available on application to the suppliers. The software runs on IBM compatible computers. The modules available are:

- general ledger and cash book;
- purchase ledger;
- fees ledger;
- direct debits;

- assets register;
- school shop;
- purchase ordering;
- payroll and pensions;
- sales ledger.

General ledger and cash book

This module provides general ledger accounts facilities, including journals, balances, budgets and forecasts. There is access to actual figures from previous years and a trial balance is always available. There is automatic reconciliation of bank accounts. Budget, financial and management reporting is available, which can be broken down by cost centre, department and type of expense.

Purchase ledger

The software can be used to record and control payments to suppliers, so that maximum benefit is obtained from offers of credit, and discounts. Payments can be made to commercial creditors, and others, such as the Inland Revenue. Full audit trails can be produced, as well as a range of standard reports. Different methods of payment are catered for, including cheques, BACS and bank giro.

Fees ledger

The software is used to produce bills for the payment of pupils' fees. Current, past and future pupils' details can be stored, and previous bills can be reprinted at any time. Different scales of fees can be used, and charges for extras may be printed on the bills. Cash receipting can be done, allowing the analysis of payments against individual pupil's bills.

Direct debits

Schools can use this software to collect fees payable by direct debit. These can be arranged using BACS or Dolphin's bureau service. Collection may be made in several ways, such as per term or in ten monthly payments. When the amount to be collected changes, letters informing payers can be generated.

Assets register

The assets register software can be used to record and maintain an up-to-date inventory of capital items. Assets may be grouped by category. Depreciation can be calculated automatically in several ways. A complete history of each asset can be printed.

School shop

The school shop module is designed to help with controlling stock, VAT and charging. Credit sales, orders and deliveries are catered for. Reports can be printed allowing the popularity of goods to be monitored, and actual stock levels to be compared with minimum re-order levels.

Purchase ordering

The software provides control of purchasing, from the raising of orders to the receipt of goods and invoices. A catalogue of regular requisition items can be set up. When deliveries are received, these are entered and the outstanding orders updated. Expenditure can be analysed by department and expense code, outstanding orders and supplier performance. Distributed access to the purchase ordering module is available.

Payroll and pensions

The payroll module records all relevant employee details. Pay may be salaried or hourly, may be paid weekly, fortnightly or monthly. Tax, National Insurance, Statutory Sick Pay, Statutory Maternity Pay and pension contributions are all automatically calculated. A variety of other payments and deductions can be made. Different pension schemes can be set up and applied to different employees. Payments may be made by cash, cheque or through BACS. A variety of standard reports can be printed, including full audit trail listings and the production of payslips. On line enquiries can be made.

Sales ledger

This software is used to issue invoices and record the receipt of cash. A file of standard invoice descriptions of stock items can be maintained. Several standard invoice layouts can be used, or users can define their own layouts.

Mentor – Academic

There are standard modules for:

- registrations and admissions;
- current pupils' records, including DfEE returns;

- former pupils' records, including governors and other contacts;
- staff records, including DfEE returns and links to payroll software;
- attendance recording;
- assessments and profiling;
- curriculum planning and options management;
- timetable generation, reporting and printing;
- examination entries and results.

Where necessary, these modules are integrated with the information used by the financial administration modules.

ERNEST CLARKE SYSTEMS LTD

103 Philbeach Gardens
London
SW5 9ET
Tel: 0171 912 0600

SPARRC (Software for Planning, Assessment, Recording and Reporting in Class)

The software helps with NC recording and reporting. Each pupil's level of achievement can be recorded in every Attainment Target. Reports can be produced in a variety of forms, including individual reports and aggregated statistical summaries. Each teacher records the information they generate on a floppy disk, at home or at work, and this is then fed into the centralised record-keeping system. The software is compatible with some other school administration software, including SIMS. The price of the software is available on application to the suppliers. The software runs on IBM compatible computers and Archimedes computers.

THE FLEXIBLE LEARNING COMPANY

15 Longpoles Rd
Cranleigh
Surrey
GU6 7JK
Tel: 01483 277020

Attainment Tracker and profile compiler

This software provides a combined central and departmental database system, designed to manage Reporting and Levels of Achievement in any number of subjects for any number of pupils. Pupils' photographs can be displayed on screen. The typical cost for a secondary school with 1,000 pupils is £175 + VAT for a site licence. The software runs on Apple computers.

Cash Tracker

This database software can be used to manage school capitation or other accounts. For example, PTA funds. The typical cost for a secondary school with 1,000 pupils is £120 + VAT for a site licence. The software runs on Apple computers.

GROUP 31

PO Box 901
Harwich
Essex
CO12 3TF
Tel: 01225 241472

Altus recording and reporting suite

The software helps with recording and reporting on pupils' progress in the NC. The typical cost for a secondary school with 1,000 pupils is £495 + VAT for a site licence. The software runs on IBM compatible computers.

HODDER AND STOUGHTON

Tests Dept
Mill Rd
Dunton Green
Sevenoaks
Kent
TN13 2YA
Tel: 01732 450111 Ext. 2175

Natprof

An NC profiling and information management system designed to meet all the requirements for recording, monitoring and reporting of assessment. The typical cost for a secondary school with 1,000 pupils is £350 + VAT for the starter pack. Various enhancement packs are available. The software runs on IBM compatible computers.

HS SOFTWARE

56 Hendrefoilan Av
Sketty
Swansea
West Glamorgan
SA2 7NB
Tel: 01792 20451

Nstore

This software is used for recording and reporting on pupils' achievements in relation to the NC in Science, Maths and English. Details on up to 432 pupils can be stored. In addition, up to 432 topics can be identified. Pupils' attainments can be recorded in relation to the topic and their personal records automatically updated. For reporting, a statement bank of around 800 statements is provided. The typical cost for 1 copy of the software is £44.95 including VAT. The software runs on Archimedes computers.

KEY SOLUTIONS MANAGEMENT LTD

Southern Division	Northern Division	Nova Timetable Systems
Number One	Wharfe House	39 Somerset Rd
The Old Yard	Ilkley Rd	Frome
Rectory Lane	Otley	Somerset
Brasted	West Yorkshire	BA11 1HD
Kent	LS21 3JP	
TN16 1JP		
Tel: 01959 565856	Tel: 01943 464104	Tel: 01373 452428

Key Solutions

Key Solutions is the collective name for a suite of software that covers a wide range of administrative and management tasks. The software was developed separately by three companies: Educational Systems Ltd, Morgan Barnett Associates and Timetabling Systems Ltd. These companies have now merged and have re-packaged their products as an integrated suite of software. This is now closely associated with Research Machines hardware, software and services to education. Almost all the software runs on Apple computers or IBM compatible computers with Windows 3.1. This facilitates the transfer of text or graphical information between the different programs in the suite of software.

The Key Solutions suite of software comprises:

- Cash Accounts
- Core Administration

- Ledger Accounts
- Library and Resource Manager
- Organisational Development Planner
- Personal Development Planner
- Premises Manager
- Staff Development and Appraisal Manager
- The Budgeting System
- Timetable Nova-T4

Cash Accounts

The software provides information on how money is being spent in comparison with budgets. The software caters for budget allocation through to reconciliation of actual expenditure. There is a full order processing facility, including an on-line catalogue. Orders for individual suppliers can be raised automatically. Each line of an order can be allocated to a different budget heading. Part deliveries and part payment are catered for. Other facilities are included for petty cash, and virement. Access can be password-protected. The typical cost for four computers is £925 + VAT. The software runs on Apple computers and IBM compatible computers.

Core Administration

The software handles administration and records for pupils and personnel. Form 7 can be generated. Basic pupil information can be handled, including medical, timetable, and special needs. Similarly, in addition to basic personnel information, details of training, qualifications, salaries, and timetable information can be handled. Updated form 7 software is issued as soon as the annual format is known. This extracts data from existing software where possible. There are comprehensive reporting functions, including mail merge and label printing facilities. The typical cost for four computers is £700 + VAT. The software runs on IBM compatible computers.

Ledger Accounts

The software provides a double-entry accounting system with nominal, purchase, sales or income ledgers, cash book, stock-keeping and inventory, VAT records and full sales and order processing. Every transaction entered has a unique audit number. Transactions can be entered in batches and posted to the ledgers when the batch has been authorised. Budgets allocated to cost centres can be compared with actual spending on a monthly basis. The software has comprehensive reporting functions, producing invoices, purchase orders, VAT returns, statements, credit notes, remittance advices, and GM Schools' DfEE reports. Nominal reports, such as Trial Balance, can be produced at any time, for any period last year, this year or next year. Transition from one accounting year to the next is catered for. Access to the software can be password-protected. The typical cost for four computers is £2500 + VAT. The software runs on Apple computers and IBM compatible computers.

Library and Resource Manager

The software manages the routine issue and circulation of books and other resources, for example, slides, films, audio and video tapes, computer software, periodicals, and audio-visual equipment. Resources can be found using title searches, and key word searches. The software handles on-line access for user enquiries, order processing, and mail merge, and can produce a variety of useful statistics. Membership numbers and book numbers can be entered using the keyboard or a bar code reader. Bar codes for membership cards and books can be printed by the software. Personnel and pupil details can be imported from existing databases. The typical cost for four computers is £1375 + VAT. The software runs on Apple computers and IBM compatible computers.

Organisational Development Planner

The software provides a structured decision-making support system for strategic planning. It provides comprehensive coverage of the whole management process and a framework for action that integrates the planning process with day-to-day activities. The software can be used to monitor and co-ordinate staff job descriptions, staff appraisals, INSET records, staff responsibilities, resource deployment, and meetings and other contacts with parents and governors. The software helps with the preparation of a structured development plan and, when used with the Key Solutions Budgeting software, a fully costed annual plan can be produced. The typical cost for four computers is £500 + VAT. The software runs on Apple computers and IBM compatible computers.

Personal Development Planner

The software provides a framework for the development of individual action plans for pupils' personal and academic development. It also automates aspects of the production of Records of Achievement, curriculum vitae, and career action plans. The software makes available a range of helpful activities for pupils and a statement bank for reporting purposes. The typical cost for ten computers is £950 + VAT. The software runs on Apple computers and IBM compatible computers.

Premises Manager

The software is designed to help senior managers organise the inspection and maintenance of buildings, equipment and furniture. It also assists with the process of tendering. Inventories can be kept and a database of scheduled inspections and maintenance set up so that actual costs can be monitored against projected expenditure. The full costs of specific events can be established, for example, the cost of remedial action due to vandalism over a given period. The typical cost for four computers is £875 + VAT. The software runs on Apple computers and IBM compatible computers.

Staff Development and Appraisal Manager

The software helps with the organisation of staff development and appraisal schemes. It covers induction of new staff, appraisal and personal development planning. Individual staff action plans, curriculum vitae, and a whole school staff development plan are produced. The typical cost for four computers is £1,000 + VAT. The software runs on Apple computers and IBM compatible computers.

The Budgeting System

The software helps prepare model budgets, monitors spending against actual budget and reviews projected budgets. The structure of the budget closely follows the CIPFA recommended format. Full current staffing costs, including salaries based on existing scales, and on-costs, can be calculated and forward staffing costs estimated. In addition, income can be estimated, recorded and projected. Inflation forecasts can be taken into account. Reports can be produced on individual budget headings and the full annual budget, including relevant graphs. The typical cost for four computers is £450 + VAT. The software runs on Apple computers and IBM compatible computers.

Timetabling Nova-T4

The software helps with timetable planning, construction and costing. Curriculum and teaching needs are matched to available resources. Construction of the timetable can be carried out automatically or manually or by a mixture of both methods. Timetables can be printed for individual teachers, rooms, pupils, and classes, and full timetables printed for all staff, and year groups. Class lists, tutor group lists, and year lists can also be printed. The software caters for the organisation of daily staff cover due to staff absence, and exam invigilation, using school staff and supply teachers to provide cover. Pupils' details can be imported from other pupil administration systems and the completed timetable transferred to other school administration systems, such as SIMS. The typical cost for four computers is £1,000 + VAT. The software runs on Apple computers and IBM compatible computers.

MEGA TECHNICAL SYSTEMS LTD

Mega House
The Grip Industrial Estate
Linton
Cambridge
CB1 6NR
Tel: 01223 893900

Recorder Assessment System

Software for recording and reporting on pupils' achievements in relation to the NC. Information can be input via the keyboard or using OMR. The typical cost for a secondary school with 1,000 pupils is £100 + VAT. The software runs on IBM compatible computers and Archimedes computers.

MG COMPUTER SERVICES

28 Poplar Grove
Allington
Maidstone
Kent
ME16 0DE
Tel: 01622 751243

April

The software can be used to generate pupils' school reports. These reports can be subject-specific, be on any aspect of school life or cover the whole curriculum. Teachers' comments can be composed using a combination of several editable statements drawn from an extensive statement bank or imported from any wordprocessor. April is supplied with statement banks for Mathematics and English. Statement banks for other subjects may be available on request. Pupils' personal information can be entered manually or imported from SIMS. Other data can be entered via the keyboard or using the DRS, CD210 Optical Mark Reader (for supplier details see Appendix 4, p. 209). The typical cost for a secondary school with 1,000 pupils is £250 + VAT for a site licence. There is a small additional charge for extra statement banks. The software runs on IBM compatible computers.

MINERVA

Minerva House
Baring Crescent
Exeter
EX1 1TL
Tel: 01392 437756

Timetabler

The software facilitates school timetabling for up to 255 staff, 383 courses, 255 rooms in a cycle of up to 15 periods per day over 15 days. Some 32,000 pupils can be registered. Resources can be allocated manually and automatically and can be re-allocated due to unusual events, for example, a room becoming unavailable. The typical cost for a secondary school with 1,000 pupils is £599 + VAT. The software runs on IBM compatible computers and Archimedes computers.

PUBLIC SECTOR SOFTWARE LTD

The Maltings
55 Bath Street
Gravesend
Kent
DA11 0DF
Tel: 01474 329932

All the software reviewed below is a development or customisation of the DataEase database. For the software to run, DataEase must be already owned or should be purchased. The typical cost of DataEase for five networked computers is £290 + VAT. The software runs on IBM compatible computers.

Achieve

Achieve is an information management system for Records of Achievement. The reports produced comply with the format of the National Record of Achievement. The typical cost for a secondary school with 1,000 pupils is £595 + VAT. The software runs on IBM compatible computers.

AIMS – Aggregate

The software helps with the administration of SATs and end of key stage pupil assessments. Data is input using OMR. A range of standard reports can be printed that meet the reporting requirements of the DfEE. The typical cost for a secondary school with 1,000 pupils is £595 + VAT. The software runs on IBM compatible computers.

175

AIMS – School

The software provides a means of managing the information a school needs about its pupils, staff, curriculum, and pupils' entries for internal and external examinations. The typical cost for a secondary school with 1,000 pupils is £895 + VAT. The software runs on IBM compatible computers.

AIMS – Workplace

The software can be used to match pupils' preferences to the opportunities offered by employers at potential work experience placements. A 'best fit' can be generated between pupils' preferences and the opportunities offered. The software can be used to keep a record of contacts between the school and employers. Appropriate standard letters can be printed for sending to employers, parents, and pupils. Detailed statistics can be produced when required. The typical cost for a secondary school with 1,000 pupils is £595 + VAT. The software runs on IBM compatible computers.

Vocate

The software provides a recording and reporting structure for competency-based assessment that meets the requirements of the DfEE, NVQ, and GNVQ, for maintaining Records of Achievement. Data is input using OMR. A variety of standard reports can be printed, including assessment outcomes for each candidate, and for a particular subject. All reports can be modified and entirely new, user-defined reports can be generated. The typical cost for a secondary school with 1,000 pupils is £995 + VAT for a site licence, plus an annual fee of £150 + VAT that includes the provision of user support and software updates. The software runs on IBM compatible computers.

RESOURCE

51 High St
Kegworth
Derby
DE74 2DA
Tel: 01509 672222

Small steps

The software provides a recording and reporting system for the NC. The Programmes of Study are broken down into a series of small steps accessible to SEN pupils. The small steps can be edited. Curriculum plans and progress reports, and an Annual Review Statement can be printed. The typical cost for a secondary school with 1,000 pupils is £199 + VAT for a site licence. The software runs on Apple computers, IBM compatible computers and Archimedes computers.

SCET

74 Victoria Crescent Rd
Glasgow
G12 9JN
Tel: 0141 334 9314

M-power

The software provides a comprehensive, integrated school administration system, including modules for pupil profiling and assessment. The typical cost for a secondary school with 1,000 pupils is £1,000 + VAT for the basic system. The software runs on a variety of computers, including IBM compatibles.

SIMS

Abbot's Rd
Priory Business Park
Cardington
Bedford
MK44 3SG
Tel: 01234 838080

Schools Integrated Management System (SIMS)

SIMS is an integrated management system for schools with a modular structure. SIMS tries to avoid the duplication of data by making information entered in one module available to other modules that may need access to it, for example, pupil information entered in the STAR module is used by the Examination module when pupils are entered for the GCSE examinations.

The typical cost for SIMS for a secondary school with 1,000 pupils is:

Core System: £1,350 + VAT
Curriculum System: £1,350 + VAT
Library Module: £800 + VAT
Resources System, excluding the Library Module: £1,550 + VAT

LEAs can buy the software for a group of schools at reduced rates. The software runs on IBM compatible computers.

Core System

This consists of these modules:

- Attendance   This module records the information required by the DfEE and produces reports to help with the monitoring of group and individual attendance patterns. The module looks for correlations between the absence patterns of different pupils. Attendance data can be entered using the OMR forms printed by the module or swipe cards. Spot checks on attendance can be organised using OMR for fast input. The module produces a variety of reports, including absence letters to parents, and the number of pupils requiring school meals.

- Examinations   This module is used for entering pupils for GCSE and other examinations. Pupils' examination entries can be input on OMR forms. The examination entries can then be prepared in a format suitable for submitting them to the GCSE examination boards using EDI. The external examinations can be timetabled in school. The examination results, returned from the GCSE examination boards using EDI, can be input, stored, and analysed for use by departments, parents and the DfEE.

- Form 7   This module produces the Form 7 report for the DfEE.

- Manager   This module is used to install other SIMS software, control users' access rights, and construct a menu system for access to other SIMS software.

- MIDAS   This module gives rapid access to all the information held on all other SIMS modules. A pupil's academic and pastoral records, attendance statistics, conduct log, assessment summary, class information and examination entries are available for review of the individual pupil's performance. There is a diary of events and a telephone book.

- Personnel   This module is used to store personal, professional and contractual information about all employees. A variety of standard and user-defined reports can be produced. The information in the Personnel module is used by other SIMS modules, e.g. Timetabling and Course Allocations.

- STAR   STAR is a database holding personal and academic information about pupils. A variety of standard and user-defined reports can be produced, including address labels. The information on STAR is shared by other SIMS modules, e.g. Form 7.

Curriculum System

This consists of these modules:

- Assessment   This software can be used to record and accumulate pupils' NC assessments. Pupils' NC attainments can be recorded and input using OMR. NC AT levels can be aggregated automatically. Conflicts are reported, for example, between TAs and SATs.

- Profiles   Reports on individual pupils can be produced, including their personal details, the curriculum followed, their qualifications, attendance statistics, and teachers' comments. Teachers' comments can be chosen from a statement bank and input using OMR. Reports can be exported to word-processing software for further alteration and amendment.

- Scheduler   This module can be used to timetable a parents evening, a careers meeting, or any similar event. Letters to parents and individual timetables for staff and pupils can be printed. Appointment times can be automatically generated, then edited later, if necessary.

- Staff Cover   This module facilitates the judicious arrangement of cover for teaching staff who are absent or otherwise unavailable. Staff absences are recorded and analysed. Details of supply staff used by the school can be stored.

- Timetable and Course Allocations   This module helps with the construction of the school timetable. Data is input from other SIMS modules, e.g. staffing information. The completed timetable can be used to update other records, e.g. pupils' timetables. Several versions of the timetable can be produced for evaluation. Timetables can be printed for individual staff and pupils, rooms, year groups, periods, non-teaching time, and vacant rooms. Class lists are also available.

Resources System

This consists of these modules:

- Equipment   This module is used to maintain an inventory of all assets and equipment. A variety of reports can be printed, for example, lists of equipment available at given locations.

179

- Financial Management System

  This module is a full General Ledger, double-entry book-keeping system, including payroll, cash book, and VAT transfers. Supplier and catalogue details are available to facilitate ordering. Related orders, and invoices can be displayed. Spending can be allocated and monitored by cost centres. Actual income and expenditure can be compared with budget profiles. A variety of reports can be produced, including audit trails, historical expense analysis, and trial balance.

- Library

  This module can be used to organise the borrowing of books and other resources from the school library or other resource centres within the school. Catalogue information can be entered using the keyboard, from Whitaker's Book Bank or from a variety of other sources. Issues, reservations, renewals and returns can be recorded via the keyboard or using a bar code reader. The catalogue can be searched by author, publisher, and keyword. A variety of reports can be produced, including overdue lists, and resource use analysis.

SOFTLINK EUROPE LTD

26 Hanborough House
Hanborough Business Park
Long Hanborough
Oxon
OX8 8LH
Tel. 01993 883401

Alice

Alice is a modularised library automation system. There are 'standard' modules for library management, reporting and utilities, circulation, enquiries (OPAC). There are also 'additional' modules for acquisitions, periodicals, journal indexing, and access to the British Library's BNB database, and 'special' modules for book reviews and fines. Bar codes on books and membership cards can be scanned into the software.

There are four standard modules, seven additional modules and ten special modules. These cost £50 to £600 + VAT per module per school. The software runs on IBM compatible computers.

SOFTWARE SOLUTIONS

Technology Unit
Technology Centre
Turner Rd
Norwich
Norfolk
NR2 4DF
Tel: 01603 620337

Asset Manager

The software provides an inventory showing the location and current values of all recorded assets. Through an analysis of periodic depreciation, a capital replacement budget can be assembled. The typical cost for ten computers is a minimum of £1,875 + VAT. The software runs on Apple computers and IBM compatible computers.

Budget Manager

Through the construction of a financial model, incorporating fixed and variable costs, the software estimates the target income to achieve break-even. The typical cost for ten computers is a minimum of £1,875 + VAT. The software runs on Apple computers and IBM compatible computers.

Client Manager

The software tracks and records client activity providing an analysis of volume and types of sales. The typical cost for ten computers is a minimum of £1,875 + VAT. The software runs on Apple computers and IBM compatible computers.

Contract Manager

The software is designed to support managers and administrators who establish bespoke services through contracts, providing an overview of resource utilisation and a comprehensive schedule of past and future contracts. The typical cost for ten computers is a minimum of £1,875 + VAT. The software runs on Apple computers and IBM compatible computers.

National Curriculum Assessment Manager

The software enables the compilation of pupils' assessments for all key stages. It assembles an overview of pupils' attainment. A variety of reports can be generated, including termly and annual reports to parents. The typical cost for ten computers is a minimum of £675 + VAT. The software runs on Apple computers and IBM compatible computers.

NVQ and GNVQ Assessment Manager

The software facilitates the recording of NVQ and GNVQ assessments. The typical cost for ten computers is a minimum of £375 + VAT. The software runs on Apple computers and IBM compatible computers.

Personnel Manager

The software stores records of all human resources, including an individual's personal details, salary details, appraisal schedule, and development targets. It assembles a comprehensive overview of a school's activities, giving warning of the need to supplement resources where necessary. The typical cost for ten computers is a minimum of £1,875 + VAT. The software runs on Apple computers and IBM compatible computers.

Record of Achievement Manager

The software helps with the creation of a pupil's summative profile in the format of the National Record of Achievement. All text generated by the software can be edited to suit individual needs. The typical cost for ten computers is a minimum of £375 + VAT. The software runs on Apple computers and IBM compatible computers.

Salary Tables

The software calculates annual salary bills from a range of salary scales, e.g. AP&T, Headteacher and Deputy Headteacher, M grade, and Soulbury. The effects of salary increases on future costs can be estimated. The typical cost for ten computers is a minimum of £300 + VAT per annum. The software runs on Apple and IBM computers.

Time Manager

The software analyses overall resource commitment using information drawn from the plans developed using Contract Manager and Training Manager. It reconciles planned time on task with that actually used and logged. The typical cost for ten computers is a minimum of £1,875 + VAT. The software runs on Apple computers and IBM compatible computers.

Training Manager

The software is designed to support managers and administrators who are planning, selling and marketing training. A variety of standard documents and reports can be generated, including promotional letters, delegate lists, and invoices. The typical cost for ten computers is a minimum of £1,875 + VAT. The software runs on Apple computers and IBM compatible computers.

SQUIGGLE

Bebington High School
Higher Bebington Rd
Bebington
Wirral
Merseyside
L63 2PS
Tel: 0151 6454145

Squiggle

The software helps with recording and reporting on pupils' achievements in the NC. The typical cost for a secondary school with 1,000 pupils is £100 + VAT. The software runs on IBM compatible computers and Archimedes computers.

STANLEY THORNES

Ellenborough House
Wellington St
Cheltenham
Gloucester
GL50 1YD
Tel: 01242 228888

TimeTabler

TimeTabler will help construct a school timetable for up to 200 staff, 200 rooms and 70 subjects in a cycle of up to 80 periods over 16 days. The software includes routines to assist with part-time teachers, staggered lunch times, and split site schools. TimeTabler monitors the choices made, warning the user if possible mistakes are made, for example, putting two classes in the same room during the same period. The user can over-ride the software. TimeTabler will schedule the timetable either interactively with the user in control, or automatically according to pre-set preferences. Printed reports include staff timetables and class timetables, in individual or whole school formats. The typical cost for a secondary school with 1,000 pupils is £445 + VAT. The software runs on IBM compatible computers and Archimedes computers.

TRELLIS

21 West Hill Rd
Brighton
East Sussex
BN1 3RT
Tel: 01273 203920

WinMATHS, WinENGLISH and WinSCIENCE

Trellis offer a range of modules for recording pupils' NC attainment. The modules are designed for use on a departmental basis first, with later integration at a whole school level. The typical cost for a secondary school is £475 + VAT for all the subject modules. The software runs on IBM compatible computers.

APPENDIX 3
Glossary

Every area of interest has its own technical language or jargon and this is especially true of both IT and Education. Technical language is helpful to experienced professionals and other knowledgeable practitioners as it helps them communicate shared understandings more precisely. However, for those training to work in these specialisations, or taking an interest in them for the first time, this jargon can be confusing. This glossary should be helpful to those needing some clarification of the technical language used by those with expertise in the managing and teaching of IT in secondary schools.

Algorithm   A set of rules to solve a problem.

Amend   To change.

American Standard Code for Information Interchange (ASCII)   The ASCII coding system is used to uniquely represent characters and other information as bit patterns or binary codes. When files are in ASCII form, they are readily transferred between different pieces of software.

Analogue   The representation of data as a range of variable voltages. Only specialist computers represent data in analogue form. Most computers represent data in digital form.

Analogue to Digital Converter   A hardware device to convert analogue voltage to binary digital numbers.

Ancestral system   The ancestral system for multi-layered file backup consists of layers of backups (copies) of a file or a disk, taken in chronological order. In its simplest form, it consists of the son (the latest copy), the father (the previous copy) and the grandfather (the copy before the previous copy). These copies are usually kept in increasingly secure locations.

Applications software   Software designed to do a specific job, for example, software for pupil attendance records, and timetabling.

Attainment Target (AT)   An attainment target is a subdivision of an NC subject into a recognisable part that can be separately assessed. IT has only one Attainment Target, i.e. it is not subdivided for assessment purposes. However, this single AT is subdivided into two themes, which may assist with the organisation of the curriculum.

Backing storage   A non-volatile means of storing programs and data outside the computer's RAM memory, for example, on magnetic disk or tape.

Backup   A backup of a file is another copy of it. The ancestral system is often used to organise multi-layered backups.

Bar code   A code represented by a series of vertical black and white lines, often used to store an identity number. Pupils could be issued with an identification card with a bar code on it that is used to store their identification number. This identification card could be read by a bar code reader when pupils register their attendance.

Bar code reader   A hardware device used to read a bar code. This could be a light pen, a laser scanner or a swipe card reader.

Baud   Baud is a measure of the speed of transmission of information over a network. One baud is equivalent to one bit per second.

Beginners All-purpose Symbolic Instruction Code (BASIC)   BASIC is a high-level language which is suitable for those learning to write computer programs. BASIC is often the first language pupils learn. It is suitable for pupils in Key Stage 4.

Binary   The base 2 number system. Binary numbers are represented using only the digits 0 and 1. This number system is easy to represent using the digital electronics found in computer systems.

BInary digiT (bit)   A BInary digiT or bit takes the value 1 or 0. Patterns of bits make up coding systems that are used to represent information. ASCII is such a coding system.

Block   A block is:
1. A section of the screen display that has been highlighted.
2. A group of records on a magnetic tape or disk that is read or written in a single operation.

Browser   A piece of software used to browse the information available on information servers on the World Wide Web or the Internet, e.g. Netscape and Mosaic.

Buffer   Extra memory that acts as an intermediate store between a sending device and a receiving device. A printer buffer is extra memory, usually built into the printer itself, which is used to hold information waiting to be printed.

Bug   An error in a computer program.

Byte   A byte is a set of bits used to represent one character. There are normally eight bits to the byte.

Catalogue   A list of all the files on a disk. A catalogue is also known as a directory.

CD-ROM   CD-ROMs are used for backing storage for computers. CD-ROMs can store text, sound, pictures, music and video. The information on them can be accessed very quickly and they have a high storage capacity. Consequently, they are suitable for use with Multimedia applications. Their appearance is similar to that of an audio Compact Disc.

Cell   The intersection of a row and a column in a spreadsheet.

Central Processing Unit (CPU)   The main part of the computer, where all the processing takes place. It consists of the Control Unit (CU), the Arithmetic and Logic Unit (ALU) and the memory (RAM and ROM). The processor box of a modern desk top computer usually contains the CPU, a hard disk and at least one floppy disk drive.

Character   One of the symbols that can be represented by a computer. Characters include A to Z, 0 to 9, and punctuation marks.

Character code   A code used to represent characters, e.g. ASCII.

Character set   All the characters that can be represented using the character code used by a computer.

Character string   A list of characters.

Check digit   An extra digit attached to a number. It is calculated from the original digits in the number, using a predetermined formula. It can be re-calculated to check that none of the digits in the number have been altered.

City and Guilds of London Institute (C&G)   An examination board specialising in vocational examinations, that also offers examinations syllabuses in GCSE IT.

Clip Art   Clip Art is graphic images or pictures that have been prepared for importing into a wordprocessor, DTP and other software. A wide range of Clip Art is available with illustrations for a range of different situations. Users can choose a suitable piece of Clip Art to illustrate their documents.

COmmon Business Orientated Language (COBOL)   COBOL is one of the more popular high-level languages used for business and commercial applications. It is not usually considered suitable for use in Key Stages 3 and 4, but may be used by pupils studying A level Computing courses.

Computer Aided Design (CAD)   CAD is the use of graphics software to help produce effective 2D and 3D designs. The graphics software used for CAD contains features not found in less powerful graphics software.

Computer Aided Manufacture (CAM)   Using a computer to control the manufacture of a product.

Computer Assisted Learning (CAL)   Using software to learn about another subject, for example, in Mathematics, using software to practise multiplication tables, or, in Geography, using a simulation program that explores the environmental and other problems that arise when controlling an oil slick in the sea.

Computer Output on Microfilm (COM)   Output from a computer written directly onto microfilm. Output in this form is compact and does not deteriorate in storage as rapidly as printout.

Concept keyboard   A flat keyboard that can be programmed to correspond to overlays with pictures or simplified keys.

Content-free software   Software designed to do a range of similar tasks, for example, a spreadsheet. Content-free software is general purpose software.

Control character   Control characters are used to control the operation of peripherals, in particular, printers. They are part of a computer's character set, and have an ASCII code. Although they are always present in wordprocessing documents, they are not usually visible on the monitor screen or printout.

Control system   An information technology system used to monitor and control environmental conditions, for example, a control system to monitor the temperature and humidity in a greenhouse, making adjustments so that these stay within acceptable limits.

Control total   A meaningful total calculated from a batch of source documents which is used to check that the batch has been input accurately and is complete.

Control Unit (CU)   The part of the CPU that controls the running of programs and the input and output of data.

Corrupt data   Corrupt data is data that has been altered so that it is no longer meaningful. Data can be corrupted by accidental failure of the software or hardware being used. It may also be corrupted by malicious actions by hackers or by viruses.

Crash   When a computer 'crashes', it stops working. Crashes can be associated with hardware failure, for example, a hard disk crash; or software failure, for example, a programming error.

Create   Set up for the first time.

Cursor   Often a rectangular block one character in size, or a vertical line, that appears on a monitor screen, often at the point at which the next character entered through the keyboard will be displayed. The cursor usually flashes on and off to attract attention.

Cursor control keys   The 'arrow' keys on a keyboard used to control the movement of the cursor around the screen.

Cyberspace   The mental visualisation or conceptualisation of the Internet.

Daisy wheel printer   A printer that has a daisy wheel print mechanism. Daisy wheel printers give high quality printout. However, they can print only a relatively restricted range of fonts. They cannot print an extensive range of graphics.

Data   Data is information in its most basic form. It can take the form of numbers, characters, control codes, and voltages from sensors.

Database   A means of storing and accessing information. The information is structured by sub-dividing it into records and fields. The stored information can be searched, selected, sorted and reported.

Data capture   Data capture is the collection of data for input to a computer. Data capture can be on-line, e.g. Point of Sale terminals at supermarket checkouts, or off-line, e.g. questionnaires.

Data logging   The use of sensors to measure environmental conditions. The sensors are connected to a computer which records the measurements made.

Data preparation   Data preparation is the conversion of written or printed information into a form that can be processed by the computer. It usually involves the entry of data, using the keyboard, from a source document to a computer-readable medium, e.g. magnetic disk.

Data processing   Computers input, process and output data. In commerce this activity is often called 'data processing'.

Debug   To look for, find and remove bugs in a computer program.

Delete   Remove. A file is deleted from a disk when it is removed from it.

Demonstration disk   A demonstration disk contains a demonstration version of software. Demonstration disks are often sent to intending purchasers so that they can evaluate the software for themselves. The software on a demonstration disk may be complete but often there is some essential feature, such as printing, omitted. This is to encourage potential purchasers to buy a full copy of the software.

Denary   The base 10 number system. This is the number system people use. The digits available are 0 to 9.

Department for Education and Employment (DfEE)   This government department was formed in 1995 by the merger of the Department for Education (DfE) and the Department of Employment (DE). It oversees the provision of education throughout England and Wales.

Desk Top Publishing (DTP)   DTP combines graphics and wordprocessing in a format typical of a newspaper or magazine with text in columns, varying character sizes, photographs and other illustrations.

Digital   The representation of data as codes made up of 1's and 0's. These can be stored in the computer as 5 volts and 0 volts, respectively, using two state, digital electronics.

Direct access   Direct access is the fastest method of accessing records in a file. The computer can store or retrieve the records without the need to read other records first. Direct access is used with magnetic disks but not with magnetic tape.

Direct Data Entry (DDE) DDE is data entry directly to the program that is processing the data; for example, using bar code readers or swipe card readers to input pupils' identification numbers to a piece of software that is currently in use.

Directory See catalogue.

Disk Magnetic disks are a backing storage medium. There are floppy disks (3 ½") and hard disks. Hard disks may be exchangeable or fixed.

Documentation Documentation for a piece of software should include a written description of how to install the software on a computer, what it does and how it is used. The manuals and on-line help supplied with a piece of software are its documentation.

Dot matrix printer A printer which has a print head consisting of a matrix of steel pins. Character shapes are made up from a pattern of dots. Dot matrix printers are relatively slow at printing but are cheap to buy and run. They can print text in draft or Near Letter Quality. A wide range of fonts and graphics can be printed.

Edit Amend, delete or insert.

Educational Welfare Officer (EWO) EWOs are responsible for pursuing pupils who do not attend school and fail to offer an adequate reason for their absence. EWOs are often employed by the LEA.

Electronic Data Interchange (EDI) The exchange of information in electronic form over a network, for example, examination entries can be sent from schools to the GCSE examination boards using EDI over the national telephone network, and the examination results can be returned to schools in a similar manner.

Electronic Funds Transfer (EFT) A paperless method of transferring money between bank accounts using a communications network.

Electronic mail (e-mail) A paperless method of sending mail, that is, letters and other documents, from one computer to another using a communications network. Schools can send international e-mail via an Internet service provider, such as Compulink. Transmission can be almost instantaneous.

Error message   A computer will occasionally detect an error when running software, and display an error message. It should be possible to find out what the error is and what action to take from the error message itself, from the reference manual or from help built into the program.

Execute   To execute software is to run or use it.

Expert system   Software that allows users to recognise particular situations, providing help and advice on the appropriate action to be taken.

Feedback   Feedback occurs when a sensor senses information about a situation that requires the computer to take action to alter the situation. The action taken changes the situation and, in consequence, the information sensed by the sensor.

Fibre optics   The use of very thin fibre glass strands to transmit information encoded as pulses of light. The underground cabling used to distribute cable television is a fibre optic cable. Fibre optic cable can transmit very high volumes of information. Television signals, computer data transmission and video conferencing are all possible using fibre optic networks.

Field   A field is an item of information within a record.

File   A file can be stored on backing storage. It may contain programs or data. A data file used with a database is likely to contain a collection of related records all of which have a similar structure.

Filename   The name of a file stored on backing storage. This should be unique.

Fileserver   A computer attached to a network whose main function is to enable network stations to access shared files stored on one or more hard disks that are accessible over the network.

Flowchart   A graphical representation of the flow of data through a computer, or an algorithm.

Font   A set of consistently-shaped characters: for example, the Times New Roman font.

Format   The format is the structure of the information, for example:

1. Formatting a floppy disk prepares its structure for use with a particular computer system. An unformatted floppy disk cannot be used.
2. The layout of a wordprocessing document.

Front end processor   A small computer used to control communications between a larger mainframe computer and the terminals and other peripherals connected to it.

Gigabyte   Gigabytes are a measure of the storage capacity of a computer's memory or backing storage. 1 Gigabyte is 1024 Megabytes or 2^{30} bytes.

Global village   It has become just as easy to use IT to communicate with someone on the other side of the world as with someone in the next room. Consequently, in cyberspace everyone lives 'next door'. This is the global village.

Graph plotter   An output peripheral that produces detailed pictures and diagrams on paper using one or more pens.

Graphic design package   A software package that allows the user to paint or draw on the screen, using a range of design tools, colours and patterns.

Graphic User Interface (GUI)   A user interface that avoids the need to remember complex, text-based operating system commands by providing a visual interface that uses menus and icons. These can represent commands, processes or objects such as floppy disks. To make a selection from a menu or to activate an icon, the user points at it and clicks a button on the mouse. Also known as a WIMP interface.

Graphics   Pictures or symbols which can be processed by a computer. They can be displayed on the screen, saved on disk, and imported into DTP software.

Graphics pad   A graphics pad is a peripheral which allows the user to transfer line drawings to the computer by drawing on a sheet of paper that is resting on it.

Hacker   An unauthorised user of a computer system who has broken into the system, possibly by discovering a valid user identification number and its associated password, or by bypassing them. Hacking is an illegal activity. Pupils should be strongly discouraged from hacking.

Hard copy   Printout.

Hardware   The physical components of a computer system.

Hash total   A total calculated from a batch of source documents that is used to check that the batch is complete. The total has no meaning in itself.

Head of Department (HoD)   The person in charge of co-ordinating a subject department in a school, for example, the HoD Mathematics.

Help   Instructions showing how to use a piece of software that are accessible using the software when it is running. Also known as on-line help.

Help line   A telephone information service sometimes provided by hardware retailers, software vendors and others. Users who are having difficulty can ring the appropriate help line for immediate assistance in overcoming their particular problem. Many help lines are free to owners of a particular product; others are free during the guarantee period; some make a charge for their services.

Hexadecimal   The base 16 number system. Allowable digits are 0 to 9 and A to F. This is often used with computer systems to abbreviate binary codes, making them more understandable. For example, the binary code, 1101 0011, is hexadecimal D3.

High-level language   A programming language that is relatively close to the English language, making it more comprehensible, for example, COBOL, BASIC, Pascal, and C++.

Icon   A picture that represents a command, function, process, device or tool.

Information   Information is data that is meaningful to us.

Information System (IS)   An information system is the organisation of human and other resources, including IT, into a coherent system for the purposeful processing of information. A school might use a Management Information System to assemble a pupil's Record of Achievement, including inputs from various sources giving the pupil's results in assessments.

Information Technology (IT)   The use of computer-based technology to store, process and communicate information.

Initial Teacher Education (ITE)   ITE and ITT courses include the Post Graduate Certificate in Education (PGCE) and the Bachelor in Education (BEd) degree. They are the courses that initially prepare students to teach in primary and secondary schools, and lead to the award of Qualified Teacher Status (QTS).

Initial Teacher Training (ITT)   See Initial Teacher Education.

Ink jet printer   A printer that uses ink jet technology. A jet of ink is squirted onto the paper to form characters. There is no contact between the paper and the print head.

Input   Data supplied to a computer system.

IN-SErvice Training (INSET)   Training that is undertaken whilst a teacher is employed by a school. INSET is often structured so that it can be completed part-time or outside of regular teaching hours.

Integrated Learning System (ILS)   A suite of Computer Assisted Learning programs that covers a wide range of studies, providing examples, demonstrations, explanations, exercises, assessment and remedial learning materials.

Interactive processing   Interactive processing takes place when the user and the computer are in active two-way communication.

Interface   The interconnection between two different systems or devices. See Graphic User Interface.

Internet   The Internet is a network of networks. These networks are inter-linked to enable communications between their users on a global scale. There is no central organisation or ownership.

Interrogate   See search.

Joystick   A lever used to move a pointer or other image around a monitor screen. A joystick is often used with computer games.

Key field   Every record in a database should have a unique key field which identifies the record.

Key guard   A metal or plastic cover that is fitted to a keyboard to prevent keys being depressed unless there is a specific intention to do so. They can sometimes be adapted to give access to some keys but not others.

Key-to-disk   A method of data preparation where data is entered at a keyboard and saved on disk.

Kilobyte (K)   Kilobytes are a measure of the storage capacity of a computer's memory or backing storage. A kilobyte is 1024 or 2^{10} bytes.

Laptop   A portable computer that is small enough and light enough to be carried around. Most portable computers have an LCD screen which folds up for use. Portable computers can be powered by batteries or mains electricity allowing their use in a variety of locations.

Laser printer   Laser printers are expensive to buy and run but produce very high quality printing. A wide variety of fonts and graphics can be printed. Laser printers are fast in comparison with dot matrix, ink jet and daisy wheel printers.

Laser scanner   A hardware device that inputs a bar code by scanning the pattern of light reflected off it by a laser beam.

Light pen   A hardware device shaped like a pen that inputs bar codes by scanning the pattern of light reflected off a bar code.

Liquid Crystal Display (LCD)   The technology used to provide screen displays on calculators and portable computers.

Load   To retrieve from backing storage.

Local Area Network (LAN)   A network with permanent links between all the hardware connected to the network. Many LANs are located in one room or in a single building.

Local Education Authority (LEA)   The body responsible for administering education at a local level.

Logic circuit   A circuit made up of individual logic gates.

Logo   From the Greek word *logos* meaning 'word'. A high-level language designed to manipulate words and sentences. Logo is an artificial intelligence language.

Machine code   Program instructions in binary code that can be executed by a computer.

Magnetic Ink Character Recognition (MICR)   A method of input where characters printed in magnetic ink are read directly into a computer. This method of input is used to process cheques.

Mail merge   The merging of a data file and a standard letter template, to produce personalised mail. Mail merge is a common function of wordprocessing software.

Mainframe computer A large, fast computer, probably having a variety of peripherals, including a high capacity backing store and terminals, and telecommunications links.

Management Information System (MIS) A comprehensive, integrated information system for management and administration. Many MIS for schools also incorporate software that has links with aspects of the management of the curriculum.

Mark sensing An input method where pencil marks on paper are detected. Their position on the paper determines their meaning. The National Lottery uses mark sensing to input customers' number choices (see also Optical Mark Recognition).

Master file A data file which is used to store most of the data for a particular application. It is updated by a transaction file.

Megabyte (*M*) Megabytes are a measure of the storage capacity of a computer's memory or backing storage. A megabyte is 1024 kilobytes or 2^{20} bytes.

Memory The part of the CPU that is used to store programs while they are running and data while it is being processed. Memory can be RAM or ROM.

Menu A list of tasks which can be carried out by a computer progam. The user selects a task from the menu.

Merge To combine one or more files into a single file.

Microprocessor A single microchip containing all the elements of the CPU. Some microprocessors have built in memory but most supplement this, using additional RAM memory.

Midland Examinations Board (MEG) An examination board which offers syllabuses leading to assessment in GCSE IT and other subjects; organises and administers the examinations; awards grades; and certificates pupils' achievements.

Model A representation of a real or an imagined system. Computer-based models can be constructed using a spreadsheet. For example, a model of predator/prey relationships may be used in the curriculum. More frequently, financial models are used in managing schools.

Modem   A MOdulator/DEModulator. Used to convert digital data output by a computer to analogue signals that can be transmitted along a telephone line and vice versa.

Moderation   Moderation is the process of ensuring that assessment has been carried out to the same standards by different assessors. This may involve assessors checking each other's work and meeting to discuss discrepancies.

Monitor   A screen used to display the output from a computer.

Mouse   A hand-held input peripheral having one or more buttons on top and a ball underneath. When the mouse is moved over a flat surface, a pointer on the screen moves in a corresponding direction.

Mouse pointer   The on-screen representation of the mouse. This can take several forms depending on the mode of operation being used. Its most common form is an arrow head.

Multi-access   When many users are connected to, and in simultaneous communication with a single computer by means of terminals, this is multi-access computing.

Multimedia   The combination of text, sound, pictures, music and video. Often based on CD-ROM backing storage technology.

Multitasking   When one user, on one computer, is apparently running more than one program at the same time, this is multitasking.

National Council for Educational Technology (NCET)   The government-appointed body given the responsibility for supporting and encouraging the use of Educational Technology in schools. This includes IT.

National Curriculum (NC)   The Programmes of Study that schools must provide that cover the whole of compulsory education, for pupils from 5 to 16 years old. The NC specifies which subjects pupils must study and provides a framework for their assessment. For example, from September 1996, pupils in Key Stage 4 must study English, Mathematics, Science, IT, Design Technology, Physical Education and a modern foreign language. Pupils will normally be assessed at the end of Key Stage 4 by sitting GCSE examinations in these subjects.

Network   A network is a system of connecting cables. For example, networks can be used to connect computers; the telephone network connects telephone users.

Network station   A terminal connected to a computer network.

Non-Statutory Guidance (NSG)   The structure and content of the NC are defined by the statutory orders which are mandatory, and Non-Statutory Guidance which is only advisory.

Non-volatile   ROM memory is non-volatile, that is, its contents are permanent. They are retained when the computer is switched off. Information stored on backing storage is also non-volatile.

Northern Examination and Assessment Board (NEAB)   An examination board which offers syllabuses leading to assessment in GCSE IT and other subjects; organises and administers the examinations; awards grades; and certificates pupils' achievements.

Notebook   A smaller version of a Laptop computer. Usually A4 size.

Off-line   Not connected to the computer or connected but not in communication with it.

On-line   Connected to the computer and in communication with it.

On-line Public Access System (OPAC)   A network station or terminal situated in a relatively public location where it can be accessed by permitted users. For example, in a library, users may be able to access the on-line library catalogue using an OPAC.

Open   To retrieve from backing storage. See load.

Operating system   The operating system is a program that makes a computer's hardware more easily accessible and useable. An operating system is always present when a computer is used.

Optical Character Recognition (OCR)   An input method that can read printed characters. Special fonts are often used.

Optical Mark Recognition (OMR)   An input method that reads marks on a document. The position of the mark is interpreted as information. For example, it is used for recording answers in multiple choice examinations, and selecting National Lottery numbers.

Pascal   A high level language named after Blaise Pascal, the French mathematician. Pascal is often used for introducing A-level Computer Science students to structured programming techniques.

Passive Infra-Red detector (PIR) A device attached to a burglar alarm system that uses infra-red radiation to detect the presence of intruders.

Password A code that restricts access to a computer system. Usually associated with the User Identification Number.

Pen An input device used in a similar way to an ordinary pen. It is pressed onto a touch-sensitive screen. Pens are often used with a GUI interface on a PDA.

Peripheral A peripheral is a hardware device that is connected to a computer system but is not a part of the computer itself. A printer is a peripheral.

Personal Digital Assistant (PDA) A pocket-sized computer that has similar functions to a filofax. They can often read handwriting.

Pixel The smallest area of a screen that can be used in building up a picture, i.e. a dot on the screen.

Pointer An arrow or similar symbol which appears on the monitor screen. The position of the pointer is controlled by a mouse.

Port A connector used to link peripherals to a computer.

Portable 'Portable' means 'easily movable'. That is, 'portable' computers can easily be moved from one location to another; 'portable' programs can be easily run on a variety of different computers.

Printout The output from a printer.

Procedure A set of instructions that performs a specific task. A procedure is a part of a computer program but it is not a complete program.

Processor See Microprocessor.

Profile component A recognisable subdivision of skills and knowledge that can be separately assessed.

Program A set of instructions used to control the operation of a computer.

Programmer A computer programmer designs, codes, tests and documents programs for a computer.

Programmes of Study (PoS)   A Programme of Study is a list of the topics that should be studied. Specifically, it is the subject content that must be covered at each key stage in each Attainment Target in each subject of the NC.

Programming language   A language that allows a computer user to control the computer, for example: Logo, BASIC, Pascal, COBOL.

Pull-down menu   A feature of a Graphic User Interface where a hidden menu can be revealed, that is, pulled down, by pointing at it.

Query   See search condition.

Random access   See direct access.

Random Access Memory (RAM)   Read/write memory within the computer's memory. RAM is volatile. RAM is used to store programs while they are being executed and data while it is being processed.

Range check   A check that a data value is within realistic limits. For example, the number of days in a month must lie in the range 28 to 31.

Read Only Memory (ROM)   Memory within the computer's memory that can only be read. ROM is non-volatile. The Operating System is often stored in ROM memory.

Real time processing   The processing of input data which takes place so fast that when more data is input the results of the processing are already available. Real time processing occurs in real time, i.e. as it happens.

Record   A record is a collection of related fields.

Record of Achievement (RoA)   A comprehensive, summative document assembled by teachers, pupils and others, that illustrates a particular pupil's achievements in a wide range of activities. It may include academic examination results, work placement records, and swimming certificates.

Royal Society of Arts (RSA)   An examination board which offers syllabuses leading to assessment in a variety of mainly vocational areas, including GCSE IT. It organises and administers the examinations; awards grades; and certificates pupils' achievements.

Run   To run a piece of software is to use it. See also execute.

Save   To record on backing storage.

Scanner   A peripheral used to input photographs, line art and pictures into a computer. It can also be used to convert printed text into a form suitable for input to a wordprocessor.

School Curriculum and Assessment Authority (SCAA)   The successor to the National Curriculum Council (NCC) and the School Examination and Assessment Council (SEAC). This body has oversight of the content of the NC and the syllabuses for GCSE, AS and A level.

Scroll   The display on a monitor screen is said to 'scroll' when it moves off the screen at the top and onto the screen at the bottom, automatically, at the same time. More accurately, this is known as 'vertical scrolling'.

Search   To look for.

Search condition   A search condition is used to determine which records are selected when searching a database. Search conditions may be simple, for example, an instruction to find the information about all those pupils whose name begins with the letter 'B'. Simple search conditions can be combined using logical operators, such as AND, OR and NOT.

Senior Management Team (SMT)   The SMT usually consists of the Headteacher and the Deputy Headteachers. In some schools, senior teachers may be included in the SMT.

Sensor   An input device used to sense physical conditions. For example, a heat sensor.

Sequential access   Similar to serial access but the data records are stored in the file in some known order.

Serial access   A method of accessing data records. In order to access a data record in a serial access file, it is necessary to start at the beginning of the file and read all the preceding records. The records are not stored in any particular order.

Software   Computer programs and data.

Software package   A complete set of programs and documentation to enable a particular computer program to be used.

Sort   To put into order.

Source document A document or questionnaire used for data capture. It is the source of the data input to the computer.

Southern Examining Group (SEG) An examination board which offers syllabuses leading to assessment in GCSE IT and other subjects; organises and administers the examinations; awards grades; and certificates pupils' achievements.

Speech recognition A method of input to a computer by speaking to it. Computers have limited ability to recognise speech. Consequently, commands are likely to be spoken in a strictly defined and restricted language. Normal spoken conversation is not usually recognised.

Speech synthesis Sounds generated by a computer which synthesise human speech. A wide variety of words can be spoken but synthesised speech often lacks fluidity.

Spooling A method of queuing output directed to a printer before printing it. For example, when a user prints from a network station, the printed output is stored as a file on the network fileserver. This file enters a queue of files waiting to use the printer. This process is known as spooling.

Spreadsheet Spreadsheets are used to calculate and display financial and other numerical information in columns. Graphs can be generated, numerical models constructed and 'what if?' scenarios explored.

Standalone A computer that is not connected to any other computer is being used in standalone mode, i.e. it stands alone.

Standard Assessment Task (SAT) An assessment task, often a written test, taken by pupils towards the end of each of Key Stages 1 to 3. For example, in 1995, there were SATs in English, Mathematics and Science at the end of Key Stage 3. It is mandatory for all pupils to take SATs at the appropriate time.

Statement bank A database of standard comments for inclusion in reports, Records of Achievement, and other documents. Statements are often identified by a number which is input using OMR. The selected statements can usually be modified, if necessary, before printing.

Stripe card A plastic card containing a magnetic stripe which stores a limited amount of data, for example, a credit card.

Surfing Surfing the Internet is the act of browsing through information on WWW information servers throughout the world.

Systems analysis and design The in-depth analysis of the software and hardware requirements of a computer-based system and its detailed design.

Teacher Assessment (TA) The teacher's assessment of a pupil's attainment. TAs are used in conjunction with SATs to assess a pupil's progress in the NC.

Technical documentation Documentation written for technical specialists, such as IT Technicians. Technical documentation contains the design of the system, program listings, error code listings, and other useful reference information.

Terminal A hardware system used to communicate with a computer over a network. Dumb terminals consist of a keyboard and monitor combination with no processing power of their own. These are often connected to mainframe computers. Desk top PCs can be used as 'intelligent' terminals. These have their own on-board processing power, and can be connected when the requirement arises.

Track A track is the path on a magnetic disk on which data is stored.

Tracker ball A hardware device with the same function as a mouse. A tracker ball has the ball and buttons accessible on its upper surface. Instead of moving the mouse to control the screen pointer, the ball is turned while the tracker ball unit remains stationary.

Transaction file A file used to store data captured since the last master file update. The transaction file is used to update the master file.

Turnaround document A printout which has data written on it and is then used as a source document.

Turtle A programmable robot with wheels. A turtle is used to learn how to control the movement of mobile robots on a flat surface. It is often controlled using LOGO or a similar programming language.

University of London Examination and Assessment Council (London) An examination board which offers syllabuses leading to assessment in GCSE IT and other subjects; organises and administers the examinations; awards grades; and certificates pupils' achievements.

Update To bring a file or document up to date by amending, editing, inserting or deleting data.

User documentation Documentation written for users. User documentation should be user friendly. It should help users install software on a computer and explain how to use it.

User friendly Easy for users to operate and understand.

User Identification number (User Id.) A unique User Identification number can be given to every user of a computer system so that it can recognise each user. Each User Id. is usually associated with a password, thus helping to prevent unauthorised access to computer systems.

User interface The way in which a computer system communicates with users. For example, a Graphic User Interface (GUI).

Utility A program which is used to do a task that is useful only in relation to the organisation and use of a computer system, for example, a utility program can be used to format a disk.

Validation A check that data is realistic. A range check is one type of validation check.

Verification A check that what is written on a source document has been accurately transferred to a computer-readable medium. This is often done by two data preparation clerks independently entering the same data via a keyboard on two separate occasions. The computer system checks to see that exactly the same data was entered on each occasion. If a discrepancy is found, perhaps due to a mistake while the data was being entered, it must be resolved before the data is processed.

Virtual reality A model world constructed using IT. The rules governing relationships in a virtual reality model may be very unreal.

Virus A virus is a computer program that 'infects' a computer system, usually without the user's knowledge. Viruses can reside in the computer's memory, on the hard disk or on a floppy disk. They may be benign but more often they cause damage. The 'form' virus, for example, may destroy wordprocessing files. When a virus is detected, it should be destroyed before further use is made of the computer system on which the virus is found.

Visual Display Unit (VDU) A keyboard and screen used as a dumb terminal. The computer's screen, or monitor, is often inaccurately referred to as a VDU.

Volatile memory Volatile memory loses its contents when the computer is switched off. RAM memory is volatile.

Welsh Joint Education Committee (WJEC)   An examination board which offers syllabuses leading to assessment in GCSE IT and other subjects; organises and administers the examinations; awards grades; and certificates pupils' achievements.

Wide Area Network (WAN)   A network spread over a wide area, possibly international, making use of both permanent cable connections and temporary connections using the telephone network.

Window   A rectangular subdivision of the screen which enables the user to look at the output from a program. There may be more than one window open on the screen at the same time.

Windows, Icons, Menus and Pointers (WIMP)   See Graphic User Interface.

Wordprocessing   The preparation of letters and other documents using a computer in a manner similar to a typewriter but with additional features.

Wordwrap   A feature of a wordprocessor. When typing beyond the right-hand margin, the word automatically carries over to the next line.

WORM (Write Once Read Many) disks   A CD-ROM that can have data written to it by the user once only. The data can then be read many times.

World Wide Web (WWW)   The WWW is a multimedia information service accessible using the Internet. Information is provided by many different organisations throughout the world.

WYSIWYG (What You See Is What You Get)   What is displayed on the screen is what will be printed on the printer. This phrase is particularly used in connection with wordprocessors.

APPENDIX 4
Useful addresses

The addresses of suppliers of software for the management and administration of a school's finances and curriculum are given in Appendix 2 (see p. 159). Below are the contact details of other organisations that readers may be interested in.

ACE centre
Ormerod School
Waynflete Rd
Headington
Oxford
OX3 8DD
Tel: 01865 63508

Information and advice in the use of IT to assist children with SEN.

Acorn
Acorn House
Vision Park
Histon
Cambridge CB4 4AE
Tel: 01223 254254

The manufacturer and supplier of Archimedes computers.

Apple
16 Roundwood Avenue
Stockley Park
Uxbridge UB11
Tel: 0181 569 1199

The manufacturer and supplier of Apple computers to educational institutions and others.

British Dyslexia Association
Computer Resource Centre
Dept of Psychology
University of Hull
Hull HU6 7RX
Tel: 01482 465589

Information and advice on software for pupils with dyslexia.

British Educational Suppliers Association (BESA)
20 Beaufort Court
Admirals Way
London
E14 9XL
Tel: 0171 537 4997

The trade association for suppliers of educational equipment, including IT equipment.

City and Guilds Institute of London (C & G)
46 Britannia St
London
WC1X 7RG
Tel: 0171 278 2468

A vocational examination board, offering syllabuses which include GCSE IT.

Compulink Information eXchange Ltd (CIX)
London House
Ancaster Square
Llanrwst
Gwynedd
LL26 0LD
Tel: 01429 641961

Suppliers of on-line services, including access to global e-mail and the Internet.

Compuserve
1 Redcliff St
Bristol
BS99 1YN
Tel: 0990 000200

Suppliers of on-line services, including access to global e-mail and the Internet.

Computability Centre
PO Box 94
Warwick
CV34 5WS
Tel: 0800 269545

A national charity that can offer advice in using IT to support people with disabilities, including pupils with SEN

Computer Education Group (CEG)
Computer Centre
Staffordshire University
School of Computing
Beaconside
Stafford
ST18 0AD

The association for people involved with IT in education, and the publishers of the *Computer Education* journal.

Concept Keyboard
Company
Moorside Rd
Winnall Industrial Estate
Winchester
Hampshire
SO23 7RX
Tel: 01962 843322

Manufacturers and suppliers of the Concept keyboard.

Data and Research
Services Plc Ltd (DRS)
Sunrise Park
Linford Wood
Milton Keynes
MK14 6LR
Tel: 01908 666088

Suppliers of the CD210 Optical Mark Reader.

Demon
322 Regent Park Rd
Finchley
London
N3 2QQ
Tel: 0181 371 1000

Suppliers of on-line services, including access to global e-mail and the Internet.

DfEE
PO Box 6927
London
E3 3NZ
Tel: 0171 925 5555

The Department for Education and Employment.

Elonex
2 Apsley Way
London
NW2 7LF
Tel: 0181 452 2444

A manufacturer and supplier of IBM compatible computers to educational institutions and others.

HMSO Publications Centre
PO Box 276
London
SW8 5DT
Tel: 0171 873 0011

HMSO is the supplier and publisher of most government publications.

IBM Computers Ltd PO Box 41 North Harbour Portsmouth Hampshire PO6 3AU Tel: 01705 561000	Manufacturers and distributors of IBM computers.
Microsoft Microsoft Place Winnersh Wokingham Berkshire RG11 5TP Tel: 01734 270526	The manufacturers and distributors of Microsoft software such as Word, and Excel.
Midland Examining Group (MEG) Syndicate Buildings 1 Hills Rd Cambridge CB1 2EU Tel: 01223 611111	A GCSE examination board, offering syllabuses which include GCSE IT.
National Council for Educational Technology (NCET) Milburn Hill Rd Science Park Coventry CV4 7JJ Tel: 01203 416994	NCET promote the use of Educational Technology, including IT, in schools. They organise and conduct research, and publish many useful reports.
National Design and Technology Education Foundation (NDTEF) The Old Chapel House Pound Hill Alresford Hants Tel: 01962 735801	A GCSE examination board, offering syllabuses which include GCSE IT.
Northern Examination and Assessment Board (NEAB) 12 Harter St Manchester M1 6HL Tel: 0161 228 0084	A GCSE examination board, offering syllabuses which include GCSE IT.

Office of the Data
Protection Registrar
Springfield House
Water Lane
Wilmslow
Cheshire
SK9 5AX
Tel: 01625 535777

The Data Protection Registrar is the
regulatory body that oversees the
implementation of the Data Protection
Act (1984).

Optech
East Street
Farnham
Surrey
GU9 7XX
Tel: 01252 714340

The suppliers of a range of CD-ROM
hardware, software and media.

Research Machines (RM)
New Mill House
183 Milton Park
Abingdon
Oxfordshire
OX14 4SE
Tel: 01235 826000

The manufacturer and supplier of RM
Nimbus computers.

Royal National Institute
for the Blind
National Education Services
Garrow House
190 Kensal Rd
London
W10 5BT
Tel: 0181 9603593

The RNIB will provide useful
suggestions for helping blind and
partially sighted people communicate
using IT and other technologies.

Royal Society of Arts (RSA)
Westwood Way
Coventry
CV4 8HS
Tel: 01203 470033

A vocational examination board, offering
syllabuses which include GCSE IT.

SCAA
Newcombe House
45 Nottinghill Gate
London W11 3JB
Tel: 0171 229 1234

The Schools' Curriculum and Assessment
Authority.

SEMERC (Special
Education Micros
Electronics Resource Centre)
1 Broadbent Rd
Watersheddings
Oldham
OL1 4LB
Tel: 0161 627 4469

Assistance in using IT to support pupils with
SEN.

Southern Examining
Group (SEG)
Stag Hill House
Guildford
GU2 5XJ
Tel: 01483 506506

A GCSE examination board, offering
syllabuses which include GCSE IT.

University of Huddersfield
School of Education
Holly Bank Campus
Huddersfield
HD3 3BP
Tel: 01484 422288

The address at which the author can be
contacted.

University of London
Examinations and
Assessment Council (London)
Stewart House
32 Russell Square
London
WC1B 5DN
Tel: 0171 753 0053

A GCSE examination board, offering
syllabuses which include GCSE IT.

Welsh Joint Education
Committee (WJEC)
245 Western Avenue
Cardiff
CF5 2YX
Tel: 01222 561231

A GCSE examination board, offering
syllabuses which include GCSE IT.

APPENDIX 5
The Internet and the World Wide Web

The Internet is a world-wide collection of interconnected networks. There is no one central organisation that owns or controls the Internet or the information on it. To connect to the Internet from home or from school, a computer, a fast modem, a telephone line, and a subscription to an Internet service provider are needed. Examples of Internet service providers are America On-line (AOL), Cix and Compulink.

The Internet can be used to send, receive and exchange information, nationally and internationally. This facility is developed to provide specific services, for example:

- E-mail. Users can send letters and other documents to each other.
- Information services. World Wide Web (WWW) Information servers give access to a wide variety of information. These can be accessed over the Internet using a WWW browser, such as Mosaic or Netscape.

Finding information on the WWW can be difficult. There is no one central organisation, or a single comprehensive directory of information servers, services or users. Information can be accessed by:

- connection to a specific WWW information server using its Uniform Resource Locator (URL);
- 'surfing' the WWW, that is, by wandering from information server to information server;
- searching for particular topics using a search engine, for example, Yahoo.

In order to surf the WWW, a connection must be established with at least one information server using its URL. Most information servers have 'hot spots' that will connect you to other information servers. 'Surfing' is wandering around the WWW by activating these hot spots. This is not always a quick or efficient means of finding information and an alternative is to use a search engine. In principle, a search engine will allow users to search the entire WWW using commands similar to those used to interrogate a database.

The URL's listed below indicate the range of interesting and useful information servers connected to the WWW. They will make useful starting-points.

SOME INTERESTING AND USEFUL INFORMATION SERVERS AND THEIR URL'S

General information

http://www.economist.com	*The Economist* magazine
http://www.timeshigher.newsint.co.uk	The *Times Higher Educational Supplement* (THES)
http://www.undcp.or.at/unlinks.html	United Nations information
http://www.timeout.co.uk	*TimeOut* magazine
http://www.csc.liv.ac.uk/users/rkl/lottery/	National Lottery information
http://www.echo.lu	EC information

Subject-related information

http://galaxy.einet.net/galaxy/Science/Biology.html	Biology
http://www.vnu.co.uk/vnu	Computing on-line
http://www.easynet.co.uk/compman.html	Computing video and book list
http://volcano.und.nodak.edu/	Volcano world
http://www.chem.ucla.edu/chempointers.html	Chemistry
http://euclid.math.fsu.edu/science/math.html	Mathematics on the Web
http://www.nmsi.ac.uk	The Science Museum
http://nmnhwww.si.edu/nmnhweb.html	Natural History
http://white.nosc.mil/physics.html	Physics page

Education

http://www.open.gov.uk/dfee	The DfEE
http://rmplc.co.uk	RM computers
http://www.niss.ac.uk	The NISS gateway
http://ncet.csv.warwick.ac.uk/index.html	NCET home page
http://www.nhm.ac.uk/	Natural History Museum
http://www.npac.syr.edu/textbook/kidsweb/	WWW front end for school pupils
http://hillside.coled.umn.edu/others.html	Schools using Internet in the USA

Shopping

http://www.bookshop.co.uk	The UK Internet book shop
http://www.books.com/	The US Internet book shop

Miscellaneous

http://www.intel.com/	Intel processor information
http://home.netscape.com	Netscape information
http://www.gold.net.online/	*Guardian* newspaper
http://mistral.enst.fr/	The Louvre gallery
http://www.easynet.co.uk/pages/cafe/gall.htm	Art galleries around the world
http://nsns.com/mix/	USA marketing information
http://olt.et.tudelft.nl/fun/bible.html	Bible on line
http://www.telegraph.co.uk/	*Daily Telegraph*
http://www.cs.ucl.ac.uk/misc/uk/intro.html	UK map and information
http://www.culture.fr/	French Ministry of Culture
http://www.eia.brad.ac.uk/rti/reports/index.html	Weather summary for the UK

Searching Sites

http://www.yahoo.com	Internet searches
http://www.lycos.com	Internet searches
http://ukindex.co.uk	Index of UK sites
http://www.ic.ac.uk/ccs/nss/jump.html	Internet sites arranged by subject
http://www.niss.ac.uk	The NISS Information Gateway
http://lycos.cs.cmu.edu/	The Catalogue of the Internet

The plethora of information available on the WWW and its anarchic organisation give rise to concerns about the validity and suitability of the information available. There is no guarantee that all the information accessible on the WWW is 'true' as it has been placed there by the various owners of the wide variety of WWW sites. The owners may or may not present what is generally considered to be a balanced viewpoint. For example, commercial companies are likely to provide particularly favourable presentations regarding the merits of the products they sell. More seriously, material unsuitable for young people is available on some sites, for example, pornography. Consequently, teachers, parents and others concerned with the welfare and development of young people may wish to make available only a selection of the information available on the WWW. This can be done by filtering the information leaving or entering browsers or sites. Filtering software will scan the transmitted information for particular key words or specific URL's and block access to unsuitable material.

BIBLIOGRAPHY

Acey, M. (1993) 'PC finds a place in a third of homes', *Computer Weekly*, 16 December, p. 2.

Allen, P. (1991) 'Information Technology across the Curriculum', *Computer Education*, no. 68, pp. 20–3.

Ankers, R. (1993) 'Tying the knot', *Educational Computing and Technology*, vol. 14, no. 6, p. 24.

Benyon, J. *et al.* (1992) *Computers into Classrooms*, Falmer Press.

Bowen, I. (1995) 'Secondary Information Technology and the OFSTED Inspections', *Computer Education*, no. 79, February, pp. 2–6.

British Computer Society Schools Committee (1995) *A Glossary of Computing Terms*, Longman.

Carr, N. (1995) 'Changes in the perception of teaching programming over the past 15 years to children aged 5 to 16 in the light of developments of hardware, software and educational thinking', *Computer Education*, no. 79, February, pp. 21–26.

Cole, G. (1994a) 'Benign big brother: a review of the Cosmex swipe card system', *Times Educational Supplement*, 17 June, Update, p. 10.

Cole, G. (1994b) 'Deviations from the Script: a review of one of the first school administration systems', *Times Educational Supplement*, 17 June, Update, p. 10.

Council of the European Communities (1990) 'Council Directive of 29/5/90 on the minimum safety and health requirements for work with display screen equipment (fifth individual Directive within the meaning of Article 16 (1) of Directive 87/391/EEC)', (90/270/EEC), *Official Journal of the European Communities*, no. 1. 156/14, 21 June.

Coupland, J. (1990) 'The implications of the NC for the use and management of IT resources', *Journal of Computer Assisted Learning*, vol. 6, no. 2, pp. 98–102.

Crawford, R. (ed.) (1994) *The Rastrick Project: Learning Materials for Cross-Curricula IT at KS4*, Calderdale and Kirklees TEC, Rastrick High School, and the University of Huddersfield, unpublished.

Crawford, R. (1997) *GCSE Study Guide: Information Technology*, Longman.

Culley, L. (1986) *Gender Differences and Computing in Secondary Schools*, Loughborough University.

Data Protection Registrar (1991) *Guidance Note 5: Registration of Local Education Authority Maintained Schools in England and Wales*, Office of the Data Protection Registrar.

Data Protection Registrar (1992a) *Guideline 1: Introduction to the Act*, Office of the Data Protection Registrar.

Data Protection Registrar (1992b) *Guideline 2: The Definitions*, Office of the Data Protection Registrar.

Data Protection Registrar (1992c) *Guideline 3: The Register and Registration*, Office of the Data Protection Registrar.

Data Protection Registrar (1992d) *Guideline 4: The Data Protection Principles*, Office of the Data Protection Registrar.

Data Protection Registrar (1992e) *Guideline 5: Individuals Rights*, Office of the Data Protection Registrar.

Data Protection Registrar (1992f) *Guideline 6: The Exemptions*, Office of the Data Protection Registrar.

Data Protection Registrar (1992g) *Guideline 7: Enforcement and Appeals*, Office of the Data Protection Registrar.

Data Protection Registrar (1992h) *Guideline 8: Summary for Computer Bureaux*, Office of the Data Protection Registrar.

Davis, C. (1994) 'Pilgrim's progress: ways to make recording and reporting pupils' assessments easier', *Times Educational Supplement*, 17 June, Update, p. 12.

Dearing, R. (1994) *The National Curriculum and its Assessment: Final Report*, SCAA.

DfE (1991) 'Data Protection Act 1984: Implications for LEA Maintained Schools', circular to Chief Education Officers, Chairmen of Governing Bodies and Headteachers of LEA Maintained Schools, 29 November.

DfE (1993a) *Statistical Bulletin 6/93: A Survey of IT in Schools*, HMSO.

DfE (1993b) *Statistical Bulletin 9/93*, HMSO.

DfE (1995a) *Information Technology in the National Curriculum*, HMSO.

DfE (1995b) *Mathematics in the National Curriculum*, HMSO.

DfE (1995c) *Statistical Bulletin 3/95: A Survey of IT in Schools*, HMSO.

DfEE (1995) *Code of Practice: On the Identification and Assessment of SEN*, HMSO.

Education Law Focus (1993a) 'Check the computer contracts', *Times Educational Supplement*, 24 September, Review (Section 2), p. 7.

Education Law Focus (1993b) 'Exemption from new law ends: the implications for colleges of data protection legislation', *Times Educational Supplement*, 29 October, Review (Section 2), p. 7.

Eraut, M. *et al.* (1991) 'Developing a whole school IT policy', *Edtech*, April, vol. 2, no. 4, pp. 2–6.

Fox, P. and Selwood, I. (1992) 'The needs of secondary school IT coordinators in the UK', *Journal of IT for Teacher Education*, vol. 1, pp. 231–9.

Fraser, K. (1994) 'Lifting the curse: M-power is being developed in Strathclyde to take the sting out of school administration', *Times Educational Supplement*, 17 June, Update, p. 5.

Freedman, T. (1994) 'What, where and when: school timetabling need not be an administrative nightmare', *Times Educational Supplement*, 1 July, p. 23.

Frost, R. (1994) 'A nightmare for truants', *Times Educational Supplement*, 17 June, Update, p. 10.

Gardner, J. (1992) 'The laptop test: a report on the first comprehensive study into the use of portable computers in schools', *Times Educational Supplement*, 6 November, Review (Section 2), p. 18.

Gardner, J. (1994) 'No pain, no gain: Northern Ireland schools are pioneering a new generation of administration systems', *Times Educational Supplement*, 17 June, Update, p. 4.

Green-Armytage, J. (1996) 'Changes in fortune', *Computer Weekly*, 15 August, p. 12.

Grundy, F. (1996) 'Gender and computing in HE', *Education News*, Apple Computer, Summer, p. 4.

Haigh, G. (1994a) 'Corridors of empowerment: administration software may appear to be making things more difficult before they get easier', *Times Educational Supplement*, 17 June, Update, p. 6.

Haigh, G. (1994b) 'Office politics: within the last decade computers have revolutionised the management of many schools', *Times Educational Supplement*, 17 June, Update, p. 3.

Harris, S. *et al.* (1993) *Software in Schools*, National Foundation for Educational Research.

Harris, S. (1994) *Schools' IT Policies*, National Foundation for Educational Research.

HSE (1990) *Working with VDUs*, Health and Safety Executive.

HSE (1994) *Maintaining Portable Electrical Equipment in Offices and Other Low-risk Environments*, Health and Safety Executive.

Library Association (1990) *Copyright in Polytechnic and University Libraries*, Library Association.

Martin, R. (1991) 'School children's attitudes towards computers as a function of gender, course subjects and availability of home computers', *Journal of CAL*, September, vol. 7, no. 3, pp. 187–94.

Millum, T. (1992) *IT into Practice*, Longman.

Milner, A. (1989) *Girls and the New Technologies*, Microelectronics Education Support Unit.

Moore, D. (1994a) 'Net gains', *Educational Technology and Computing*, vol. 15, no. 3, p. 30.

Moore, D. (1994b) 'Choosing a CD-ROM drive', *Educational Technology and Computing*, vol. 15, no. 4, p. 30.

NCC, (1990a) *Technology: Non-Statutory Guidance, IT Capability*, NCC.

NCC (1990b) *Technology in the National Curriculum*, NCC.

NCET (1992) *Choosing and Using Portable Computers*, NCET.

NCET (1993a) 'Management of IT and cross-curricular issues: investing in IT, guidelines no. 2, formulating a plan', *Directory of Information*, vol. 3, MAN 3.65, NCET.

NCET (1993b) 'Management of IT and cross-curricular issues: choosing and buying a portable computer', *Directory of Information*, vol. 3, MAN 6.21, NCET.

NCET (1993c) *Portable Computers in the Curriculum: the PLAIT Research Project*.

NCET (1993d) *Software in Schools: a Synopsis*, NCET.

NCET (1994a) 'CD-Recordable (CD-R)', *Directory of Information*, vol. 3, NCET, March.

NCET (1994b) *Attracting Girls to IT: NCET/WIT Development Project*, NCET, December.

NCET (1994c) *Differentiation: A Practical Handbook of Classroom Strategies*, NCET.

NCET (1994d) *Directory of Software for Assessment*, NCET.

NCET (1994e) *Integrated Learning Systems: A Report of the Pilot Evaluation of ILS in the UK*, NCET.

NCET (1994f) *Making the Most of IT*, NCET.

NCET (1994g) 'Management of IT and cross-curricular issues: CD-Recordable (CD-R)', *Directory of Information*, vol. 3, MAN 6.57, NCET.

NCET (1994h) *Using IT for Assessment: Directory of Software*, NCET.

NCET (1995a) *Approaches to IT Capability: Key Stage 3*, NCET.

NCET (1995b) *Managing IT: A Planning Tool for Senior Managers*, NCET.

NCET (1995c) Mathematics: Approaches to IT Capability: Key Stage 3, NCET. This is one of a series of NCET booklets. Others include those for: English, Science, DT, and modern foreign languages.

NCET (1996a) *Delivering IT Capability*, NCET.

NCET (1996b) *IT Disability and Lifelong Learning*, NCET.

NCET (1996c) *Gender and IT*, NCET, June.

NCET (1996d) *Information Sheet on IT Policy: How to Write a Whole School IT Policy Document*, NCET.

Norman, S. (1993) 'Guidelines on computer software', *Audio Visual Librarian*, vol. 19, no. 1, pp. 42–4.

OFSTED (1995) *Information Technology: A Review of Inspection Findings 1993/4*, HMSO.

Philips, A. (1993) 'Football crazy, football sad', *Times Educational Supplement*, 24 September, Review (Section 2), p. 1.

Riley, J. (1993) 'IT Budgets: spend shift', *Computer Weekly*, 21 January, p. 26.

Research Machines (1995) *Budgeting for IT: A Flexible Approach to Financing your School's IT*, Research Machines.

Research Machines (1996) *Special Educational Needs: A Practical Guide to IT and SEN*, Research Machines, May.

SCAA (1995a) *An Introduction to the Revised National Curriculum*, SCAA.

SCAA (1995b) *Key Stage 3 Information Technology: The New Requirements*, SCAA.

SCAA (1995c) *Key Stage 3 Information Technology and the National Curriculum*, SCAA.

SCAA (1995d) *GCSE Mandatory Code of Practice*, SCAA.

SCAA (1995e) *Subject Criteria for Information Technology*, SCAA.

SEAC (1990) *National Criteria for GCSE Technology*, SEAC.

SEG (1995a) *GCSE Information Systems Syllabus*, SEG.

SEG (1995b) *National Curriculum Certificate in Information Technology Syllabus*, SEG.

SEG (1996a) *GCSE Information Technology Syllabus*, SEG.

SEG (1996b) *Information Technology (Short Course) Syllabus*, SEG.

Steadman, S. *et al.* (1992) *CD-ROM in Schools Scheme*, NCET.

Stebbins, R.A. (1996) 'Physical context influences on behaviour: the case of classroom disorderliness' in M. Hammersley *et al.* (ed.) *The Process of Schooling*, Routledge and Kegan Paul, p. 208.

Strack, G. (1992) 'The pick of the crop: what makes a good classroom computer?', *Times Educational Supplement*, 9 October, Review, p. 17.

Tinsley, J. (1994) 'CD-ROM and Photo-CD', *Hotshoe International*, no. 68, p. 28.

Tizard, J. (1988) *Girls and CDT*, Bradford LEA.

Watson, D.H. (ed.) (1993) *The Impact Report*, King's College, London.

West Glamorgan Centre for Computer Education (nd) *Educational Software Evaluation Report*, West Glamorgan Centre for Computer Education.

Yeomans, D., Martin, M. and Williams, R. (1995) 'From vertical to horizontal? A longitudinal study of IT in 10 schools', *Journal of IT for Teacher Education*, vol. 4, no. 3, p. 329.

INDEX

access to IT resources: equal
  opportunities 89–90; hardware 70–1
action statements 43–4
administration and IT: advantages of
  IT use 131–3; disadvantages of IT
  use 133–5; selection criteria 135–7;
  software 126–30, 159–84; useful
  addresses 207–12
ancestral system 80–1
assessment 17–25, 30, 38–9;
  evidence 18; GCSE 143–58;
  mapping of subthemes 19;
  moderation 22–5; record keeping
  18–20, 30, 38; reporting 18, 22,
  30, 38; whole school IT policy 30,
  38–9
audit 37

backing storage 56–9
backup copies 80–1

CD-ROM 59
Computer Assisted Learning (CAL) 74;
  evaluation training activity 108–12;
  for Special Educational Needs (SEN)
  98; software 74
coursework (GCSE) 143–58
curriculum models 11–16; cross
  curricular 12–14, 17, 20, 30–3, 34;
  hybrid 14–15, 21–2, 30–3, 36;
  subject 11–12, 17, 30–3, 36
curriculum organisation 38

Data Protection Act (1984) 35, 41,
  139–41
disaster recovery 35, 41

e-mail 62, 213

equal opportunities 35–6, 42, 86–101;
  gender bias 87–8; monitoring 88–9;
  role models 90–1; Special
  Educational Needs (SEN) 97–101;
  training activity 120–1
examinations (GCSE) 143–58

fileserver 62
finance software 129
floppy disk 56–8, *58*
funding IT 37, 43

GCSE: IT syllabuses 10–11, 143–58;
  assessment records 22; hardware
  requirements 52–3; software requirements 73–4
gender monitoring 88–9
general purpose software 73–4, 130
glossary of terms 185–206

hard disk 56–8; hard disk drive *57*
hardware 31–2, 40, 52–72; access to
  resources 70–1; backing storage
  56–9; PC characteristics 53–6;
  planning activity 112–17; purchase
  and replacement 65–7; review of
  provision in secondary schools 64–5
health and safety 83–5; legislation 85

INSET 36, 42
Internet 62, 213–16
inventory 70
IT in school administration 126–41
IT policy (*see* whole school IT policy)

Key Stage 3 17–22
Key Stage 4 22–5
keyboard 55–6

221